Traveling Light

Moving Our Awareness Beyond the Five Senses

Jennifer Shoals

ISBN: 978-1-7341987-1-3 (sc)
ISBN: 978-1-7341987-4-4 (e)

Library of Congress Control Number: 9781734198713

Shoals, Jennifer.
Traveling Light: Moving Our Awareness Beyond the Five Senses / Jennifer Shoals.
— Thunder Bird.

1. Transcendence 2. Consciousness 3. Personal Growth 4. Channeling I. Title

Books may be ordered through booksellers or by contacting:
Thunder Bird
PO Box 776
Grand Marais, MN 55604
www.jennifershoals.com

The author of this book does not dispense medical advice or prescribe the use of any technique as a form of treatment for physical, emotional, or medical problems without the advice of a physician, either directly or indirectly. The intent of the author is only to offer information of a general nature to help you in your quest for emotional and spiritual well-being. In the event that you use any of the information in this for yourself, which is your constitutional right, the author and the publisher assume no responsibility for your actions.

Cover art: Jennifer Shoals, with Maryl Skinner and Denny FitzPatrick of M Graphic Design

Printed in the United States of America
Lightning Source / IngramSpark

With immense gratitude for all our Teachers,
reaching across the veil
to share the wisdom of the Universe

For my father,
who came to see the light of God in every person

And for Amy, Debi, Christy and Steve,
whose steadfast support has carried me
through times of thin faith

Contents

Introduction

Space — The Final Frontier

Our everyday connection with reality occurs through the five senses. We use our five senses to create the conditions that allow us to live in a physical body and to make choices that will assure our survival. That is the vital role of Ego. Infusing this physical context is Life Force, an energy that characterizes us as being alive. This is the arena of Spirit.

We can nurture the energy of Spirit by expanding our consciousness, by moving our awareness beyond the five senses. Many people have experienced this through prayer or meditation or contact with Nature. They describe it as relaxing and nourishing. It does not occur by leaving the body, but by fully integrating a grounded physical experience with an expanded spiritual experience. This deep state of alert relaxation is called transcendence.

Channeling is a spiritual connection that occurs during transcendence. The channel is simply an energy pathway. Many people channel energy while they work. Painters and musicians are good examples, as are dancers and actors. Some athletes and scientists are, too. Channeling is what happens when someone is "in the Zone." It's about opening to the mysteries of the Universe and allowing that in.

Channeling is not something new. Connecting with ancient wisdom is a very old communication skill. We are here today because our ancestors were very tuned into the energies of the natural world. They had to be, in order to survive. When we connect with the energy of the Universe now, we are practicing skills that we once had, skills that have been drowned out by the noise of technological society.

This is a book of channeled writing. While I channel, I type, and a rich stream of helpful wisdom is generated. When I am open and accepting of this information, its flow increases. When I judge its contents or insert my own agenda, the flow stops. Clearly, it is not something that I control. It is something that I allow. It's an intuitive process.

I began channeling in the 1990s. I did not understand it as channeling then, but Spirits began to visit me. Over time, they helped me to heal significant personal trauma. In 2005, a Spirit Teacher came to me and asked me to write a book. Even though I had no idea what the book would be about, I agreed.

Over the next several years I recorded hundreds of channeled interviews with many spiritual guides. I call these guides The Teachers. A Teacher appears to me as a specific person. I see them with my mind's eye, hear their voice with my mind's ear, and interact emotionally with their personalities during our conversations. You will be introduced to each one as they appear in the book. Their words appear in italics. I do not edit their words.

The Teachers are my ancestors. They arise through cellular memory, which has been transferred through many generations of DNA coding. Every single human is the product of common ancestors across hundreds of thousands of years—we *are* all related, and we all have access to many Teachers. The Teachers who visit me are the voices of a variety of people from different cultures, age groups, genders, and historical times. I do not represent or speak for any of these groups. The Teachers speak and I record their words. Our intention, together, is to foster greater understanding.

I also communicate with Universal Wisdom, which is the aggregate of all the wisdom in the Universe. I do not see or hear it, and it has no personality. It comes through me as energy in words. Another term for this is the Collective Unconscious. Occasionally, I have also been in the presence of God. This is a very intense experience, one of magnified mega-radiance, so powerful that it is difficult for the human body to integrate. The Teachers are the spirits that support God. They act as God's intermediaries.

I realize that the use of the word God may be uncomfortable for some readers, especially those who have been harmed by organized religion. I use the word God in a very broad sense, to mean all of the energy of the Universe. See Chapter One of this book for a more detailed explanation.

After many years of recording channeled interviews, the Teachers instructed me to publish a book. I was told by the Teachers that the purpose of the book would be to foster communication. It would disseminate the information contained in the interviews to a wider audience. The book itself would also serve as a physical object, a point of connection encouraging people to discuss the topics it contained. *Grandmother Dreams, Conversations Across the Veil*[1] was published in 2012. It focused on the spirit-fed life.

The Teachers continued to share this kind of information with me, both during and after publishing. *Traveling Light, Moving Our Awareness Beyond the Five Senses* is the second book in this series. It outlines how our lives interact with the Universe, and encourages us to invest in our own intuitive process of transcendence. It supports Spirit manifesting on Soul Path.

In a physical sense, the title *Traveling Light* implies that we have less baggage, that we are living a life that is not heavy with misdirected ego. In a spiritual sense, *Traveling Light* describes the awareness of ourselves as spiritual energy in motion—we are the journey of a spirit traveling the earth, we are *light* that is *traveling*. We can encourage these improvements, both physical and spiritual, by *Moving Our Awareness Beyond the Five Senses*.

A third book, *The Next World*, is in progress. All of the books are part of a series called *Inspiring Deeper Connections*.

In all of these books, the Teachers appear to be sharing information with *me*. As you read along, however, always understand that the word "you" applies not just to me, the receiver and recorder of

---

[1] Shoals, Jennifer. *Grandmother Dreams, Conversations Across the Veil*, Balboa Press, 2012.

these conversations. It also applies to you, the reader. Always insert yourself into the discussion. The Teachers are speaking to everyone.

There are several ways to read these books. They can be read in the traditional way—front to back, starting at page one and going to the end. The information in the books can be complex. I have found that it is helpful to read the book out loud, either with another person or in a group. You can also use the "Book Fairy" technique: open the book at random, wherever feels right, and just read that page. Many readers have told me that they use this method and always find something helpful.

According to the Teachers, a change is occurring in the energy of the Universe. They refer to this change as The Shift. Humans are part of the Universe so we, as a collective, are also transforming our energy vibration. Our species is moving forward in spiritual evolution.

Humans have a specific purpose, a niche in the order of the Universe. We are beings that are capable of cultivating Love.[2] Universal Love is an energy vibration, a resonance. It is magnified when it is transferred through the physical medium, when it is expressed in compassionate action. The Teachers are asking us to cultivate and share this energy.

All of the major religions start with this idea. The Teachers' directive, however, is not religious. It is spiritual. It is open to everyone. You can follow a structured religion, or not. You can practice rote rituals, or not. What is being requested of us is a spiritual energy practice that transcends religious boundaries, that is expansive and inclusive.

As you read this book, it is important to keep your energy open to feelings. Making a spiritual change is not something that is done by thinking about it. Intelligence, the ability to solve problems, may help you reach greater understanding. But consciousness, the ability to feel, is how changes are made.

---

[2] There is a difference between *love* and *Love*. Lower-case-L love is a sentimental, conditional state which we refer to when say "I love baseball" or "I love chocolate." Capital-L Love describes a state of spiritual connection. It is the kind of Love that Mother Teresa expressed—inclusive, compassionate and unconditional.

The Teachers would like us all to practice opening our energy state, to develop a communication pathway to a broader level of wisdom. It is a place where we connect with our ancestors and receive their assistance. Creating this state means cultivating the ability to be both grounded and expanded, simultaneously.

Being grounded means that our physical body must be a welcoming place for Spirit. It requires us to bring awareness to how we function in our everyday lives. It means that we recognize the choices we make, choices that become either supports or obstacles to spiritual experience. The difference between making choices that feed the ego or that feed the spirit is outlined in *Grandmother Dreams*. There, the Teachers use a train metaphor.

A train is a physical object, just as our body is a physical object. Without fuel, the train will not run, it is an empty hull. Without an energy presence, our body will not be alive. Our Ego's actions are the fuel for our physical presence. We make choices that maintain that train in good working order, or not. Our ego follows through either in service to Spirit, or in service to self.

Choices that serve our Ego tend to be destructive over time. They are motivated by a short-term desire for pleasure or avoidance of pain. If we habitually make these kind of choices, we feed addictive behaviors. The train's engine, our body, will run poorly or burn out. On the other hand, choices that serve our Spirit tend to be nourishing over time. They are motivated by a long-term desire for clear connections to self and others, and to the larger context of Life Force. This is the trajectory that aligns with healing, compassionate action, and the Love of the Universe. When our physical presence is fueled by spiritual choices, we travel well on the track that is our soul's path.

The Teachers want us to have a personal connection with the Love of the Universe. They want us to access the layer of conscious reality that is realized when we open to the world beyond the five senses, and to use this increased awareness to live in harmony with each other and the planet. In other words, the Teachers support us in traveling our Soul Path.

Another way to understand transcendence, to be simultaneously grounded and expanded, is through the integration of Point and Zone. Concentrations of energy show up on the radar of our five senses as objects. An object appears as fixed and stable. This is what the Teachers call a *Point*. Objects do not stand alone. They exist in the context of the space around them. Each Point is located within an area of shared space which the Teachers call *The Zone*.

Humans, for example, are Points. We are physical objects. Each of us is separated from other humans by the space between us. Three people sitting in a room are three objects, or three Points. They are separated by the space between them. The room where the people are sitting is in a building, which is an object. It is separated from other buildings in the neighborhood by the space around and between them. The neighborhood itself is a Point, one of many neighborhoods, within the space of a city. The city is a Point, surrounded by the space of a continent which contains many other cities. The continent is a Point on the planet. Our planet is an object that is part of our solar system. Our solar system is a Point, which is part of our galaxy. Our galaxy is a Point, surrounded by the Universe. You can see that everything that is a Point is also a component of a bigger Point, which is a component of an even bigger Point. *Everything* is both itself, a whole, and also a part of a something else, another whole.

Every thing is a Point, and every thing is also made up of Points. Let's look at humans again. Our body is a Point. It is made up of organs, which are Points, with space between them. (If there was no jiggle room, we would be unable to move). Each organ is made up of cells, which are Points. Each cell is made up of molecules, and each molecule is made of atoms—which are all Points, all surrounded by space. Recall the diagrams of atoms from high school science, showing a nucleus with orbiting electrons. The particles are tiny, orbiting in huge amounts of space, just like planets orbiting in a solar system.

What connects all of these points, both inside and outside our body, is the space surrounding them. The three people in a room share the space of the room, which is connected to all the space in the neighborhood, on the planet, and inside of atoms. The objects may be seen as separate, but the space within and between every Point is shared. It is continuous from one part/whole to the next part/whole. Whether it is the space within a neighborhood or a human, within a solar system or an atom, it is all the same shared space. This continuous space is called the Zone, and it is the "place" where energy transfer occurs.

The Teachers are encouraging us to expand our energies into the space around us, into the Zone. The space between Points is where energy transfer occurs—energy transfer between humans, between humans and other sentient beings, between The Teachers and ourselves. This is the "place" where Spirit travels. It is not something that can be intellectualized, or figured out with the brain. It is felt as an intuitive vibration, and allowed as an act of creativity.

As we become aware of the energy in our bodies, and become aware of how we move that energy, we can be intentional in its vibration. We want to move positive energy without the expectation of return or reward. We want to move positive energy within ourselves and others because the act of doing so improves us. It is not just something to think about, it is something we do. It is an action. It is a lifestyle. The Teachers are encouraging us to engage in a life of spiritual purpose.

We are coming to the end of a long period when humans have prized rational and intellectual functioning at the expense of the creative and intuitive. Communication technologies and the realizations of a shared planet are turning us into global citizens. We are moving away from individual achievements and toward collaborative energies. This is the kind of movement that aligns with The Shift.

Universal Wisdom describes it this way: *People will need to learn how to talk with hearts—Honesty, Openness, Speaking Truth. These will all be necessary. Civil face-to-face dialogue will begin.*

You can begin your practice right now. Every time you are with another, think: Face-to-Face, Heart-to-Heart, and Spirit-to-Spirit, My

Center Meets Your Center in the Space Between Us. Reach deep, into that which you know is possible, and into that which you do not know. Accept the Mystery and let it guide you. Help yourself into the new world.

"We're on a mission from God." ~The Blues Brothers

~ 1 ~

The Nature of God and the Universe

There is a beautiful organization to our world. It is evident everywhere in Nature. No two snowflakes are alike, for example, but the creation of each one follows an underlying energy pattern. The source of this pattern remains a deep mystery and creates a fountain of human questions. What is God? Where do we come from? Why are we here? What happens when we die?

Organized religions attempt to answer these questions. Religions, however, are often constrained by history, group behavior, and political structures — they can limit spiritual evolution by reinforcing Ego. Individual growth can and does occur within religion, and it also occurs outside of it. Development of a spiritual identity without Ego requires a very broad perspective, because Spirit exists in a much larger context. Its realm is Nature, Life Force, Timelessness, and the Universe.

This chapter explores the nature of God and the Universe. The information is intended to help us expand our understanding of our place in the cosmos. It is an invitation to see ourselves, both individually and collectively, as companions of the Creator.

Before we begin, we need to recognize the importance of words as symbols. They borrow historic meaning from their linguistic stems, and create emotional attachments with their ongoing use. The meaning of some words can vary widely under different circumstances. The word "God" is one of those words. For those who have been harmed by organized religion, for example, God is a powerfully negative word. But it is still just a word. I use it because, unattached to religion, it is a term that Westerners immediately recognize as a deep reference to spirituality. Substitutes do not confer that depth. In my books, I use God as an inclusive word. It describes an immense collective of energies. The following conversation explores this broader definition:

I think of the Universe as the All, the Void, the Infinite Everything. And God is…the White Light of Love, Immeasurable Radiance…These words are just weak attempts at definition. How are they connected? Are God and the Universe the same?

Universal Wisdom: *No. They are not the same. There are some differences It is time to understand some of these differences. It is not so important to define them, but understanding a framework will aid comprehension in the future.*

First, we will talk about what God is. God is a force, a form of energy. God is all of the energies of living combined. Not just humans, but all living combined. And not just the present, but all lifetimes and layers combined. God is very powerful in this way. God is all of the knowing and also all of the unknowing, all of the action and all of the action not taken. It is why what you choose to think and feel and do is so important — it all adds into the whole which is God. It is constantly being formed. You are wondering if God is passive or active energy, and the answer is Yes. We will talk about that another time.

Right now, we want to focus on the relationship between God and the Universe. The Universe is Everything. It is the living and the nonliving and more than that as well. There is so much that humans will never see, because you are blinded by the dream of physical reality that you function in. This is not a problem, it is a gift, because there is so much richness to the experiences you share with God when you are in physical form. It can be a problem when you forget that there is existence beyond the physical dream. This is the process of addiction that was discussed in the first book.

The purpose of this work is to help people come back to the awareness of a world expanded beyond the physical dream. Not to discard the physical world, but to include it and move farther into other realms, across the veil. To develop the ability to cross the veil and come back, to share the wisdom gained and integrate it into the physical world — to impact the physical world with the wisdom gained from spiritual travel.

When spiritual travel occurs, the energy that you travel with is God. The "place" that you travel is the Universe. They are all interwoven, since God exists in the Universe and the Universe feeds God.

I am feeling a very intense sensation right now. It is something I call Love and Let Go — transcendence, but with much more energy. I am totally grounded and also highly expanded. It is energy concentrated through my belly, a psychic-physical energy that is distracted by intellect.

Spiritual travel is not an intellectual process. It is readily available to those who are already intellectually inhibited — animals, children, low-IQ and other mentally challenged individuals. Adults who have been socialized to worship the intellect have a harder time grasping the skills of spiritual travel. They must learn to let go of intellect, and develop other pathways in order to access the deeper functions of the mind.

What can be done to develop these pathways?

Regular practice — at least daily — which involves the movement of energy and increases the awareness of that movement. Walking, relating to Nature, T'ai Chi, yoga, dance, meditation, and many others. These are all well-known vehicles. They are useful if they are done with the awareness of energy and energy movement. Once you are connected to this awareness, it is not that far to move energy in spiritual travel.

It is important to realize that this is not something that you control. It is something that you allow. It involves surrender. When you are moving energy in this way, when you are traveling with God, you will receive feedback from the Universe.

I have noticed that sometimes when I relax and connect, a little image of a Buddha pops into my awareness. It is actually a Buddhist Lama, the Holy Man who came to me at the end of the last book. When I connect spiritually, he smiles. He is happy with my progress, happy to see me. I am happy to see him, I smile too and we both feel energy enriching around us.

This is feedback, of course. Very specific to you, because you are traveling already. For most people, it may not be so direct. It is important to recognize the sensation of connectedness, so that it becomes familiar, so that you can come back again and again.

Of course, it will change as the path becomes wider, but it is important to have a connecting place, something that tells you when you are there. A Home to return to. As you spend more time connected to this Home, it will become more and more obvious when you are not there. Being disconnected is uncomfortable. This is a good sign.

God is the energy of spiritual travel....That is amazingly simple and powerful. I believe that you can create an intention (sometimes called prayer), which at its root is about creating energy. It is creating and channeling energy into the Universe, not for a specific outcome, but adding to an energy manifestation. I can't be attached to the outcome. I just need to be ready to recognize the manifestation whenever and however it appears. I am creating an energy pathway and then traveling on it as it manifests.

Maybe that is why God is both passive and active — because there is the active creation of the pathway, and also the passive acceptance that the specific manifestation is out of my control. I actively accept something that feels like the energy fit I am opening to, the harmony of the energy vibration. Is there anyone to comment on this.

A'riquea:[3] *Yes. This is the area that I work with. I am involved with Intimacy, which describes connecting points of spiritual energy. Humans tend to think of intimacy in human terms, like sex, because that is the most immediate physical sensation. Intimacy is difficult for humans because it involves an intensity which few are skilled at managing. You gravitate towards it and are also frightened by it. The only way to become skilled in Intimacy is to approach it and learn about it. Mistakes will be*

---

[3]**A'riquea** is a beautiful young black woman with rosy cheeks. Her voice is soft and gentle. She often teaches me about intimacy and connecting the points of spiritual energy.

made, because that is one of the ways that learning occurs. Remember that Fear is a Tool.[4]

We can discuss that more another time. Right now you are interested in the nature of God energy. God is energy. As you know, God is not an entity or a personality—those are human constructs. God is energy. It is the energy of One Love, the movement of Life Force, the white light of Pure Radiance. It is beyond your capacity to comprehend in human form. Only when you are outside of human form can you truly join God.

That does not mean that you cannot experience God while you are in human form. You can, and you must. That is your Purpose—to find God's Pure Love on Earth. To use your physical form to move God energy. Through yourself and others. These are the connecting points I was talking about. To become capable of embodying this Love energy and moving it towards others. This energy movement is what is needed in the Universe.

One way to do this is through prayer. Unfortunately, "prayer" has become a passive concept. You may actively pray, for healing, for world peace, for a new job, but it ends there, with the act of creating the prayer. Praying may be active, but then it is just given away, it disperses into the Universe, passively awaiting the action of "God" to work on it. This is not the way it works.

Prayer creates an energy which must then be tended. It is true that you cannot direct the exact outcome, because this energy will come into contact with other energies along the way. Once you create it, it does not belong to you alone. This is why we have been talking about a sea change—many humans need to be doing this kind of work in order for the energy to hum up, to harmonize into a greater good. This is why it is so important to transfer the energy to others. You cannot just sit on your cushion and pray for a better world and then hope it happens. You have to pray on your cushion to get yourself centered and energized. Then you have to take that out in to the world and move it. Bring it along, keep

---

[4]*Grandmother Dreams*, p. 148: "Fear, itself, is not a bad thing. It can be a tool. The realization of fear is, literally, a call to attention—pay attention to what is happening and shift your attention, not away from it, but towards something else. Fear is a notice that disconnect is occurring. It is a reminder to reconnect. To reconnect, not with ego, but with Spirit."

it active and moving — taking compassionate action because it creates larger harmonies.

People can get all tangled up in compassionate action as a feather in their cap, a medal on their sleeve, a boost to their identity. But this kind of work is really about letting go of all these identities. Remember that the ego has to serve the spirit, not the other way around. So you use your physical form as the vehicle for moving spiritual energy. In order to do that, the physical form cannot be draining energy into itself, feeding the ego. Let your masks fall away. Let your spiritual core open up. Let your spiritual core be the point where God energy moves to and from the Universe. Be a point that concentrates energy by moving energy.

You cannot control this energy, you can only be a clear channel for its movement. The energy is God when it is moving. God is the movement of Love energy. You must be a clear point, which is passive. And you must move energy, which is active. So you see, God is both passive and active. You can Be God and you can never be God.

There is one more thing I would like to talk about. You may not understand this right now. That is fine. Just listen. I want to tell you about the End Times. Yes, I can sense your dread. You really do not want to hear about this. You can only think about destruction. But that is why you need to hear this.

The End Times are really a description of a spiritual way of being, not a physical Armageddon. One reason why many Christians are so threatened is because there will be an end to the power structure that has kept them in place. You can see this already, with the poisoning of the Catholic church around sexual abuse. The church cannot profess to embody the Love of Jesus and also turn a blind eye to victims. Other Christian churches are losing membership because the church's dogma has become an obstacle to the spiritual evolution of the masses.

Any movement toward spiritual growth must include the churches, not exclude them. This will be difficult for you if you have a negative reaction to Christianity. It will be important to focus on the commonalities: Jesus is Love. You do not have to take Jesus as your savior, but you do have to let Love into your heart. One can ask, "What would Jesus do?" and have it mean "How can I move Love?"

You have been thinking about the Bigger Tent, which is inclusive. This is a good direction. Many Christians, however, feel threatened by this because they have used the security of human-gospel to create an isolated bubble for their egos. All you can do is keep asking for Ego to be in service to Spirit. The church is a conglomerate of Ego, it is a human construct. Do not use "The Bigger Tent," because it has political implications. Use "The Bigger Church." Let go of your reaction to "church."

Do some dictionary look-up here, and talk about that.

There are multiple meanings for the word "church." I find I have many judgments about these concepts, but I'll go point by point and see where that takes me:

The first definition of church is a building or location. It could be for any religion, since it's where people worship together. It could be someone's home. It is very nice outdoors.

The next definition of church is a religious service. I start to get uncomfortable here, because I think of the "service" as a set of rote sayings. They could be a framework for growth, but more often seem to be a comforting ritual — I'll say this and you say that and aren't we all one big happy because we both know the lines. How the service is used is very important. Service to the church, or service to the greater good?

Next we get to church as the clergy. It's not a bad idea to have someone who is knowledgeable, who can be a teacher or consultant or guide. It seems dangerous, however, to believe that another human being is somehow closer to God, or that someone else has be a conduit for my own spiritual relationship with God. True spirituality is primarily personal.

Then we get to church as authority and also the aggregate of its followers. These describe the physical arrangement, the political structure, the human organization. This creates the religious family, with both the safety and dysfunction that that allows.

The dictionary also lists a common idiom — right church, wrong pew — which is used to indicate that somebody is correct in a general way but wrong in a particular way. A church is right in a general way when it's about Love and compassion. But it can be wrong in a particular way when it's about a specific religion — making it about who's right and who's wrong, my way or the highway. This is what fundamental religions seem to be about — more about The Church (exclusive) than the True Love of God (inclusive). One serves Ego, the other serves Spirit. In reality, they are probably both in operation, which is confusing to everyone.

I was raised in a Christian church, but got bogged down in the tangle of rules and egos that were running the show. My own spirituality was more fluid and expansive. I was connected primarily to the Spirit World, and often felt lost in the Physical World. It seemed that these were two separate things that could not be joined.

I had been influenced by the notion that physical manifestation is some kind of illusion, ready to disappear in a poof to make way for the reality of the Dream World. The Dream World seemed more attractive, because it was so inclusive and nonjudgmental, less harsh in terms of consequences — consequences like illness, injury, hunger, exclusion. It is important to realize that the Physical World and the Spiritual World are actually joined in the same moment in Space. They occupy the same Zone. It is all one together.

When the Physical and Dream worlds are concurrent, it means that the spiritual is present in all physical events. I had chosen to forget the pleasant things about the physical world — health, healing, growth, inclusion, intimacy. Was I experiencing more of the negatives because I was so much more willing to see them? Did I somehow imagine that we are here to experience suffering?

But our lesson isn't about suffering. It is learning how to place both suffering and pleasure in the context of the whole, and then return to a state of balance. That is seeing the Universe in everything. I would like to hear more about the integration of the physical and the spiritual, the Universe in everything.

Universal Wisdom: *There is much to talk about here, some things which you are not ready for yet. Today we will limit our discussion to the Universe. Look up Universe.*

The Universe has been expanding for about 13 billion years, and is believed to be at least 10 billion light-years in diameter. It is all of the existing matter and space — the whole ding-dang-deal, infinity, everything combined. The word comes from Old French or Latin, and is a combination of "uni-" (one) and "versus" (turned). What does that mean, "turned"?

It means that the One, who is known to you as God, is turned, turned inward into itself. Turned so that the radiance is concentrated and magnified, magnificence returned upon itself.

Each one of us is capable of this on an individual level, taking the radiance of the spiritual world into the core and returning it into the world, a cycling and recycling that increases its intensity and power. Made In the Image of God, made with the ability to concentrate and radiate spiritual energy. Made with the ability to heal and cleanse with the intensity of the White Light of Love, to take the rainbow of available energy and concentrate it into Radiance.

This is the action We are requesting. Crossing the Veil affords the opportunity to incorporate all of the light mediums. Maintaining the illusion of the physical world alone creates a limiting factor, excluding the full array. It is time to incorporate the Dream World in with the Physical World, to manifest the unity of the Universe in physical form. When this is accomplished on a grand scale, other worlds will be visible, other worlds that will illuminate the physical world in a way not seen today. These experiences cannot be demonstrated now, they are beyond the current abilities of Humankind.

Remember your own journeys across the Veil, when your body was disassembled and then returned. This is one of the ways that Humans will learn to travel, to experience Space in a more direct way. This kind of travel allows more Light to enter into the spaces of the physical body, to create a kind of healing and reorganization that will advance evolution. The spiritual needs to become integrated with the other planes of functioning, daily functioning.

You experienced the sickness of disconnection in humanity recently while you were in the airport. [It felt like a massive swarm of people just feeding their egos.] *There is a huge change to be made, a giant*

Shift. It is understandable that you feel overwhelmed by this task. Do not let that limit you in your work. Although you may feel isolated, you are not alone.

As you work, you will come into contact with others doing this and similar work. It is important to allow yourself to be supported, in whatever way that is offered. Some people can not be with you now because they have their own work. It may be useful to agree to support each other. Move carefully, in case time frames do not match up right now. Things come together when they will, not when you choose. Practice Trust and Patience. That is not the same as avoidance or procrastination. It is important to understand your own task and commit along that path.

I have to say that, even though I understand the directive, it feels a little like evangelism or proselytizing. What is the difference.

Those words have negative connotations because they are used in a religious context. They are an attempt to get other people to join an organized religion. There is no religion here, just personal spiritual practice. There is nothing to join, no dogma to accept, no authority to bow down to. There is only the spiritual experience. The movement of energy in a spiritual dimension. The inclusion of the spiritual in the physical world, the integration of the dream with the waking, walking the road of Love.

This is all for now. Move about in the physical world, go outside and walk, integrate this learning into your physical body.

～

If the Universe is Everything, is that where we come from? How is it that we enter into physical form? A friend of mine was present when her mother passed on. She described a grimace on her mother's face, which transformed "like the northern lights" and then relaxed. She also described the sound her mother made, which was a moaning similar to that made by women pushing a baby out during birth. These are obvious parallels between birth and death.

It reminded me of my own psychic trips through the tunnel towards the white light, the physical disassembly that occurred as I went through. I am wondering if the tunnel is the same, just going different directions. I am also reminded of the indigenous practice of keeping a spirit fire at both a birth and a death, to assist the spirit in its passage.⁵ If the spirit enters when a baby is born, why wouldn't it also be present in the womb? Is there someone to talk about this.

Healing Indian Grandmother:⁶,⁷ *The Spirit is present in the child in the womb, but it is not well attached, because the baby is in a dream state, sleeping, and spending much time in the Spirit World. It is contact with the outside environment, after birth, that encourages the spirit to make its home in the body. The Spirit Fire encourages the spirit to stay in the body. It is a beacon to the physical world. Not just the fire itself, but the intent of those who light and keep the fire, making a commitment to the responsibility of safe-guarding and supporting the spirit on its physical journey.*

A baby is in a vulnerable state, completely dependent on others to support its physical existence. This is also why it is so important that a baby be nursed whenever possible—the mother's milk feeds the baby's spirit by giving it energy from the mother's body, making spirit connections. The connections come through the milk itself, but also through contact with the mother's body.

The mother's heartbeat is the first drum that the baby hears and feels. As you know, the drum moves Life Force. Moving Life Force keeps it clear and energized. Life Force maintains its vibrancy through movement. A baby's body is not organized enough to do this on its own. It needs the mother's heart as a reminder, as a mover. It needs the mother's milk for spiritual replenishment. It needs the commitment of the firekeepers to maintain its Home. This will place a baby well on this earth, prepared for the journey of Life. This is part of your work, to bring this practice

---

⁵In some indigenous cultures, a ceremonial fire is lit when a woman goes into labor, and maintained for a prescribed number of days after the birth. A similar fire is maintained when a person dies. It can be seen as a kind of portal to the Spirit World. Parallels in Western culture might be prayer vigils or wakes.

⁶There are several terms used to identify the people who were already in North America when Europeans arrived. Politically correct labels vary over time and geography. I use the term 'Indian' because, as of this writing, the indigenous people I know prefer that term

⁷**Healing Indian Grandmother** is a short, indigenous woman from the Southwest. Healing is her lifework.

back to The People. It is not the only work being done, but this is part of your work.

A'riquea had more to add to this:

Humans are on an interesting journey. You start out coming from the Spirit World. Your physical body grows around your spirit while you are in your mother's womb. This is your first opportunity to be bathed, in physical form, in the Love of God. It is something that Spirits desire, the opportunity to feel this. It is why you choose to come in.

The developing baby is open to this experience in every way. Other energies impact the baby as well: the mother's feelings, and energy from the environment around the mother. These kinds of effects continue during the birth and after the baby is born. There is always an interplay between the baby's energy and the energy around it. This interplay continues throughout a person's life.

One reason that Life is made this way is so that each person can have a unique energy impression. No two people will be the same. Everyone has gifts and losses. Your work while you are in human form is to use your unique energy impression in the best way possible. This involves finding your spiritual passion and expressing it through compassion. The way in which you make your way through your own unique energy maze leaves an energy impression on the Universe. This is what is meant when it is said that your learning goes back to the One. Everything that everyone is learning in physical form is available in the infinite energy field of the Universe. You contribute to it and you are bathed in it. You have access to it. There is not a separate individual in the world. The energy is in constant motion.

Humans are often distracted by the desires of the physical form. This kind of information is like chatter, like static on a radio station. In order to access the inclusive field of all energy, humans will need to find themselves in the field of All-That-Is. This is like tuning in to a radio station. You are more likely to be a good listener if you are a clear channel.

You are wondering where love fits into this. Little-L love is the opportunity for humans to express and receive the vibration of Love. There really is no difference between the two. Humans, however, are always practicing. Mistakes are made. The love/Love is given and withdrawn, it bathes and then dries up. The challenge of the receiver is to be open to the Love of others, and then to stay open even when it is removed. The ego tends to see the removal as a personal threat, and tries to build protection against the pain that is felt.

Everyone, on their human journey, has to figure out how to become open to the Love of the Universe. This is the greatest Love, and it is unconditional. It is always present. Once this is experienced, it is easier to forgive the imperfections of other humans. Early unconditional love from a parent or caregiver boosts a baby's ability to recognize spiritual Love. This can also be a barrier to discovering Universal Love in adulthood, if the person comes to believe that this Love always comes from another person.

Only under significant circumstances can another human provide truly unconditional love. Being parented without unconditional love can encourage a child to put up barriers, but it can also enhance the ability to find spiritual Love in the Universe, outside of their strings-attached relationships with others. So you see, it is not that one way is better than the other. It is up to each person to find their way within their own circumstances. The circumstances are all different. The outcome — opening to spiritual Love — is the same.

This is a good application of the One Mountain idea: some people are walking, some are riding a donkey, but everyone is climbing the same mountain. We cannot judge others for the way they are traveling. We can smile when we meet them on the way. Have joy in your heart at the opportunity to make this journey. Believe. In the Love of the Universe, and in the journey that opens to it.

Babies are born into the world as spirit beings. As children grow, their free and exuberant energy shows us that they are still clearly connected to the Spirit World. It seems unfair that some children's lives are so difficult — neglected, unsupported, abused. All children need our support and Love. I was wondering about that, wondering about childhood, and this is what I heard:

Universal Wisdom: *Childhood is a Dream. It is a continuation of the before-birth dream. After birth, it is a series of Now moments.*

Children live in the Now. Adolescence is a waking up from that dream. It is the realization that the Now moments add up. Without spiritual guidance, adolescents can be trapped into social definitions of what it is to be Human. These social definitions are a kind of surface identity.

One of our tasks is to sort through our childhood and make adjustments. There are two sides to the coin of childhood: joys and losses. It is important to hold to the edge, which is Life. We connect to others' lives when we see that we all have joys and losses. When we celebrate the opportunity to feel both joys and losses, we are accepting the gift of physical manifestation. Then we can use the sensations of these feelings to foster compassion and Love, and we can take compassionate action to make a better future for today's children Now.

It cannot be stressed enough that spiritual experiences form the basis of healthy living. Children need to be touched by the world of Nature, a world that accepts them as they are. Adolescents need to be able to place themselves in context, to know that each person has purpose and meaning. Adults are responsible for creating the environments where these things occur. Elders provide guidance for all. This is the way that harmony is established. The current structures are out of balance. Too many people, at every stage, are being encouraged to feed their own egos.

Remember that the ego is a vehicle for movement of the spirit. It is a means, not an end. Spirit makes the choices, and Ego carries out those choices. Humans need to be rethinking their place in the Universe. Humans need to see themselves in context. There is a hunger for this way of living. Every decision needs to be based on the needs of your children's grandchildren.

The number of responsibilities that are presented to us in the physical world can be overwhelming. It is easy to become lost in a barrage of decision-making, and I often wish for a simpler life.

Universal Wisdom: *This is how the world turns. You would like to have some down time, some time when you don't have to cope with transformation. You do have that, you just don't see it. It is in all of the moments between the changing. It is in the changing itself. It is the present.*

What tires you out is worrying about the future. Or linking your present to your past. Staying in your belly is about being in the present.

The Now Moment. It is the only thing that is true and definable. The rest is all just being created by your perception.

The gift of understanding that the Now Moments add up is that you have the opportunity to be aware that you can affect your Now by being in it, or not. The more you avoid the Now, the farther away you get from being able to be present. Then you have less influence on the bigger picture that is all of the Now Moments added up. Choosing to be present in the Now means that you are making the best use possible of your energy and your intention.

You can belong to the bigger picture of your life by owning every moment that goes into it. You will have no regrets if you have been fully present. You will embrace the future if you see that it can be as beautiful as the Now. The Now exists in your center, your core. It is the gateway to the Universe. It is the movement of energy between Points. Points that are within you and Points that are in other dimensions. This is the focus of the third book. Before you can do this, you will need to practice being present in the moment, in the Now. Because that is the springboard for moving in other dimensions.

There is breath, and physical movement, and interaction with others, and it is all occurring in the Now. Be present to it. Be. Practice centering in your belly.

Our lifetime is a continuation of our spiritual existence before we took on a physical body, and also the aggregate of choices made while we are in a physical body. What happens, then, when we let go of our body?

A friend was distraught at the recent death of someone close to them. After posing the question to several clergy, who had no real answer, the person asked me: where did my friend go? Basically, what happens after you die? My immediate thought was that the physical elements of the body lose their integrity and begin disintegrating, releasing Life Force.

But where does the Life Force go? Into the Zone? How does it get picked up again? If the person I am dissolves, how can there be Spirits or Teachers who are reaching me across the Veil? I understand that they are presenting themselves with a form I can comprehend, but how is it that they have personalities?

Universal Wisdom: *There are many levels to the Life Force that make up a human, a spirit-walking journey. Remember that a human is a journey, an action. It is the traveling of a spirit on the human path. So there is the Life Force of the spirit and there is the Life Force of the physical body. As was discussed another time, the body itself is many spirits—many cells and cell components and molecules, each with their own Life Force. So there is the physical effect, at death, of the body losing its place in the music, no longer able to harmonize and communicate with itself. The separate instruments that make up the band no longer play together. They move apart and can continue to play separately, although this does not have the greater harmonic effect of playing together. The separate instruments go back in to The Zone.*

(That is why it is so important to keep the physical body tuned up and in good health—the components want to play together in physical form in such a way that they are in clear contact with the Zone, where they came from and where they have the cleanest connections, unhindered by physical effects such as gravity.)

When the physical body disintegrates (dis-integrates), the components return to The Zone. This is the easiest part of death to understand. Humans are exposed to birth and death in the physical world. Physical death is observable. Death is understood as one thing ceasing to Be. But there is, as we discussed above, more than one "thing" involved.

A human life is a series of choices. Each choice, conscious or unconscious, creates an energy effect in the Universe. Humans are making choices all day every day. Some of them seem small, some very large, in terms of the effect they have. But it is all additive. "Personality" is not just the material, the baggage that one starts out with, it is also the accumulation of choices over time. Each choice leads a person down a path of their own making. Certainly, humans are born into an environment of circumstance, but they make choices within that environment.

Remember the contract you come in with: to keep shining under the circumstances. Everyone does their best. Some are more skilled than others. The challenge is to see through the temptation to be passively directed by all that exists around you, and to recognize yourself as your own creator. And then to make positive choices that will move you on your spirit path. A lifetime of choices create an energy pathway that is unique to each person. When the person "dies," when their physical body can no longer support a physical presence, there remains an energy pathway that is unique to the individual. This energy pathway joins the multiple dimensions of The Zone. As the physical form falls away, it loses the baggage of the Ego. This is when the spirit becomes enlightened (en-light-en-ed—it becomes lighter in physical weight but it also releases personality). A good example of this is when Peter came to you after he died. Talk about that.

My friend Peter avoided his Earthly pain by using alcohol, and this destroyed his physical body at a young age. He came to me a few days after his death. He was very happy to have been released from the pain of his physical body, he was giddy with the thrill of it. And he was also able to clearly see the opportunity he had missed in human form. He told me that our true purpose in life is to "find God's Pure Love on Earth."

I gained more understanding into what happens when we die, when I was given the gift of witnessing of my own mother's passage. Here is how it happened:

I was informed of my mother's death while I was on a multi-state bus trip with 50 high school students. Her death was completely unexpected. She had Parkinson's and was receiving supportive care in a nursing home, but her disease was not advanced and she had not been recently sick. In the space of one or two minutes, she just died, and no one really knew what had happened.

When I heard the news I felt a sudden, strange shift in reality. I needed to be alone. The only place I could go was the toilet cubicle in the bus, where I stood for half an hour, praying and centering. By the time I got home and left again to be with my family, all of the funeral planning had been done. I'd come in to the process late. I hadn't had any time with my mother's body before she was embalmed, and I felt a strong need to be where she had last been present.

Late that night, after everyone else had gone to bed, I went to my mother's empty room at the care center. I closed the door and laid on her bed. I cried a little, but mostly I was struck by my mother's view from that bed. It did feel like prison, which she sometimes called that place. I was glad that she was done with it and that her exit had been mercifully fast.

While I was lying there I began to see her form, dimly, up in the air. She seemed unaware that I was there. She had her hands out in front of her, and she was looking at them, looking at the palms, as if they were something foreign that she was trying to figure out. She was gently turning around in circles, as if she was dancing with her hands. As I lay there watching her, she came down to me and began brushing my legs, from my hips down to my feet with whispery sweeping motions. It was clear that I should move my energy into meditative Love and Let Go, transcendence, which I did.

After I had meditated for a short while, my mother became a wispy concentration of white transparent vapor. I have seen other spirits leaving their bodies, while working as a nurse and an EMT. My mother's appearance was similar. She was a vague misty cloud about the size of a human, but shaped like an elongated teardrop, with a condensed and rounded "head" leading and a wispy tail trailing as it moved.

My mother's spirit traveled out of the room and went down the hall along the ceiling. It came back to me and went down the hall again, many times. She seemed to be asking me to come along. I wasn't done in the room yet—I knew that I would never be coming back, so I stayed a little while, touching and smelling her clothes. All the while, my mother's spirit continued to travel back and forth between the room and the elevator.

When I left the room I closed the door, and let her lead me. I opened the heavy hall door and made sure her spirit got through it. We stood together waiting for the elevator, and when it came I made sure she was on it before the doors closed. We traveled together through a maze of connected hallways on the way to the building where I was staying. It was night time, dark, quiet.

Several times I wondered if I was imagining my mother's spirit, if I was making it up. Just like meditating for channeled writing, when I doubted the experience it left me. When I meditated and trusted, it was there. I couldn't look directly at her spirit, but I was aware of it and its movements out of the corner of my eye — zooming along the ceiling of the hallways. I made sure she made it through every locked door. When we got to my building, I realized that she was going to see my dad.

In the elevator of his building, she began to materialize. I saw her standing in the corner, looking much younger and wearing the blue and white coat that she often wore when traveling. She looked relaxed and unconcerned, but also somewhat curious about her surroundings, as if she was trying to figure out her presence there. She wasn't communicating directly with me, but I was able to see her because I was in a meditative state.

When we got to the door of my dad's apartment, she became agitated. She was desperate to see him but didn't know how to get in. She had materialized and did not know how to get back to her spirit form. I sure didn't know, either. I showed her the wide crack under the door, telling her that she would need to get in that way. It was well after midnight. I didn't want to knock on the door and wake my dad at that hour, trying to explain what was happening. And I was completely exhausted myself. So I left my mom crouching by his door, encouraging her to figure it out on her own, and I went to bed.

The next day was the funeral. On the way there I saw her in the car, sitting in the back seat next to me in her materialized form, again wearing her traveling coat. We did not interact. She had that same relaxed and curious affect as the day before, when I first saw her. She was looking out the window at the world, detached from it. During the funeral I saw her in her white wispy spirit form, above her casket, way up in the church's cathedral ceiling. Her spirit form was lighter and less dense than the day before. It was flying up there like a bird.

The next time I saw her was the following day, in her hometown, at the mausoleum where her physical body was to be interred. Her casket was to be placed in a drawer there, near her parents, with an empty place waiting next to her for her husband. While our family was there, the casket was placed in the front of a little chapel, with a high ceiling and tall glass windows looking out over a beautiful scene of summer trees. During the brief service, I saw her spirit form near the ceiling, above her casket. It was even lighter then, barely visible.

At the end of the service I saw her spirit outside the window, in the sky just above the roof of the chapel. It hung there briefly, and then there was a sudden silent transformation. Her spirit form dissolved into millions of tiny, shiny particles, like crystal glitter. The glittery particles floated together, and then one by one they disappeared. Like little lights winking out, they were being reabsorbed into the Universe. The last I saw, there were a only few left. I knew they would all soon be gone.

My mother walked on in the spirit world. My own interaction with her was minimal. I only helped her to leave her room at the care center. After that she managed it all herself. Because I was open to it, I was gifted with witnessing her passing into timeless eternity. It was beautiful and easy. Peaceful.

~

Apparently, not everyone who leaves the physical plane makes a clear transition to the Spirit World. One night, as I was lying in bed waiting for sleep, a grandmother I had never met (who passed a half century ago) came to see me. She wanted me to go with her. Her face was continuously morphing into a black-and-white mask. She was trying to keep her "normal" face in place, but the mask kept appearing.

My grandmother took me by the hand and led me into a black mist. I was not sure it was a good idea to go into that black mist. Every other time I have crossed the veil, I went into a white mist. This black mist was thick, smoky, sooty. Grandmother was insistent. Eagle Brother, my husband in the Spirit World, was nearby. He looked skeptical, but I went ahead and followed my grandmother. She led me through the black mist into a giant cave.

The cave was crowded with many thousands of other beings wearing masks. The masks were all black-and-white designs, stylized dogs and other animals, constantly morphing in shape. The throng of beings ringed a large opening in the floor of the dark cave, maybe

100 feet across. In the middle of this opening was a giant fire, with flames shooting up toward the high ceiling. The beings were drawn to the flame, but kept their distance from it. They were milling at the fire's edge, mumbling and groaning.

Through some invisible communication, I became aware that these beings were lost souls, and the flame was The Fire of Lost Souls. I was somewhat distressed to realize that my grandmother was a lost soul. I kept asking how a soul could become lost, but there was no answer. I stood with her at the edge.

Then, I don't know why, but I leapt headfirst into that fire. I was engulfed in a feeling of freedom, and came out of the flames shiny and burnished, like a statue of a Buddha. While I was in the fire, I could see my hands glowing green, something I have been shown in other visions — that there is a gift in my hands. When I came out of the fire my hands continued to glow green, but were also covered in the black mist.

I came out of the cave and my Eagle Brother was there, lying on his back in the clouds with his arms folded behind his head, a playful smile on his face. He seemed amazed that I would have risked going into the fire and amused at my return unhurt. His smile said: see how you are, fearless and strong. He showed me how to use an edge of broken glass to scrape the black mist from my hands.

While Eagle Brother was helping me, my grandmother flung herself headfirst into the fire. She did not come out. I could see her in there, and she was smiling. Something was happening that was helping her. Maybe she also had the feeling of freedom that I had? I want to ask: how does a soul get lost.

Healing Grandmother: *A soul gets lost when it is detached from the body at death. You are thinking that that is what death is, when the soul leaves the body. It is not quite so simple as that.*

The Spirit is in the body during Life, it comes and goes during sleep and other travels. The Spirit is attached to other worlds while it is in the body. It is in many places simultaneously. The Soul and the Spirit are not the same thing. Remember that the Soul is the path that the Spirit is traveling. It is a much larger energy. One of the tasks of manifesting as a Human is to learn to live a spirit-serving life. When that occurs, the path of the Spirit will be streamlined. The Spirit will travel its Soul Path in a way that provides clear energy for other dimensions.

Sometimes there is a disconnect from the soul path. This can happen in several ways. The Spirit may miss the track, the path, when it leaves the body. It may be distracted or disabled at the time of the transition. It is not generally something that is chosen.

What you witnessed at The Fire of Lost Souls is not a permanent location. It is an opportunity in Space, an opportunity for Souls to regain the path. You were able to leap into The Fire and come out again because you are not a Lost Soul at this time. Your grandmother has been lost for many years. She needed you to come with her to The Fire. A healing has taken place. This will vibrate along your ancestral lines. It will help you in your own healing, although you will not see it for some time.
Rest now.

~

When I am at pow-wow, I feel my spirit traveling the soul path. I am living outdoors, in an environment of respect and honor for the Earth and all beings, dancing and socializing. After a few days, the drumming and singing enters my bones.

Eagle Brother[8] came to me one night at pow-wow, after everyone had gone to bed and it was very quiet. I saw him disappear ahead of me through a hole in the darkness, and he asked me to follow him. We came out of a tunnel into a cave. Migizii Niikaan crossed the cave and climbed up onto a high shelf of rock on the other side. He asked me to follow. The shelf was a resting place for the ancestors, the ones who had passed on. What was left there were their bones.

Migizii Niikaan carefully handed me a long bone. The bone guided me to move it. I held the bone horizontally and pressed it to my forehead. I brought it to my lips and kissed it. I held it across my chest, my heart. I held it at my belly. Then I turned it vertically, and held it against my shin. It matched my shin, and I knew that

---

[8]**Migizii Niikaan** (**Eagle Brother**) is my spiritual husband. The story of that marriage is told in Chapter 5.

my own bones are the same as these bones. My bones are the gifts of my ancestors. I held the bone even with the ground, along my foot, and knew that when I am dancing, my ancestors are dancing also.

Bones are an amazing part of the body. They are the hardest elements, and provide the structure of the skeleton, while at the same time their soft insides create our blood. Bones are also the permanent part of the body — when a person passes on and the body disintegrates, the bones are what remain. When I practice energy movement in the morning, I am aware of white energy being created and emitted through my bones.

Migizii Niikaan is before me, with his arms folded across his chest, one hand stroking his chin. He is looking at me thoughtfully. The hand on his chin points to the typing keys.

What you want to know are things that cannot be shared right now. I took you to the bones because it is important that you understand the respect required in dancing. You have come to this in steps. First you understood the energy movement of turning the circle. This year you felt the shift, the gratitude for being alive.[9] Now you will think about the gifts of your ancestors, and how to honor them in a good way. Life is short. It is important to enjoy it and use it well.

I want you to know this: I want you to know that when this life is done, you will want to know why you did not appreciate it more. This is the reason that people are afraid to die. Their spirit knows that this is a limited opportunity. It seems so hard, but really it is so simple. To Love. That is all there is. To Love.

He motions to me that we are done. He smiles, and jumps a little to his left, his head breaking the surface of something that appears to be water, even though it is a vertical surface. His body follows his head, splashing through that surface. He smiles and waves to me as he swims upward in the water. I am watching him go, as through a

---

[9]As I danced in the circle that year, I felt the familiar turning of the circle and the healing of my body. After several rounds, however, I also began to feel a huge gratitude for the opportunity to be on this Earth. I danced with joy and appreciation. I usually hear "kiss, kiss, kiss..." as my toes touch the earth in front of me. This time, I heard "thank, you, thank, you, thank you..."

plate glass window. He swims up in the water. When he reaches that surface he breaks through into the sky and becomes the bald eagle. The eagle flies upward, continuing the journey. The eagle flies higher and higher, until he comes to the divider between sky and space. The eagle bursts through that divider in flames, and I see the white wisp of smoke that I have seen when other spirits leave their human bodies. The wisp of smoke remains visible momentarily, and then dissipates. There is only the night sky then, full of stars.

And here I am, standing on what I think of as the surface of the Earth, which is really the bottom of an ocean of air. And the only thing I have to do is To Love.

~

According to the Teachers, we have a purpose during our time here. We come into this world with a contract, to Love as much as possible. We have good intentions, but then we get distracted by the physical world, where we have to learn to function.

I have to wonder how specific the contract is. Do we actually choose the kind of experiences we will have while we are here? Or is it all just a giant flow, created by everyone's constant choosing, and we make use of opportunities for learning? If all of the Life Force we create goes back to God, where do we come from before we come here? So many questions! Is there someone who could speak about this. *We are wondering why you think that you need this information. How will it help you?*

I can't believe that our lives are so minutely orchestrated, so predestined, that we would be given a specific lesson to learn from, and that that is happening continuously to everyone on the planet at the same time.

That kind of thinking just seems to create a vehicle for guilt — if I have been given this pain for a reason and I don't figure that out, then I am not doing my job. It implies that if I could just figure out the lesson then I wouldn't be given this pain — pain is a punishment. It seems to me that pain is just part of living. It is the loss and grieving of physical living.

A'riquea: *Suffering is not a punishment. Suffering happens because hu-*

mans feel a certain kind of permanence from living in the physical world. There is the appearance of solidity, and Time—the focus of the Points. When this illusion is shattered, it is disappointing. It would be less disappointing if humans could focus on Space, because then the Points would be seen as relative and un-fixed.

It appears complex, although really is not. It is very simple, but difficult to comprehend when thinking is limited to a linear pattern of Points. Space is the Home you seek. Humans have a great deal of focus on the material world. You will experience greater health when you are able to return beyond the five senses, to place yourself in Space.

You are putting the "Contract" into a linear pattern—a contract like you would sign for legal purposes in the human world. But you will have to be able to understand the dimension of Space if you are to understand the contract. The contract is a connection between Points. Not so much about the joining of the points, although that occurs, but the points themselves are not fixed. They are moving energy points.

Think of a shoal of fish. Each fish is a moving point, but the shoal of fish is itself a moving point made up of fish. Each individual fish is also made up of energy points, or "pixels" (such as organs, cells, atoms, etc), which are actually prisms. The fish together in a shoal make an energy prism, and the shoal is a prism in something even bigger, like the ocean. It goes on and on, in both directions, infinitely. That is why the points cannot be the only focus. There is also the energy that joins them, like a rainbow arching through Space. And there is not just one rainbow between any two points, but infinite rainbows. Luminous threads, weaving the Universe. The contract has to do with these threads.

Recognize the looping thread of energy that is your life. Your current place on the loop, this lifetime, is like a cocoon on the thread. The looping luminous thread of Life is Soul Path. Except that since you are made of many beings in many lifetimes, the inheritance of genetic material, you are the coming together of many luminous threads. The ancient teachers talked about this with Carlos Castaneda's Don Juan.

The contract is a journey, it is the traveling of the light. It is not so much the light or the path, but the motion. You are a Spirit Walking Journey. A Spirit is walking in the human world, and you are the journey made by that walking. You come with the intention of making a Holy Journey, a pilgrimage of sorts, to create Life Force while you are in physical form. The physical form, however, creates many obstacles that make this Holy Walk difficult. But Life Force created while in the physical form has much power, and that is why the Journey, the contract if you will, is undertaken.

And, as you already know, the Life Force to be created is Love. That is the purpose unique to human form, why humans have importance in the Universe. The presence of physical consciousness makes the creation of Love possible. Love, Compassion in Action. You feel most spiritually alive when you are on The Journey.

∽

When Life Force is in motion, luminous energy pathways are created. In a teaching vision, I was shown these pathways in my own body. The threads were long, graceful, and floaty—reaching out into the world like fly-fishing line cast out into the breeze. The energy threads originated from energy spools in my joints and my chakras.

The threads need to be free and traveling, and this cannot happen when the spools are immobilized. Where the spools in my body were snarled up, my energy was restricted. Those spools were like thread in a sewing basket, with the loose tails all tangled up together. The tangled threads limited the movement of the spools.

The biggest snarl was in my abdomen, right around my navel. When I placed my attention there and loosened up the energy, the spools wove a beautiful golden mat, an indigenous design, round and rich. I heard it being called a "God's Eye." It was six or seven inches in diameter, glowing like threads of gold in the sunlight. I saw another smaller Eye at my forehead, about an inch around. Looking again at my navel, I heard the words: when you see this again you will know where you are. It is some kind of energy point. I'm not sure what to make of this. Does anyone have a comment.

The Grandmothers' Circle:[10] *You do not need to understand everything*

---

[10] **The Grandmothers' Circle** is a group of women who have supported me in the healing of significant trauma. In my visions, I often find them at a fire circle in the

about this to know it is a power wheel—when it spins, you will be able to experience new energies. The location of the wheel is the same as the connection to what some call the Universal Mother, but that is a laden term. Especially in your case, we can sense your distrust.

Think of it as being connected to The Void, the place where everything ultimately comes from. You are capable of that connection, and it is very powerful because it connects you to every thing, including every one. It is not "just" on the spiritual plane, either. You have somehow decided that these are separate, when of course they cannot be. We exist in many worlds simultaneously. If you are disconnected in one dimension, then you are disconnected in others.

You are correct, that part of your disconnect is currently "chemical," that you are going through the unpredictable changes of menopause. But these "chemicals" are not the cause. They are changes that you have not yet adjusted to. Energy shifts. You are actually coming into a powerful time of your life, but the upheaval required to get there is unsettling. Keep paying attention. Don't get too wrapped up in any one thing—that is where the snarls of energy threads get started, because you focus your energy there.

You need to find a way to stay centered, a way to let things flow by you. Not without your attention, but without the emotional attachments. It would be a good time to get as much sleep as possible, to let your spirit do its work in concentration during that time. Let go of some of the details, especially at work, and just enjoy people and relationships and Space. Cultivate Space. Be happy for the things you have, especially whatever time you have with your children. Don't work so much around them—play with them!

And what about the God's Eye.

Right now, be an observer. You will be shown.

I wonder who has spoken to me tonight.

We're all here, the Angels you wish for.

Now I am crying, to find that there really is support in the world for me. I knew that, but now I feel it. It's not easy to let myself believe

---

forest. The circle appears deserted, but when I seat myself, when I take my place, the Grandmothers instantly appear.

it, because that would mean that I could lose it—which reveals my own fear and mistrust.

You don't have to trust for Us to be here. You don't have to think that you deserve Us. Angels are dancing in the Eye of God. Always. Let Us in. Don't just do it for yourself, do it for Everyone. Let Us in. This is your connection to The Void, inside and out.

And when I breathe and let it happen, they are in all of the space, Continuous Space, inside and out.

∾

I began to realize that the spools, the source of the luminous thread energy, the place where the angels dance, was in my cells. The spools were generating strands of DNA, constantly unwinding and sending flags into the world. It was important for the spools be able to spin, to move and flow.

One night, I was lying in bed thinking about Carlos Castaneda's discussion of filaments.[11] These energy filaments are connecting dimensions and are present all around us. He spoke of a joining point in the back of our bodies where the filaments meet, in each person, called the assemblage point. As I thought about the filaments joining behind my own back, I was suddenly able to sense them. They were shooting out of the back of my body, golden, joining at the assemblage point. It was almost like lying on a bed of nails, although it was not painful—I was aware of the energy from every luminous thread. The filaments joined, at the assemblage point, from my own body and also from the Universe.

I would like to ask about the threads and the spools and anything related to that.

Universal Wisdom: *It is correct that the threads are related to DNA, but it would be limiting to think that they are the DNA itself. The function of DNA is to carry and tell the story of Life. That story is not static. It is changing all of the time in response to interactions with the environment. In part, this is what has supported evolution.*

As you know, nothing evolves on its own. There have to be things for

---

[11]Castaneda, Carlos. *The Art of Dreaming*, New York: Harper Collins, 1993.

it to eat, which have to be evolving at the same time. And there have to be other things as well, like interplay with germs, parasites, predators, and toxins, that are not so strong as to wipe out the organism but enough to strengthen it. And there also must be things that feed the organism, like sunshine and fresh air and nutrients and others to reproduce with. All of those factors, helpful and harmful, are evolving too. It is all dancing together.

Every time a thread is cast into the world, it interacts with the world and sends information back to the spools. The spools sense the information and make adjustments. The spools want nothing more than to keep sending forth information and to make adjustments. That is their purpose. That is Life Force in motion.

The spools can be shut down, or at least limited in their ability to spin and be free, by too many negative experiences. Or, in many cases, by the perception that experiences are negative. Perception involves the complexity of reacting and the process of learning. Negative perceptions can be unlearned. This is something that you are just discovering, that it is possible to change direction and learn a new way to see things. Your negative perceptions have clamped down the expression of the spools. Not completely, for then you would die. But you have created many slow deaths of spool behavior by choosing to continue negative thought patterns.

Think of the spinning of the spools. Say that a positive direction is the way the sun turns. (You could call that clockwise, but that is a very limited description of this spinning. More on this later, but it is like the difference between a circle and a sphere in dimensionality.) Relative to each other, positive is one direction and negative is another. Exerting negative energy slows the positive spin, like putting the brakes on. If enough spools are limited in their spin, then this will affect the kind of experiences that are possible, because under the braking effect fewer threads are set free. Or their range is limited.

When the threads are infinite in their movement, then joy is felt. Freeing the movement of the threads will bring you into greater contact with other Life Force energies. And this is your purpose — expanding Life Force. You have felt the expansiveness of the thread reaching out towards the possibility of human love. Imagine the effect of multitudes of threads moving that way in the Universe.

There are infinite multitudes of threads traveling through the Zone. The assemblage point is a way of concentrating connection with them. The threads are what does the traveling in the Zone. Points are places where they concentrate. True Life Force does not stop in the Points, Points are places that it moves through. Movement is key. Traveling in the Zone, Movement in the Sea. That is why Life is constant change. It has to move. There is constant interaction. The spools want to express Life.

Remember your admiration of the plants in your garden, how much desire there is in their growing, and your love and tending is all it takes to help them blossom and fruit more fully. The spools want to express Life. Let them. Help them. Love them.

I would like to hear more about the spools.

First, be aware of the spinning. See how it feels when the spools are spinning freely.

It feels like a turning. When I allow them to spin counter-clockwise, I become free and expansive. This is the Let Go part of the simultaneous Love (center) and Let Go (open) in my meditation. I feel a deep sense of well-being and connection with the Universe, with Universal Love. I can make the turning go the other way, putting on the brakes and shutting down. I begin feeling disconnected and anxious. Then the energy moves up and out of my pelvis, straining upwards toward my head. Head space. It feels tight, restricted, a clamping down or closing in of energy. This seems to be the opposite of what was said about sunwise (clockwise) being positive.

It doesn't matter which direction is which, as long as you know which direction frees Life Force for you. This is your homework, to practice this. Practice releasing the threads when possible. Your threads want a direction, but not necessarily a landmark. A landing point would define and limit its travel. Practice not-knowing. Having a landmark can come later. What you are practicing is allowing the travel, putting something forth without expectation or control. Let the threads travel. Let your Being travel with the filaments.

Once I began to practice this, I became interested in related metaphysical ideas. I started reading about the Theory of Everything, a concept that would explain the intersection of general relativity and quantum mechanics — something that has, so far, been elusive to scientists. I also read about String Theory, which seems like a parallel to Castaneda's filaments. As I was reading, I could see the Library Man getting very excited.

Library Man:[12] *This is very important information. It is not easy to distill it into a few thoughts, because everything is so connected, and related. You will listen while I talk, because you cannot be interrupting with questions about things you do not understand right now.*

I am struggling to stay well connected — some of it is lack of practice, most of it is physical imbalance....

Yes, well, you have asked and let us go ahead.

So. What these mathematicians and physicists and other scientists are interested in is some kind of Unifying Theory, something that ties it all together in a neat equation that explains all of the complexities at once. This is admirable, because it is possible. Everything is possible, of course.

There is something to learn from this. What we want to learn is how to make these connections that take us further into the Universe. And we would have to describe the Universe going both inward and outward from the human perspective, the Universe being absolutely everything that there is — a daunting task. It requires that the observer somehow be removed from the equation. That is why this kind of learning, across the veil, is so important. Because you can receive information that does not come through your own ego.

The thing that I want to talk about today is Light. This is critical. Light is currently seen as a visible effect of energy. Some of it is visible, yes, yes. Humans are visual beings. The light bouncing off of objects has informed the human physical experience. It is relied on as a kind of proving.

In our culture, seeing is believing.

---

[12] **The Library Man** is a Teacher that I first met during the writing of *Grandmother Dreams*. He is an older man in a lab coat, with wild white hair and a thick Germanic accent. He is surrounded by a library of jumbled paper stacks and books. During our visits he explains metaphysics and the scientific underpinnings of spiritual concepts.

There will be no interrupting.

So. What we want to do today is show that Light is not the thing that it has been defined as. Light is another dimension. Yes, you are cognitively shocked, because you have never thought about this before. Do not be concerned. Just carry on.

Light is not the thing it has been defined as. Light is another dimension. Light is something made visible that is coming from another location. Of course, this location is not a point in space, it is another space created by shifted coordinates. As if you could pull back a curtain and light came streaming through the crack. Except that the curtain is not a three dimensional object. It is a layer of coordinates that exists simultaneously in every aspect of the perceived three-dimensionality of your world. Everything "exists" in all of these locations simultaneously. So that when humans observe Light they are actually experiencing energy from another dimension. So you see, Light is the source and energy is transferred through it. Everything that you "see" is energy from other dimensions.

For there to be a Unifying Theory, which really just describes a way of looking at things, for there to be a Unifying Theory there would have to be the ability to experience these other dimensions. This is not impossible, but it cannot happen while in the physical state of the body. One would have to have the ability to leave the body and travel using the mind. Not the brain, but the Mind. You experienced this at the end of the first book, when a Dalai Lama helped you to journey. The cloud of stringed light around your brain is your mind. It extends well beyond your physical body.

Ah, yes, the strings. The filaments. The strands reeling off of the spools. Not just in your Mind. These strings are filaments joined through a common energy pathway. They travel through multiple dimensions simultaneously. They are constantly picking up and expressing energy. When a string loops through a crack in the curtain — the veil — its light is visible. Light is its source. Yes, people will want to know this: How can Light be the source of energy. Then you have to know what Light is. Light is the Radiance. Light is what happens when Life Force is in motion. It is Creation.

Remember some time ago, in the first book, when we discussed the

Sea of Movement. Movement. In motion. Traveling. I cannot say this enough — the quality that we are exploring is motion. So much of science, so much of the human need to define and understand, is based on the capture of a static Point. This is a very masculine, a very left-brained way of seeing the world. The way of Motion is feminine, right-brained, fluid. It is what happens when fluidity is not only allowed, but experienced.

Here is an example which illustrates this. You enjoy dancing, because that is a right-brained activity — unstructured, irrational, movement flowing with the music. The music is made by musicians, who are using left-brained techniques to play their instruments, but what is created is a right-brained flow of creativity, being in the Zone with the other musicians and creating an in-the-moment experience. Humans have been given this gift of right and left thinking. Of course, we know that it is not so black and white, but it is a useful way to describe what is going on.

I want to go back to the science of all this. Some ideas need to be turned around in order for new thinking to emerge. I want the mathematicians and physicists to try some new angles. Work on Light being the Source and energy being produced by it. Try to think of fluid dynamics in the realm of Light. Continue trying to define the coordinates for other realms.

Earlier, Universal Wisdom said that "the function of DNA is to carry and tell the story of Life." And *tell.* The strings spooling out into the Universe are DNA telling the story. I sense that telling a story is not a static event. The story is being created as it is being told, and as it comes into contact with other stories/strings/events. That is how healing in the present can heal the past and the future, because it changes the story.

I have also been told that the lives of the Teachers leave a trace in Space, like an indented line in gel, and that is what I am having contact with when we meet. So the environment of the Universe has a fluid gel quality, rather than an airy quality. Is that right?

The Library Man is sitting across the room in an easy chair. He has his arms folded across his chest, looking out the window in a thoughtful moment.

I am not sure what to tell you about this. I want you to continue to be

*curious and keep learning, but I'm not sure this is the track that you
need to be on. I am challenged to meet your curiosity but also to keep
the information on track. Curricula versus curiosity.*

*Well, since you have asked, we will explore this, and see where it goes.
Yes, the* DNA *is telling a story. It is not just* DNA, *because all of Life is a
story in progress. But* DNA *is the measurable item that humans understand
as being the foundation of the story. Of course, there is much more to it
than that, because what is the* DNA *itself made up of and where does it
come from. It really goes much deeper than you can imagine. But we can
use this* DNA *example as a place to start out. Going the other way would
be starting in, and now you have begun to be curious there.*

Let us continue with the DNA. *It has been compared to a computer
program. It is really more like a blueprint. It is a map that is more than
three-dimensional. It is a work in progress and always will be, because
that is its nature. It is something that is in motion and always affected
by the things it comes into contact with. It is a blueprint. It is a map of
everything that has come before, with a plan to build on that and make
adjustments as they are needed to be effective in the next situation.*

*The blueprint is there, and then the building occurs. Many things
can affect the building process. When we look at something like a human,
we can see that physical factors like nutrition and toxins can affect how
the building happens—the resources that are available to build with.
People are starting to recognize that there are emotional and psychic
factors involved also. It all boils down to energy. That is what nutrition
and toxin and Love and trauma all are made of—energy. Blueprints
may have resilience to some factors or to many. Not all blueprints are the
same. They are, of course, designed through their heritage.*

*But humans are not the only thing creating a story based on a blue-
print. So is every living thing. And every thing is living. Rocks, soil, the
Earth itself. Even the plastic bottle that has been abandoned in the ditch is
made up of some kind of cells with a blueprint. Nothing is ever "dead," it
is only transforming to another state. All of these blueprints are interacting
with each other. The blueprint itself and also the processes of building and
transforming are all interacting, so that one thing is affecting every thing.*

What we want humans to understand is this connectedness. Everything is affecting everything. The choices that humans make affect everything else, which in turn affects humans. And not just humans as an aggregate, but also each human. Each human is making choices all of the time, creating a story which is spooled out into the Universe. Even if the story is crushing the inner state, it is having an affect on the Universe and the story of Life. The reason that humans need to hum up and learn to communicate with other dimensions now is multipurpose.

There is much destructive human energy on the planet at this time. Destructive energy aimed at the Earth and also at other humans. Some of this is mindless, but that does not mean it doesn't have a negative effect. Mindful compassion is needed to correct this imbalance and move humans into a more productive role on the Earth. In the absence of such a shift, the Earth will rebalance itself. Humans will not be winners in this rebalancing. This is already occurring.

So, one reason to move into multidimensional experience is to improve the environment that humans must survive in. The other reason is because The Shift is already occurring in other dimensions. We have touched on this before. Humans want the security of maintaining a reality based on the five senses. It is a limited experience. Moving beyond the five senses is a shift from stability toward growth. That is what evolution is — the adjustment of what is built on the blueprint. The story is moving into the next chapter. This is an exciting time. The New Wave.

I am excited to be in this awareness. It is also sometimes frightening, because there still seem to be many who think this is crazy.

Universal Wisdom: *You have not spread out very far yet. You will find more connection in the bigger world.*

It is interesting to be connected to a Native community, where many people have understood this kind of spiritual communication for a long time, but are also skeptical of a book written about it. I am also in the "white world," where people are interested in the book but totally confounded by the idea of transcending. Two sides of the same coin. I am seen as crazy in both worlds.

The white world sees you as crazy. The Native world is more open-minded, but nervous about your intent. Patience is needed. It is right that you are moving slowly.

I have felt like the hurry-up market slam, the make-a-big-splash-and-make-big-money part of publishing these books is a very consumerist approach. It does not apply here.

That is right. You are reaching a different group of people. This will have to seep through the cracks.

But these books are to help white culture make a shift?

Everybody needs to think about this. When you participate in Native culture, you will be traveling the path and strengthening your connections. You will need this strength when you travel the white world — you will feel like a foreigner there. It could be tempting to get sucked into the Ego-gimme of mainstream culture without the foundation of a true spiritual journey. Tread lightly in the Native community, your presence is enough. As you know, you will also have to be careful with status-seekers in the broader world. You will need some financial backing, and it will be important to be mindful about where that comes from.

Is there any more to learn today about the telling of the story.

The story is Life, it is everything in motion at once — the past, the present and the future. It is everyone and everything, being constantly created and re-created. There is no true moment when anything stops. It is always moving. Like a river is made of water but it is different water all the time. Like a wave, which is made of water and is also part of the bigger body of water — it is water drops, and it is a wave, and it is the ocean, all at once. The New Wave.

The **Library Man** returned to me again, seated in an easy chair. He appears agitated, pointing his finger at me.

You think that you already know the answers to many questions.

(I am ready to be defensive, but I know that is not helpful. I did feel confused yesterday, trying to write while distracted, and sometimes wondering if I was feeding the words rather than letting them flow. He seems somewhat satisfied with this response, but still irritated).

You cannot be learning unless you are ready to suspend your idea of what it is you are learning.

Now, we have work to do and it is important that you are not inserting yourself into the words.

Is there something from yesterday that we should go over again and repair.

No. We will move forward.

What we are going to talk about today is related to the discussion of DNA and spooling. There is more to say about that. You had the experience of energy strings spooling out from your body, spooling out into space like a fishing line being cast.

I'd had a brief but intense connection with a stranger. After we parted, I felt grateful for the interaction. I felt the blue lines of energy reeling out from my body, into the world, to wherever this stranger had gone. I had a freeing feeling when I let the strings go, when I did not need to know where they went or where they landed.

I want you to think about theses lines, about the lines created when the strings were cast out.

They were not so much cast out, like being thrown. It was more like they were being created by my body and they were seeking freedom in their own energy. The lines were light and flexible, like a spider's thread. I did not control their movement. They went high into the sky, looped and bounced by the air currents. They went out past the horizon and it made me happy to see them going, wherever they were going. It opened me up.

This is something you need to understand, these lines. These lines are created by your own energy, the energy of your intentions. The reason those lines, that day, were so light is because you were feeling connected to someone that you thought you would never see again. You experienced an intense connection and then you both went your separate ways. Neither of you knew what the other person's life would look like in the future.

Suddenly, I am feeling the heaviness of having connected joyfully and then been left behind, anchored to a small town and my small life, having been affected by a passerby. I feel some shame creeping in.

Now you must examine that. Where does that come from.

That comes from my ego, my need to belong in the world. It hooks into an old story of abandonment, of not being seen or cared for by my own mother. It retells that story in another framework.

Exactly. So the blueprint of your birth was built on by your early experiences. Once that framework is in place, you are continually building on that again. You have no other framework to use. It is part of your cell structure. But the ego, the physical manifestation, is only one framework. There are many frameworks, existing simultaneously in the same space. As long as you function only in the five-sense world, that is the only framework you have to work with.

Another way to function would be to make contact with a spiritual framework, which is available in the same space but in another dimension. The spiritual framework is much more fluid. Both of these frameworks, and many others, are available at all times. You can choose which framework to operate in. They are separate, but also connected and overlapping, so that work in one can spill into others. These dimensions do not operate at the same "speeds", the same vibrations, so that some changes do not come through immediately or completely. But the energy contact is there.

When you first spoke about the spooling and the freedom, you were in the spiritual framework. When you began to feel the abandonment and shame, you were in the physical framework. You choose which framework you function in. You can choose healing (spiritual) or stuck-ness (physical), being open or closing down.

I can see these multiple frameworks. It is like viewing a hologram, with the blueprint beneath them and then these frameworks superimposed over each other, different but visible in the same space. The space is blue, with light white lines forming the blueprint and the frameworks, and there is also a grid below that that looks kind of like graph paper.

The grid is there also. It is the most basic structure in the Universe. It is the patterns that are observed in flower petals, ice crystals, atoms and molecules. It is the perfection of Life. Life is always in motion, making blueprints and frameworks, and other things we have not gotten to.

When energies align correctly, the patterns of Life are created. This is the foundation of The Shift. Life Force is generated in these patterns. They are beautiful and perfect. Some imbalance is necessary, to keep creating new patterns. Too much imbalance pulls energy away, and the patterns become distorted, more difficult to arrange. The energy of Life Force is diminished.

The current basis of The Shift is to create more Life Force energy. Compassionate action by humans is a powerful generator of Life Force. It aligns human function with the grid. The Earth is rebalancing herself in this time also. She is so large, her shifts appear huge to humans. She is taking care of herself and her need to align with the patterns that create Life Force. Human concerns are a small factor in her activity, but positive human actions can magnify Life Force in a way that helps her alignment.

I hear you wondering about Life Force itself, and this is a bigger topic for another day. For now, settle into the information we have already talked about, especially the blueprint and the frameworks. See the hologram in your everyday life and choose which framework you operate in. Be the hologram. Understand how you create your frameworks, how they interact. Place yourself in the grid that generates Life Force. Feel Life Force moving, through you and to others.

Thank you so much. I look forward to seeing you again.

We are working well together. It is appreciated.

~

I was lying in bed one night when my mind filled with images of all of the people I have known over my lifetime, starting in childhood and coming right up to the present. They appeared as visible threads, without emotional attachment, weaving together parts of my life. I could see the threads flowing from one to another, connecting through time and context.

I thought about how I was connected to all those people. I wondered where any of them might be now and what they might be doing, even those who had passed on. I saw how all of them wove their way through my life. And I wove my way through their lives. We are all woven through each other's lives—it's all a big connected web. My present is connected to my past, which is their past, which is part of their present. And it isn't just those people, because they are connected to other people. And it isn't just people, because all of those people were also connected to the energy of places and events. Energy. A giant web of energy.

This made me think about people and their *internal* energies. My daughter and I were looking at pictures of the human eye, the iris, magnified many times. It was kind of scary, to see what things in our bodies look like from so close up, a view we are never able to actually see ourselves. It was also fascinating to try to comprehend the beautiful and complex world that exists right under our skin, in our bodies, every second of every day, and we just cannot see it. It's not something static. It's an amazing and productive motion, it is what keeps us alive. It goes infinitely inward, into the molecular and subatomic worlds and beyond.

I was thinking about that, about the energy web inside my body, and I was shown a view inside of humans that was kind of like looking at that iris. I began to be able to "see" inside each person I encountered. What I saw was a complex web, like a honeycomb. It was each person's unique personality and circumstance and experience. I saw how each person was doing their best to make sense of and work out their presence in the world. I was seeing yet another web. This one was internal, weaving the pattern of each of our lives.

I carried that awareness with me through cancer treatment, a process during which almost all of my physical presence was burned off and I experienced myself as the web of my mind only. Chemotherapy stripped away my previous life patterns and placed me in closer contact with the person who the creator meant for me to be.

I am intrigued by this web making and remaking—the web of my mind, webs made of people and their experiences. All of the energy in motion and being connected. It's like a matrix.

Universal Wisdom: *Look up matrix.*

There are two related definitions. A mathematical matrix is an organizational structure in which two or more lines of communication may run through the same individual. A biological matrix is the substance between cells or in which structures are embedded. It comes from older words that mean "mother" or "womb."

So it's the space between everything. We are back to that. And lines of communication are energy in motion, running through a person, who is a point in the space. It sounds like the relationship between Space and Points and Energy.

This seemingly complex arrangement is really very simple, because it describes everything. There is energy moving in the points and also in the space around the points. Energy is always moving. It is moving in many ways, that are both seen and unseen. You are noticing the unseen. This is what people call The Mystery. It is creating the vibrations of the Universe. You are having a hard time holding this vibration right now, because your body is tired from the chemo. Chemo is a very powerful drug. It is attempting to upset the vibration of cancer cells. It cannot help but upset the vibration of all your other cells. You are doing well to work at keeping as much alignment as possible in your body during this process.

But I am confused. Of course I want to protect my health as much as I can. Doesn't that also create a richer environment for the cancer cells?

Cancer cells are just normal cells that have lost their place in the music. Everything you can do to harmonize the music in your body will allow cells to join in and not develop into cancer. Cancer cells are not something separate, some invaders that appear out of nowhere. They are everyday cells that have lost their way. They are following a program that does not add to the harmony. Your job is to create as much harmony as possible.

So the chemo is destroying any cells that have already lost their way. It is difficult for me to understand how the chemo is not also creating more dysfunctional cells in the process. Everything seems so out of whack.

You are right to question this. The chemo is only as effective as you are strong. You have to be able to withstand the chemo. You are strong, but so is the chemo.

And are there other choices I could make to help myself.

Keep yourself open. You will know when something hits the mark. Keep wading along. You do not have to fight against things that don't work for you. Just wade along and let them flow past you. Use your energy to build the resources that support you. This is how you take care of yourself.

I have spent a lot of time and energy in my life fighting against the difficult things. I see how it is better to let them go, reach for that which is positive.

Keep the stream in mind. Energy is flowing. What you hold on to will define where you are. It's not that you want to ignore negativity, you just don't want to hold onto it. Even positivity is not something to hold on to, because everything changes over time. But you do want to focus your own energy there, connect with it. It is about energy connection. Energy is everywhere, in everything and everyone. You have the ability to choose what you will be aligned with. Let yourself feel. It will all come to pass as it should.

The matrix describes multiple dimensions existing simultaneously in the same space. "Dimensions" are just specific arrangements of points in the matrix. When we place our attention somewhere, we are choosing certain coordinates in the matrix of possibilities. We sense three-dimensional objects, for instance, because they occupy a predictable set of coordinates. We form our "reality" and its effect on us according to where we choose to place our attention. We can sense other dimensions that occur in the same location by shifting our attention to other coordinates. This is what occurs in meditation, channeled writing, and other forms of transcendence. Energy, like the Teachers, exist in these "other" dimensions and are available to us when we learn how to shift our attention there.

~

I dreamt several nights in a row about fish, fish that were trying to speak to me and get my attention. When I awoke I thought about fish in previous meditations, where the fish were messengers, moving between Points of Time in my body—their movement was telling the stories of cells, my DNA. This time, when I opened my mind to the fish, the following vision occurred:

I see the brightest fish from yesterday morning. She turns and dives below the school of her fish-mates, deeper into the water. The flick of her head invites me to follow. We are under the water, looking up at the surface, made up of the breaking planes of light where the water meets the air. The world below, around us, is denser. The water both carries and muffles sound. It is another world.

The fish is next to me, looking me in the eye with mischievous energy. She veers away swiftly. I am to follow. We are swimming through the water easily, our sleek bodies sliding along, supported all around, nearly weightless. It is a joyful experience.

Through the murky light ahead a giant fish approaches, its toothed jaws wide and menacing. We dart away to a rocky area by the shore, where it is too shallow for the big fish to follow. The water here is bathlike, lapping against the warm summer rocks. The little fish looks at me expectantly. Suddenly there is a commotion in the shallow water, with human feet plunging along and a duck's wings frantically windmilling away from shore. We slide farther out from the rocks toward the edge of the deeper water. Constant vigilance is required, and I am glad to have an experienced fish to follow.

She turns to me, so we are face to face, head on. Her eyes roll up and around, constantly scanning the environment. So, it is not that easy to be a fish. It is not all weightless and slippery acrobatics. She nods her head. She turns and swims along the edge of the drop-off. I follow her tail fins, grabbing bits of floating food with my lips as we go.

She rounds a corner and we are in a big bay, with wide open sky above us. We leap high into that blue sky, and become giant fish breaching and diving among the fluffy piles of white clouds. I feel huge, as if the sky is another ocean, and I am a whale in it. My fish friend is far ahead of me in the distance. I try to follow but am entangled in the clouds as if they were a fish net. I break free and swim fast, but I cannot find my friend.

I swim along in the upper atmosphere, seeing tiny airplanes moving below me. Now I come to the surface of the atmosphere, where the air meets Space. I swim through and float in the random gentle currents of the Universe. There are stars all around me. I see the sun in the distance, feel its heat and light. I am pulled into the orbit of the sun and swallowed by the blinding burn of its surface. I am consumed by the fire, becoming first a fish skeleton, then just a pair of fish eyes. I continue to burn. Finally, I am a collection of

brilliant rainbows, illuminated by the sun's glare, washed together like wind chimes in a gentle breeze. I laugh out loud, and my sound waves briefly scatter the rainbow chimes until they drift back together.
The Fish: *This is your spirit form, the form you become when the fish of Time cease to travel in your body, what you are after the death of your physical form.*

The rainbow crystals will eventually drift away from each other, traveling out in the Universe to become part of other fish. Each one is a tiny replica, carrying information from the original fish. When the rainbow crystal becomes part of another form, its information is accessible. Access only requires a match with the energy state of the original. All of the fish are made up of rainbow crystals from all of the other fish. In this way, the human history and the human present and the human future are all contained in any one fish. It is the old and the new, constantly being remade. It is the Codes For Living, available to those who are listening with their attention.

So you see, you are the body in which the fish swim, and you are all the fish that are swimming, and you are the rainbow crystals which make up each fish, and all of the rainbow crystals of all the fish. You are all of these things at once. You can choose where to place your attention. For the best outcome, you will want to place your attention in the rainbows. Be the rainbow, shining and moving. Be yourself and everyone else, simultaneously. Be the energy of the Universe in the body of a human. Vibrate. Create Harmony.

It's not too late. But you cannot get there unless you open. Open Up.

I had no idea where we were going today. I have opened up and look where we are — a beautiful place of calm and wonder.

"The fairest thing we can experience is the mysterious. It is the fundamental emotion which stands at the cradle of true art and true science." ~ *Albert Einstein*

~ 2 ~

Expanding With The Shift

The Universe is not static. It is constantly changing and evolving. According to the Teachers, a significant change is now occurring in the energy of the Universe. They refer to this change as The Shift.

The Teachers are encouraging us to actively participate in The Shift, to embrace the energy that exists both within and beyond our five-sense reality. They are asking us to align our energy with The Shift by expanding our awareness, and including ourselves in a larger context. They would like us to learn how to place our attention in the Zone, in shared space. When we are able to move our energy there, we will evolve into the next layer of consciousness.

Universal Wisdom: *We have talked about a change coming. This is not news. Many people know this already, many people sense it. What they don't know is what the change is. There is much discussion about the nature of the change. People assume there will be a physical calamity of some sort. That is already happening, and will continue, on the physical plane while the planet rebalances. These changes will, of course, require many adaptations. But this is not the monumental change that is on the way. Planetary rebalancing is a parallel, which is helping some to wake up to the other changes that will be necessary.*

The monumental change that we are discussing is a functional change. For the purpose of simplicity, we will call it The Shift. The Shift is a rebalancing also, but it is occurring in another plane, another "dimension" if you will. Dimensions are interconnected, so changes in one will ripple into others. Because it is happening where humans cannot "see" it, there will be confusion and irritability. Humans will feel The Shift but not be able to explain it in physical terms.

The Shift is necessary for cosmic balancing, there is no choosing whether you will participate or not. It will occur. It is beginning already. People who are tuned in will be able to understand the changes. People who are tuned in are those who are Loving the Universe.

Tuning in is required. This is a connection to what you call the spiritual world, God. It is not a religion or a religious dogma. It is not a follower-leader situation. It is about personal connection with the Love of the Universe, traveling in the Zone. It is not just about heart connection, it is about Heart Open with Support of Spirit. Mind is the tool, not the medium. So, you see, it is a deeper level than most of your culture now allows. People will have to drop expectations of themselves and others in order to reach these levels. There will be a time of great learning.

The great teachers of this time will be women. It is the time of the pendulum swinging back. It will be important to hold up that which is valuable in the feminine without trampling that which is positive in the masculine.[13] Mistakes will be made.

Cosmic balancing means that energy is moving in multiple dimensions. This is not just an idea or a concept. It creates some disruption in what we are used to feeling physically. When we feel the changes of The Shift but do not understand them, remaining at the level of the ego, we react blindly. We become uncomfortable, irritable, defensive. **Universal Wisdom:** *The Shift is a realignment, of sorts. Some other dimensions are clearing space and moving energy through. When your body is centered, you are really integrating all of the parts of it into a cohesive whole. Under those circumstances, the space you occupy is more open, less cluttered or chaotic. When the space is clear, there is a greater ability to accommodate changes in concurrent dimensions.*

Irritability is created by defensiveness. You feel energetic ruffles and

---

[13] It is important to understand the terms "feminine" and "masculine." They are not gender descriptions, like "female" and "male." They describe a collection of qualities. Like yin and yang, they refer to essence.

move to protect yourself. You gather your energy into the point which is yourself. This condenses your own energy and obscures the common space. It makes it difficult for energy to move through, and the ruffles feel bigger and more disturbing. A negative cycle can be created: more tension, more disturbance, more tension. It takes a lot of energy to maintain this defended state.

Allowing disruption is required to provide the environment for creative thinking. Allowing disruption is also required to provide the environment for physical evolution. The New Wave is not just a change in thinking. It is necessarily a change in Being. The physical body is going to have to reorganize. It has to be able to accommodate greater and greater amounts of Space. You will not be able to tolerate that when you are resisting the physical change. That is why you feel irritable. Instead of keeping your body tuned up, you are reacting to the energy ripples with defensiveness. You need strong physical exercise every day. We have talked about this before. Exercise keeps your body tuned up to the higher vibration of the spirit.

Your spirit is participating in The Shift on multiple planes. It has difficulty reintegrating into your physical body when the body is vibrating at a lower level, when it is sluggish from lack of movement or poor diet. It can also be disconnected by the frenzied energy of stress. Taking care of your body and your psyche are a spiritual responsibility. Not just a spiritual directive or a set of religious rituals — you want to choose this because it creates the environment for evolving into the next layer. It is time to do this. It is time to direct your life for this purpose.

All of your choices need to be made towards spiritual resonance. And that includes the small choices that you make all day every day about what you put in your body, how you move your body, how you interact with other people, the direction your thoughts go. These are all examples of Ego in correct position, carrying out the choices that Spirit makes, for optimal survival and also for evolution.

You will have to make choices about things that you did not see coming. It will be easiest when you have paid attention to the maintenance of your physical energy. Love yourself the way you want to be Loved. Remember that you are Life Force in motion, you are God in

physical form. Celebrate your abilities by using them. Make sure you are
celebrating Life. Open Up.

We are being asked to allow disruption in our thinking and our behavior, because this will create the opening for new energy vibrations, including our physical evolution. Although it starts internally, it is not something that we do in isolation. The Shift includes a change in the vibration between ourselves and our world.

The Library Man: *We need to talk about this. You have been thinking that somehow you can control the outside world by modifying your connection to it. This is only partly true. One thing you are missing is the idea that there is an interaction between you and the world. It is happening all of the time. There is no stopping it. The energy is continuous and in motion, through all things at once.*

Many people are feeling heavy right now. They are being weighed down by an energy that is much greater than they are aware of. There are changes occurring. Everyone is being asked to become more aware of the Earth, to pay attention to the ground that supports you.

The Earth is going to be communicating with humans. Some people are already listening, some that you know have been listening for a long time. The Earth is opening up. It will be important to join the vortexes and help move the energy. This is both work and celebration.

A vortex is a swirl of movement, places where concentrated energy moves in and out. The human body has energy vortexes. These are sometimes called *chakras*. The Earth also has energy vortexes. Indigenous peoples have honored these energy centers by holding ceremony there.

A pow-wow circle can be this kind of ceremony. Drumming and dancing in the circle turns the Wheel of Life, enhancing all of the participants — drummer, singer, dancer, family, community, spirit world, planet, and the balance of Life Force. It is mutually beneficial. Dancing in the circle is one example of actively participating in the bigger context of concurrent dimensions.

Universal Wisdom: *The Shift has occurred. It will be creating ripples.*

This is difficult for humans to process. Humans do not have the tools for integrating this. There is increased tension, increased irritability. Negative response. It is what it is. As you have seen, you cannot control the behavior of others. Sometimes you do not have the skills to control your own behavior.

You have been comforted by pow-wow music and Native languages. This is because it brings you back to a more ancient vibration, one which connects with the Universe. The Shift in other dimensions has a vibration similar to this, they fit together harmoniously. This is The Shift that we have been asking humans to make. The Shift is movement into the world beyond the five senses. The ancient vibrations had this. It is time to be there again.

The old ways connected humans with the cycles of Nature and the Universe. It is not that there weren't distractions, but the distractions—hunger, weather, predation, illness—required a greater tuning in order to survive. The distractions today are somewhat enriching, but do little to aid direct survival—electronic gadgets, empty foods, mindless media.

What has brought human culture into your current position was a mass movement, and what will get you out of this position, into a more harmonious position, will also be a mass movement. Many people have to make this change. You are currently feeling powerless in the face of the "Male Machine," the masculine agenda towards profit and control. As long as you are small, you will feel powerless. It is time to accelerate your connections with others who are moving on this path. Do not lose sight of your goal to make new connections. Encourage others to be making connections. Keep talking about it.

There are many ways to be working right now. They are additive. Speaking and behaving in a Loving Way are the most important things you can do. Expanding the circle of people you interact with in this way increases that energy. Do not be afraid to talk about the movement needed. You will be surprised at how many people are already interested. This is who you want to interact with—those who are interested. You have been thinking that you need to somehow convince those who are confined in their security bubbles. What you really want to do is encourage those whose bubble is already flexible or expansive.

In everything you choose, ask yourself, "Is this moving me along my spiritual path?"

~

When I think of moving along my spiritual path, it is easy to believe that everything will be all roses and rainbows. But learning how to adjust my energy, how to actually evolve, can be a rough road.

One time, for example, I had been challenged by depression for several weeks. I could feel it sinking in deeper and deeper. At first, I would bump into it, like coming around a corner and coming up against a brick wall. After a while, it started creeping, like a mist, around the corner and reaching for me. I experienced negative thinking loops. My usual anti-depression methods — exercise, gratitude, green foods, meditation — didn't help.

Eventually, I just gave in. I realized that sometimes this happens, and it doesn't last forever. It would leave me eventually. That very night I started to feel better, like the mist was retreating. The next morning I actually felt a little burst of happiness when I woke up. I improved throughout the day and felt quite good by the next evening. I went to bed and fell asleep fairly easily. But then I was jolted awake several times during the night, jolted so hard that my arms and legs shot out. I was highly anxious.

I wonder where this is coming from. I also wonder if I am sensitive to some kind of larger energy change. I am wondering about the shifts occurring in other realms that can be felt here.

The Library Man: *You are wondering about this, and that is a good thing, to be wondering instead of reacting. It is true that something is happening on another plane. If you talk to others, you will find that many people are feeling this. It is important to stay grounded now. Not just today but also in the future. Many things are going to happen that you will find difficult to understand.*

You can help yourself by reminding yourself that this is the way it is. It is not supposed to be some other way. Something is shifting. Humans are anticipating this shift and don't know what it is, so that has added a lot of fear and anxiety. Some people will not make good choices during this time of stress.

Can you tell us something about The Shift.

It cannot be explained in a way that humans will understand.

Can it be explained to our spirits.

Spirits already know about this, because Spirits are participating in this shift. It is why humans feel uncomfortable, because their spirits are involved in a change process, and their spirits are at least partially attached to the physical form of human bodies. This is the vibration that is causing concern. But it is also the reason to weather the shift, to ride the flow that is occurring.

Shifts are occurring all the time. As you know, that is Life Force — change. The current shift is close to the vibration of physical form. That is why it is more easily felt.

Riding the flow, going with it, allowing it, requires a certain amount of physical grounding. That feels a little more difficult in the face of some of the reactions I feel — depression and anxiety.

Note, however, that this has occurred primarily in thought form. Not that there aren't physical manifestations, such as the night awakenings you describe. It will be important to temper your reactions to these manifestations. Do not be drawn into thinking that something is wrong. Be aware that something is different. Be curious and pay attention. There is much to learn.

This is very helpful.

It is emotionally difficult to watch news of the wars in the Middle East, even though I am physically distant from these events. What about the people who are there, who are directly exposed to the effects.

The people in these areas have been exposed to significant threats and losses for a number of years already. Events are intensifying there, and so are effects. They, obviously, have greater challenges in staying grounded, not buying into the conflicts created by government politics. These people have the opportunity to Join Hands in Peace, to choose Ego in correct position to Spirit. There are many challenges ahead.

The most important thing you can do is stay centered and spiritually connected. Global events are well beyond your personal control. Remember that you draw energy to the place where you rest your attention.

I was thinking about health, how important it is to recognize what is healthy in your body. Certainly, to listen to the parts that are experiencing pain or illness, and help them find a healthy direction. But it is also important to pay attention to what is in good health and working well, to strengthen that so that the less-well parts have something to lean on while they repair, so that the less-well parts will have a path to follow.

Yes. This is the same for mass identity, and environmental health, as well as personal well-being.

Westerners have been problem focused. We have been missing the fact that the problem is part of a larger whole, a whole which includes strengths as well as problems. The two are tied together. I can think of many situations where a person or group has become their problem. The problem is their life, instead of being part of their life. In some cases, what is good has been overpowered and forgotten.

The Library Man is sitting at a table with his papers. He is not looking at me, but waving the back of his hand in my direction to shoo me away.

That is enough for today. You will have much to think about. Come back tomorrow.

Thank you very much, Sir. I appreciate your attention.

Yes, well this is my job. And I am happy to do it.

He tries not to smile, but then laughs. I have to smile and laugh, too. Life is good.

~

Functioning in the five-sense world requires a lot of attention. There is much to take care of every day. It is easy to become driven by a task-master lifestyle. The more I feed that way of being, the more I feel disconnected from my spiritual process. When I have no time or energy for my spiritual process, I tend to cover up that lack by reaching for distractions, like caffeine or alcohol or media. This focuses my energy away from my spirit path even more.

Universal Wisdom: *There is not much to say here until you get reconnected. Because that is what has happened, you have become disconnected. Too busy and then loading on a toxin. We do not leave, we are always here. The connection is fuzzy, however.*

Yes, it feels difficult to sustain.

Do not focus on that, because then your energy will go there. Focus on what you want to do to bring yourself back. Getting outdoor exercise is a good idea. Sleep is a good idea. Find a way to relax at work. It's true that your workload has increased. But your attitude has shifted to accommodate that, instead of making the work accommodate you.

I did notice that trap — the more work there is the faster I go and the faster I go the more work there is. It's a killer cycle.

Yes, and what is getting killed off is your spiritual life. It's why you feel so dead — you are trying to be a physical presence only. That is like running a marathon during hibernation. It is a poor fit. You need the input of spiritual energy. That is what connects you to purpose and to others and to your own path. These things will all be obscured if you are not feeding Spirit.

Ego in service to self. That feels like survival mode.

And that is what makes you feel so tired. Like growing a plant in a dark closet.

Focus on what feeds you spiritually and go there first.

Ego in service to Spirit.

Maybe I can put Spirit into those tasks. Go to the grocery store and choose things that will feed me well. Do my recycling because it is good for the planet, and good for me to keep clearing space. These things help me feel better. Focusing on accomplishing the tasks does not.

Be careful, though. The busyness can easily take over. Stop to think about your motivation for each thing you do. If you are doing it to get it done, then it is a task. If you are doing it to improve your life, then it might not be a task. Make sure it hums up your energy. Love what you are doing. Stop doubting and start doing. You will know how to proceed when you have eaten the fruit of living.

I went to the Sunday morning gospel hour of a nearby music festival. The music was fabulous — groovy, positive and uplifting. I felt my body opening up to the Universe and vibrating in bless-ed energy. A Teacher came to me and spoke about managing my physical presence in a spiritual way.

Church Mother:[14] *You can not have everything you want all at once.*
(She has her hands together in her lap, with the fingers of one hand
circling the other wrist. She waves a finger back and forth at me while
her hand still circles her wrist.) *You gotta be willin' to work for these
things. And I do not mean "work" like toil and trouble makin'. I mean
"work" like mind your manners, and live in a Godly way, and be thankful
for whatever it is that you do find. Life is goin' to reward those who are
payin' attention. Not pushin' and pullin' through life. But bein' aware.*

*See, that's what you been doin'. You been tryin' your best, and that's
good. But you been draggin' around a bunch 'a stuff that don't belong to
you. Somebody gave you their mess and you took it on.*
I just heard this: "If you can't let go, at least loosen your grip."
(She looks away and waves me off.) *See, that's part of what I'm talkin'
about. You are so busy telling your story that you can't even see the parts
that ain't yours. You're telling these stories all mixed up with yours.*
Hmm. And how would I tell my story without other people in it.
(She leans in closer to me.) *That is exactly what I'm talkin' about.
What is your story without all that extra in it? What is your story??*
That would have to be where I came from, the original seed of God.
(She is smiling and nodding.) *Mmmhhmm. That's right. That's where
it starts. And then you come into this place where they give you a physical
body.*
And then all Hell breaks loose!
(She points at me, chuckles.) *That's kinda funny. 'Cause that is just what
happens. That's what Hell is, being stuck in this physical business without
having spiritual attachment. You gotta be bringin' that seed along, the
memory of that seed, into everything you do. You gotta grow that seed,
love it up and give it what it needs, talk to it, invest in it.*
I can see that plant growing in me, its vines and leaves looping all
through my body, and golden rays beaming out from them.
*Bein' outside, workin' your body and keepin' it strong — that is the air
and sunshine that plant needs. Bein' with family and friends and sharing*

---

[14] **Church Mother** is a religious elder. She is a round, big-armed black woman,
wearing a light-blue dress patterned with small flowers.

social times — that is the fertilizer. Taking care of your feelings, showing your Love and receiving it too — that is watering your seed. Your Being is the soil this seed grows in. Your spiritual life is the root of it all. Nothin' good happens without those roots.

That seed is just waitin' to grow. That is what it wants to do. It will try hard even if you don't. Because that is its job, that is what it was made for. You are the gardener. Don't be thinkin' there is some kind of short cut, because there isn't. It takes Love and attention for plants to be strong and healthy. Do your job.

'Nuf said.

I love Church Mother's teaching. It is very down to earth, bringing it home through the example of gardening. I am challenged, however, to understand the position of churches in general. Rather than put the human body in a spiritual context, traditional religions tend to demean our physical presence. How can I support my spiritual development by making better use of my physical presence?

Universal Wisdom: *Energy is moving all of the time in order to evolve. The purpose of Tradition is to keep the foundation, so that ancient wisdom is not forgotten. It is true that each person has their own view of this process. And each community tends to have their own common threads. But be careful about thinking that you can interject something yourself. You are, after all, outside of these communities. You have traveled there, but you have not lived there. There are many more underground currents than you will ever see.*

The most important thing you can do is value each person's perspective, and try to discern the common threads. You will come home to this one day, probably when you least expect it. In the meantime, you must remain humble and aware of your intention. Personal gain is a poor intention. Consider what you are cultivating in your garden. Not just what seeds you are planting, but how you care for what germinates. You, of all people, can benefit greatly from the grounding that comes with intentionally decreasing your speed.

Please say more about "decreasing your speed." I assume it is partly in reference to the ADD monkeymind of my chemo brain?

It is that. But that is just the most obvious expression of this speed. There is also a slowing down that needs to occur in order to synchronize better with the Spirit World, the world of Space and Zone. The physical body needs to hum up to a higher vibration in order to join the vibrational level of the Spirit World. But in order to then expand into the Zone, your activity level needs to decrease. In some ways, cease. This is a difficulty faced by Westerners today. They are moving so fast all day long that when it is time to slow down, it is impossible to do so. Like humming up physically, slowing down energetically also takes practice.

To bring it back to gardening, you can not go out there and work as if you are completing a task. You must be present there with all of your energy. You must be clear and open to what the plants and Nature ask of you. You must put into the garden that which is already at work there. Your energy must add to the process and enrich it. It can not be distracting. You will want to slow down to the energy pace of the Zone.

When I have been there before, in the Zone, there is a slow-motion, timeless quality to it, as though it is thicker than "just" air.

Yes, you are practicing now: see how your energy settles into your belly, away from your thoughts.

That is where connection to the All That Is takes place.

That is where, and how, the ancestors move.

I see a dancing circle. It is night, very dark, and someone in a white buckskin outfit with long fringe on the arms and legs is dancing, their head bowed. It is a man. Dancing in the night.

He is dancing for The Night, for Moon, and the many stars, for everything that is visible and not visible at night.

It is very beautiful. I feel the night sky filling the interior of my body, and I become **Star Sky Forever.**[15] I had forgotten about this part of

---

[15] **Star Sky Forever** is a name that was given to the Universal Me that is beyond Ego. I met this part of myself when I made a pilgrimage to Wounded Knee in South Dakota. Weeping at the cemetery, with my face on the ground, my white-skinned outer body asked forgiveness from the brown-skinned people who had been murdered there. In that moment, my white skin peeled away to reveal a brown layer underneath, Brown Being, my connection to all our ancestors. And when my brown-skinned ancestral self granted compassionate forgiveness for the unforgivable, the brown layer peeled away to reveal the entire Universe inside of

me, this way of Being. And here I am. My hands are tingling with the multitudes of stars filling my body. My body, that is not really my body, but an expression of the Universe. Not inside out, but Outside-in. Flawless connectedness.

~

In order to move our attention beyond the five senses, we need to be able to accept that there is more to the Universe than we usually perceive. There is energy all around us. Paying attention to this energy, and how we are aligned with it, can lead to a shift in our behavior.

Animals are especially aware of energy. Cesar Millan, who is known as The Dog Whisperer, uses energy awareness in his work. His entire foundation for training is that the dog is a pack animal, and that the humans in the dog's life must behave as pack leader in order for the dog to be a follower. The pack leader behavior is based on nonverbal communication, on energy. In only a few days of using his practices with my rescued dog, she became calmer and her severe behavior issues decreased. I was stunned at the changes.

Then I heard a radio interview with Louise Booth. Booth's son, Fraser, was a child with autism. He was severely disabled, unable to interact with anybody or anything. A cat named Billy made the first contact ever with Fraser, and went on to teach Fraser basic activities like how to climb stairs and how to take a bath — all through non-verbal communication.

These examples demonstrate energy communication — communication beyond our five senses — in action. "Other" dimensions are readily available to us. We have only to develop or improve our skills in order to access them.

I see **The Library Man**. He is licking his thumb and touching the edges of his papers thoughtfully. He taps their bottom edges together on the table and looks at me.

These events are catching your eye because you are ready to hear more and

---

me, the One With All. I then appeared as the infinite night sky full of stars, and was given the name Star Sky Forever.

it is not happening. We would like to see you on a more regular basis.
[I begin to interrupt to try to explain how chemotherapy is a barrier
to my energy, but he holds his hand up to stop me.]
*There can be no excuses, really, because the work must continue on. It
is time to work on your focus. Remove some of the other things that you
are doing instead of the work. You have more time on your hands now.
It would be best to use it effectively.*
Yes, I [he holds his hand up again.]
*Even stopping to discuss it is wasting time. There is only Now, and doing
it. The time is gone by for processing.*
Is there something you would like to talk about right now.
[He is filing his papers among books on a shelf, and looks at me with
a sideways glance.]
Yes. We will begin a discussion of Range.
[I look at him quizzically, and he responds with exasperation.]
Yes, Range. [He swirls his finger above the keyboard and points. I
am to type.]
*There is a range of behavior in communication. Humans are used to
relying on the spoken word, which is more about training than instinct.
There is always energy around the words, the energy of intent and interaction. These are things that people sense, but often discount because they
are not used to incorporating them. They feel the energy but let it bounce
off of them. They are also not used to speaking with intent. There is so
much useless chatter, generated by the ego and the head.*

   *Humans have gotten trapped by their brains. The brain is not what is
in charge in a balanced person. This is directly related to the information
from The Dog Whisperer. We can manage ourselves and our interactions
in great measure by paying attention to what our intent and our energy
is doing. This is very important. Our intent and our energy set in motion
the vibration that we will be expressing during an interaction. That
vibration begins internally. Is the starting point of our energy clear and
harmonious? Is there a feeling of peace, or of disturbance?*

   *These are no small matters. Cultivating harmonious interaction
within ourselves will necessarily translate into our actions. Words are
actions. Words are actions that affect those who receive them. The speaker*

is responsible for what the listener receives.
Talk about your experience today.

As I participated in this new energy interaction with my dog friend, I became very aware that I had a similar relationship possibility with myself. If I could be an effective pack leader for all the cells in my body, then I would be creating a harmony that would encourage health and discourage cancer.

I was cross-country skiing out in the winter woods, and used the rhythmic motion of my body to practice the harmonic alignment of my energy. As I practiced, I felt my cells following this energy by lining up in a harmonious formation. Then I sensed the non-follower cancer cells lagging behind my body, out of formation. Unattached, they eventually drifted off into the woods along the trail, to get reabsorbed by Nature. It was a very pleasant feeling, both to be aligning in a harmonious way and also to be letting the cancer cells drift away. There was nothing dramatic or violent about it. The cancer cells just didn't belong in the arrangement and the healthy cells did.

Creating this inner peace was not difficult. There was a clear cord of energy in my core, just inside my spine, which created the Leader position. All the other cells either fell into place around it, or didn't. Very simple and very effective, like rearranging my energy pattern with my dog. I refocused my attention, and that created a shift in my energy.

And this is the kind of shift that humans need to be addressing spiritually. It is an alignment that promotes energy movement. The first steps seem difficult, because they appear to be far beyond everyday experience. It does require a change in everyday experience. People cannot keep doing the same things and expect a different outcome.

I feel fortunate that cancer has allowed me to change my daily pattern. How could others choose this.

There are upheavals on the way. There will be opportunities for humans to change. People are going to have make changes. They will need to be able to see how to change. This is one area of your work, to help them see guidelines for change. It is both an exciting and a dangerous time. That is the definition of opportunity.

[He is fingering his thick white mustache. He has been turned to the bookshelf during this discussion. It is as though he is choosing the next topic.]

Yes. Well, that will be all for now.

[He is lost in thought, but then turns and shakes his finger directly at me.]

You must stay on track. Do not be diverted by frivolous activities.

I felt a positive shift after addressing my relationship with the animal in my life, and that led to a shift in my relationship with the cells in my body. I began to practice this energy shift every day and tried to hold the sensation for longer and longer periods. It reduced tension and aided inner peace.

This definitely holds me in the present, in the Now, where everything is happening. I feel centered and expanded, very much the same as the Love and Let Go meditation that I use with channeled writing, although there is a little more rational concentration on the present. I can see my core, which is a luminous white cylinder of light, about the same orientation and dimension as my spinal cord, but shifted more into the center of my body. It has "fingers" of energy, also white light, extending out into my body like fibers. I do not have to be practicing energy alignment anymore to be able to "see" this reality. It has just become part of my energy body.

∼

Making The Shift is not just a thought process or a personal exercise—it also requires active participation. After years of writing *Grandmother Dreams* and several more years learning how to publish, for example, The Teachers told me to go out and use the book to move information. I felt lost and overwhelmed at this directive. I was more comfortable just continuing to write about my spiritual experiences. **Great Grandfather**[16] is pointing at me:

---

[16] **Great Grandfather** is my paternal Grandmother's biological father. He is an indigenous person born some time in the mid or late 1800s. His teachings are often brief, with little room for discussion. He speaks at length in later chapters.

You think that all of this is amazing, and you have spent quite some time here reporting about it. There is much to be done. (He is sweeping his hand across a sky of clouds.) There is much to be done and sitting here is not getting that done. It is not all about recording the diary of your life. You need to get up and move. Move the information that has been given to you. Yes, you are afraid, because you are not used to talking about this. That is not a reason to not do it.

He is sitting next to me now with his arms folded across his chest. He is irritated with me.

Not so much with you as with the lack of understanding by the people who should know better. The ones who are talking about this all the time, but they are keeping it to themselves.

Where would I find these people.

He looks at me with surprise and anger, like I have been eavesdropping.

This is not for you to know yet. They will come to you when it is time.

I asked who I should be talking to and he stood up in frustration, walking away toward the horizon.

I know the answer. I was looking for support or confidence-building, easy answers. I just need to take my books everywhere and talk about them, even though I am uncomfortable. This is what The Shift is about — adding to change in the broader world, not just sitting home and thinking about it.

Great Grandfather is still walking away, but he has turned back a little and is waving his hand for me to come along and join him. I will quit writing now and just go with him. As I catch up, he has his hand out from his side and I slip my small hand into his big hand. I am the child, skipping alongside the Grandfather she loves, happy to be with him.

The directive to go out into the world and actively support The Shift does not require banners and bugles. Our actions can also be silent and indirect. In the following experience, I was able to share with someone very quietly:

I had been the labor assistant for a young mother's beautiful birth.

A week or so later I sat with the little boy while his mother took care of something in another room. As I held him we stared at each other, going deeply into each other's pupils. I whispered and encouraged him on his Earthly journey, acknowledging that he had just come from the ancestors, a beautiful place which he could have with him his whole life. I encouraged him to be aware that there were many people who were ambassadors of the ancestors, who would always be around him — all he had to do was be open.

We practiced being in the Zone together. He looked astonished, intent, comforted, relaxed. He spoke aloud to me as he could. His mother came back in the room remarking on what an amazing exchange must have happened, how he had never "talked" so much or with so much animation, even to her. I shared our conversation about the ancestors with her. I went away feeling refreshed, having made contact in the Zone, connected.

There are many places in the world where we can connect. Like this little boy, we will need to be open and seek them. And in the mean time, we must trust that we are meant to be on this journey, even when we feel lonely.

Universal Wisdom: *We want you to know that we are with you, even when you feel alone. The physical world is not as separate as you sometimes think it is. The energy of the ancestors permeates the physical world. That is part of what keeps it in place. Remember Life Force. Life Force is the fuel for all of the processes in the physical world. Yet it originates beyond the physical world. The worlds are interconnected in ways that you cannot yet understand.*

Part of what needs to happen in The Shift is for humans to acknowledge this ancestor-energy, which is perceived as beyond the veil, and bring it into fuller contact with the physical world. To act with intention and cross the veil, in both directions. Traveling both directions will create an energy pathway. That pathway is lightly used at this time. It will become a super-highway. And then new developments will be possible. The energy pathway has to be developed for these other things to occur. Bringing your books out will assist the process of traveling.

Prioritize Zone in all you do. This will not only improve your function through practice, it will also bring you in contact with situations that diminish your obscurity, the loneliness you feel. Like the interaction with our baby. We are pleased that this contact was made. It will increase the Life Force that this child is open to.

Make these connections with other children, who are still open to the wonder of the Dream World. Adults also have this capacity. But as you have found, many have become strangers to the Zone. The directive to stay silent will help you. You need not practice verbally, directly, in order to make a difference. Just maintain Zone and meet others who might go there too. This is an energy practice. Some will be able who cannot verbalize this connection. Words are not required. Eyes, feelings, connections. You know how to do this. Sometimes you get disconnected, distracted by the physical world. That is temporary. You can always come back to Zone. That is your true Home.

Our good work, our purpose on Earth, is to increase Life Force. Humans have the capacity to do this through Love, by moving Love in compassionate action. What is the relationship between moving Love and The Shift?

Universal Wisdom: *Moving Love creates a vibration. It is energy moving in the space between Points. Space is shared by multiple dimensions simultaneously. Positive changes made here will affect change in other areas.*

Why would humans care about that.

Humans are moving toward a leap in evolution. The leap involves expanding beyond the five senses.

I guess I am assuming that people will want to know why this is important, why they should care. I accept it completely, because I know how it has helped me to move forward in my own life—to recognize when I am reacting out of Ego, to let Spirit do the choosing. I feel more balance, more open to other people, more compassionate about how things are and what my place in the world is. I recognize the importance of connecting spiritually. The physical/Ego/pleasure path is a dead end when that's all there is, but it's a fabulous gift when it is put in the context of a spiritual life.

We are all looking for purpose in life. We know it is not what TV is selling us, and quite a few are turning away from the dogma of formal religions. We all have a purpose, and it is to move Love.

Yes. And to go back to your original self, the you who is connected to God, to the great mystery, to All That Is.

The change we are being asked to make is not about fixing a goal and then marching towards it. That is a linear process. What we want to be doing is opening to a new way, which is nonlinear — it is a spacial process. It is moving our attention away from Time and in favor of Space. To open up and step into the unexpected.

A'riquea: *That is how this works. Traveling in other dimensions is like stepping off a cliff into thin air. Except that there is no gravity involved, and there is no danger of harm.*

I have been excited to see mainstream films lately that are beginning to address these other dimensions, but disappointed that these dimensions are always made to look scary and dangerous.

This is what most people think of the unconscious, that it is a hiding place for monsters. This is partly true. If personal fears and feelings have not been addressed, the unconscious will provide a place to meet them. But, as you have seen, there is also help available. It is not just the unconscious of the individual mind that is opened up. There is also the universal mind.

Multiple times I have been shown the grid, the matrix, that includes multiple dimensions using the same coordinates.

This is the next place, the next step in human evolution.

I feel that I am closer and closer to it all the time. My life is moving in that direction. I am curious about the energy that is shared between dimensions. If we are sharing the same coordinates, and energy is moving in multiple directions, in concurrent dimensions, what is the outcome for any dimension? I have been told that one of the reasons that humans need to take this next step in evolution is because there are energy requirements on the other side.

I have lost verbal contact. I feel myself on the other side of the veil. The environment is glowing, light blue, and very thick. I am trying to move my body, and I am mired in thick blue gel. It is even filling my nose and mouth, although this does not matter because this is not a place that requires breathing. I am suspended in this blue gel. If I travel without my body, then the gel is thinner.

There are stars all around. I am traveling with just my mind. My mind is a halo of particles with red trails. The particles are interacting with the gel, and with other particles, creating spherical ripples where there is contact. My ripples are coming in contact with my own ripples, and there are other ripples and other waves. There is energy in motion everywhere. I can hear it, almost like the cacophony of a symphony warming up their instruments. There are also the sounds of Nature, like wind and water rushing, and birdsong and animal roars. So it is everything. It is the Everything. The All That Is. Each ripple is like an echo. Somewhere in here is Silence, also. So it is just everything. And then I can choose what I focus on, where I place my attention.

A'riquea is looking quietly on. She opens her mouth and in I go. Now I have crossed the Veil. I am A'riquea's body, her presence. I can see out through her into her world. I see the hard-packed sand of the village, the strong walls of the thatched huts, the brilliant colors of the people's clothing. We are smiling, and clapping our hands together in rhythm with the drums. There is singing, the high nasal of women. It is a happy sound.

There is a nice fat baby playing in the dust. The baby is clapping hands too. Each clap makes a little puff of dust. I am entering the space between the baby's clapping hands, entering the little cloud of dust particles. I am a speck of that dust, that old old dust. Ancient. The dust that came from the making of the planet, that came from the cosmos.

The energy around me has organized into a wavy line. The line swings and vibrates in its waviness, gradually reaching a higher and higher frequency until the wave is a straight line. The straight line is like the string on an instrument. It is plucked, a cloud of particles puffs off of the string, and the string vibrates, waving, until it appears to come to rest. Looking very closely at the string, I can see that it never actually comes to a stop. It is always vibrating.

The string is made up of particles that make it appear to be solid but, microscopically, it is made of particles, particles that are constantly in motion, particles that have a great deal of space between them. That space is the doorway into the next reality.

Step into the space and open up.

I step into the space. All of the "particles" in my body expand, and I experience the space between them. My outstretched hands and feet are in distant galaxies. My heart is a sun. My head is thrown back in the glory of it. I lie on my back, floating. My mind, the red trails and the particles, has fallen away. I see it below me, blinking and spinning. I am enjoying the feeling of all the space in my body. I want to remember this feeling. I want to recreate it later, a sensory memory guide for the future.

Another day, I was told a story that encouraged me to continue moving my awareness. The story explains why we want to travel in this way and shows how one thing transforms into the next, without us knowing what that next thing will be.

Ronnie Wall: [17] *This is something we need to tell. We want to tell people about how it was before the rocks came into the soil. You can look out now and see rock walls all over the surface of Ireland, but it was not always that way.*

There was once a lot of soil, and it had been placed there by the ocean that once covered this area. When the ocean receded then there was this big pile of mud. No one could be living here. It was just all mud. So the rocks lined up underneath the land, and this allowed the soil to be drained, so now there was a place to stand. But nothing could grow there, because the ground was so compacted. So those rocks came up, through the soil, which is really quite amazing because they had to travel against gravity to do it, didn't they. Those rocks came up through the soil, and in that way they allowed the soil to breathe. They created cracks and pockets and tunnels with their movement, and the soil then could take a breath.

---

[17] **Ronnie Wall** is a red-haired Irish farmer who is my very distant relative. He speaks with a thick brogue, and often explains the relationship between spirituality and the Earth's energy.

Now people are complaining about those rocks — that there are too many and it's awfully hard to farm. The rocks brought the grass, but few are acknowledging that, just complaining about what are we going do with all these rocks. The rocks just keep coming. Maybe someone needs to go down there and tell the rocks that they've done a good enough job already, and aren't we pleased with that.

But, you know, it's the same way with the mind. Right now people's minds are all covered by ocean. They don't want to wash the waters away, because then what would they do with that big pile-of mud. But it all works out. Because there will be the rocks to come and help the soil breathe. And then what? What will happen when their are too many rocks? Well, then the next thing will come and won't you be surprised by that.

Or, you could just keep floundering about in the water. Things are constantly in motion. If you deny that, you might be left behind and drown. Best come up on the land and warm yourself on the rocks. It'll be raining before you know it.

~

There are barriers to changing the human mindset and allowing new ways of seeing. The vast majority of our culture is working hard to keep the lid on the box, to keep one view of reality in place. There are many people outside of the mainstream, however, who already accept alternate realities. There is also scientific information that shows there is more to reality than what is usually perceived by humans.

The magazine *Discover* explores science, technology, and the future. The July/August 2013 issue, in an article called "Darklands of the Cosmos" (p. 90), discussed the non-observable world:

"We think of ourselves, and the world immediately around us, as something special. And by extension we regard our kind of matter — atoms, molecules, rocks, water, air, stars and all the other things that interact with visible light — as the most important kind of matter in the universe. The only matter that matters, as it were.

"Science tells us a starkly different story. Last spring, the European Space Agency's Planck spacecraft completed an ultra-precise, 15-month census of the composition of the universe. The kind of matter that we can see makes up 4.9 percent of the total. Another fundamentally invisible type of matter vastly outweighs it, accounting for 26.8 percent. (The remaining 68.3 percent is an even more baffling component that consists of formless energy: That means more than two-thirds of the universe has no substance at all.) … We could be sitting right on top of a whole shadow galaxy and not even know it."

This article gives some support to otherwise subjective sensations and ideas—almost 70 percent of the Universe is made up of energy that we don't understand.

The Library Man is standing at the bookshelf, fingering his mustache thoughtfully.

We would like to say more about this. It is a topic of interest. It is a topic of interest because there are cracks in the boundaries between these realities. This is a good thing. We want the cracks to occur, so that humans can begin to see across. There are difficulties with this, of course. People may begin to feel unhinged, and this does need to happen, but people will need to have a context to place this in. There needs to be a place to go with the changes once they occur.

The Awakening of Humanity.

Yes, of course. But what does that mean in the five-senses world. What are the applications. Channels need to be created that allow this flow to have a direction. How to cultivate compassion so that it creates a flow. We have talked before about these paths—that right now there are just rabbit trails, but eventually there will be superhighways of communication and travel across the veil. Obviously, this is a ways off. It might be worthwhile to be thinking about trickles.

Use the example of fluid dynamics. Trickles can join streams, streams can join rivers. Eventually there will be oceans. Not in your lifetime. This is good for you to know, this context of the work. Right now we are working on springs bubbling to the surface. This is why it is important to stay focused. Because it will be easy to get pulled off center, when there is more around you that does not support the work.

You were looking for a more concrete lesson today. That is just not where we are at the moment.
He is shooing me away. We are done for now.

There *are* concrete examples of energy streams joining to powerful effect. The night of the presidential election in 2012, I cried with relief. So much seemed to be hanging in the balance. I was heartened to think that the Rainbow Coalition (black, brown, female, gay, poor, environmental) had joined forces to push back the Great White Oppressor.

I know it's not that simple, but it is possible to turn in a more positive direction—to work to provide rights and opportunities for all, put the planet before profits. I was rereading a section in *Grandmother Dreams* about oppression,[18] and it occurred to me that part of The Shift is about creating this New World.

If larger numbers of people move towards Love and Compassionate Action, then these are the kinds of things we might see. Being aware of The Shift is a beginning. Coping with vibrational changes follows that. As more people open up, a positive mass movement is possible.

Moving Love and Compassionate Action both come from and result in the awareness that humans are more alike than different. We all come from the same Creator. The Blood of Brotherhood is in my cells and in the cells of every human being. We are connected by the human family tree, but also by the web of Life, the continuity of the Universe. All of Space is continuous, inside and outside of my body, inside and outside of everyone's bodies—and we are all connected by that shared space. No wonder we can communicate across dimensions!

There definitely are people who are interested in making these kind of changes. They have read *Grandmother Dreams* and ask me how to

---

[18] *Grandmother Dreams*, pp. 79-85.

travel across the veil. These are skills that can be learned. It is important to understand, however, that it is not just about learning skills or techniques—life changes have to be made in order to accommodate this kind of energy work.

A'riquea: *Of course, you can not ask others to do what you are not already doing. So awakening is something that you model. You can teach by Being. You have seen this already. People see you or read your book and they naturally want to be able to do that too.*

It's important to sort out the smaller desire to speak across the veil from the bigger need to awaken the spirit. That is why they ask you about technique. They want to know how to do this. The better question is what is this that they see being done. Travel across the veil provides the transportation to a new place, but living in the new place is what is desired. It is a move. A move of consciousness into another level.

People can want to learn how to travel, but they also need to want to make the move in awareness. It is a new way of Being. As you know, it is a beautiful place of centering. Getting there, however, requires a shift. It requires giving up the security of knowing, of feeling safe in your ideas and thoughts and beliefs. In order to shift, one has to let go and embrace the mystery. It is not possible to live in two places at once. There can be a transition time, but eventually the new Home has to be the residence.

Making the Shift is not something that we can just layer onto our already busy lifestyles. It is a new way of Being. We want to have our energy aligned, with Ego and Spirit balanced, so that Ego is serving Spirit and not itself.

If I ask "am I traveling my soul path by making this choice," I am tempted to be motivated by the greater good, and I will almost always put the needs of others ahead of my own. But this can be draining over the long term. When is it in the interests of the greater good that I do not push my own needs away? When do I show compassion for my own self? Are needs the framework I should even be working with?

A'riquea: *This is actually a difficult topic to address. There are so many factors involved, it is not easy to distill into a few statements. I think that what you want to be thinking about is how you are moving in the* *world. Is your movement balanced. Are you making choices that help others and help yourself. There are so many choices every day and they are all interconnected with other choices.*

I'm thinking about an example such as what I choose to eat. If I choose a given food with awareness, I need to be thinking about its nutritional value, and also how much it costs and whether that affects what I can choose in the future. I want to be aware of where the food came from, whether it was it grown in a good way, how the people growing my food are treated, how it got to me, and what I am supporting by choosing this food and not another. Am I choosing this food because it really feels like the right thing to eat now or because I have some emotional need that this food is going to meet? I have gotten off track talking about this when I want to be listening. Excuse me.

We're doing fine. These are good questions. Every choice you make is like a pebble in a pond. Even not dropping it in the water is a choice.

It seems that what you are trying to straighten out is what it would look like to be on your Soul Path. This is a bigger context than just meeting your needs. What if the example you gave was about spiritual practice, spiritual food. You have gotten distracted by thinking of Me in the context of Ego. We would like you to be thinking about this in the context of Spirit.

You are making good choices in your daily life. You can also be making those kind of choices on a bigger scale, choices that place you in position to expand your spiritual life. There are choices to be made that will ripple out into the field of humans and the Universe. The Creator is waiting for this to occur. Things have been lining up to make this possible. At some point, you will need to make a change that will turn your life. Yes, cancer has accelerated the possibilities, but it is up to you to manifest the needed changes. It is time to become a mouthpiece, a teacher.

I have no doubt that I am being supported in this. I can see how I have been stuck in the daily routines of work and mainstream culture that reduce my opportunities. I have been thinking about setting goals for My Life After Cancer. Maybe I should be thinking about setting goals for My Life *With* Cancer.

It is not about cancer at all. Cancer is just the catalyst for rapid change. It is up to you to grasp the possibilities and move.

I see the possibilities. So far, though, I have not been able to see how to make the changes. I feel obligated to work, for social contact and income. I do not want to let go of the spiritual opportunities there. I do understand that there are bigger arenas for this kind of work. I have been afraid of that because I know it will lead to a bigger opening. And I can't seem to let go of the need for some kind of financial security — needing to know ahead of time how this is going to work out. I am afraid. Of course, the antidote to that fear is Trust.

Trust is important. You have come all this way and it has worked out. Think about the first day you agreed to write Grandmother Dreams. *You had a title and an opportunity. You did not know what the book would be about or how it would change you. What if you had not accepted that unknown challenge. We are asking you to make another commitment.*

The thing we would like you to do now is go out into the wilderness. Not the wilderness of Nature, but the wilderness of Mankind, of Humanity. There is great need and the time is right. Even though you are afraid, you are ready to do this.

I had to follow through on what was asked of me. I began moving *Grandmother Dreams* out into the physical world. But I felt mentally weak and unprepared. My memory and attention had been damaged by chemotherapy. Can I assume that **The Teachers** will be with me when I go?

Yes, we will be with you. Remember that these are all topics that you enjoy talking about and learning about. This is an avenue for meeting people, for forming relationships. We want you to get comfortable putting yourself out there, being a vehicle. You will need to get used to being in motion, winging it. This is just the beginning.

The channeled writing process has been about placing my Ego in correct position. Putting myself out in the world challenges that. It is easy, when alone, to sink into the Great Mystery. It's not so easy to put myself out there, front and center, in public.

There is something else here. Believe that you are just as important as anybody else, not in an ego way but in a spiritual way. All humans are spirits in physical form, making their way along a spiritual path that is obstacled with physical objects and feelings. Placing yourself in context is also about seeing this spiritual path through the maze of physical form. They go together, the two things, the spiritual path and the physical path. This is what we have been talking about when we say Spirit and Ego. They are two worlds occupying the same space.

Your directive is to help illuminate the spiritual world within the context of the physical world. Humans want this spiritual contact, but they are losing track of how to be with it. Your job is to make a place where it can be felt, and to make a place where they feel capable of making that contact themselves. You are the example, and you are the teacher. The first book is a way to start thinking about The Shift, to start thinking about how we order our lives.

Besides channeling, then, I am also being asked to function this way in a much larger context, to allow the direction of my spiritual path to move this information into the wider world through these books. This requires a lot of letting go. I have to disregard cultural pressures to keep me behaving in a predictable way, one that relies on the masculine priorities of self and achievement. Without that familiar structure, there are times when I am confused about my path.

I see an Indian Courier of the 1800s. He is wearing white man's shoes. He is **My Great Grandfather as a young man.** He is out in a broad meadow, sitting under the hot summer shade of a tree.

There is a time for everything. Sometimes it is hard to know until the time comes, so thinking ahead about it is not helpful. We want you to make these connections, it is an important time in white-Indian relations. (He looks over his shoulder watchfully.) You know my work, bringing messages to my Indian relatives, walking invisibly through the white world. You have an opportunity to do this also, in another way. You will be one who brings the messages to our Indian relatives through what appears to be the white world. Indians will be surprised to see that this is available to all, that there is a common language.

Whites can learn to communicate with the Spirit World, because it is their inheritance also. Whites have different obstacles to overcome, one of which is believing that this communication is possible. Most Natives already believe this, even if they do not currently have the skills. So you see, there is a bridging. There is no limit to who can access this communication. You are in a position to bridge both worlds.

(He glances over his shoulder again, as if concerned about how long he stays.) *You will see who comes to you, what you will be asked to do. Remember to create a space for opportunity, a space of freedom and ease. Hold that space and enjoy what comes in to it.*

(He is getting up.) *I must go now.* (He reaches out to shake my hand firmly.) *We are in this together. We are on the same team.* (He pulls me to him for a light embrace. I smell the rich perfume of his leather vest. We look each other directly in the eye and smile. He gives a quick Whoop and lopes away into the sun-heated forest.) I have good work to do.

≈

Our current culture is organized around masculine principles, and we are used to having our sense of reality stabilized in these predictable forms. We rely on our five senses to prove the findings of science, for example, and formal religion often tells us exactly what we have to believe in order to belong. We need to be able to shake off these cultural limits in order to explore and make deeper connections.

Universal Wisdom: *Spirit wants to transcend—that is its purpose. Transcending fulfills its purpose. Many humans sense that their physical beings want to expand. They have been crushed into a small space by cultural learning. What they want is more space. They want to expand and allow more energy to enter the space between matter. This is only possible with transcendence.*

Action based on the five senses is the arena of Ego. The world that transcends the five senses is the arena of Spirit. It is based in the ability to feel and integrate energy.

A'riquea: *Your ego's needs are not the same as your spirit's needs. Your ego wants to belong, it wants praise and approval. Your spirit wants there to* *be more Love. As has been talked about before, Love is a vibration. It is something you can feel.*

Philip Shepherd talks about the brain in our belly — the gut instinct that is different from cranial thinking.[19] The enteric (belly) brain is actually a network of neurons lining the abdomen. This network perceives, thinks, learns, decides, acts, and remembers all on its own. The world can be seen and felt through this brain in the belly, a different experience than being filtered by the brain in the head. The brain in the head breaks down information into little bits. The brain in the core perceives the world as a whole.

Belly perception is what we think of as intuition. It's what the term "gut instinct" refers to. It is how this meditative writing occurs. For me, it is concentrated in the base of my spine. It's why I was led to Sparkle Lake, the grounded center in my pelvis, during the first book.[20] It requires that the cranial brain (the head) take a secondary role in the process. I assume that this would also be the way that Spirit would be aware of the Love vibration.

This is correct. There is much emphasis in your culture on Love as something that occurs through the heart. The heart is a feeling organ also. But it is not meant to manage the processing that is required to sense Love vibration. This is something that is done in your body. It is why it is so important to limit the use of toxins — they cloud the body's ability to read the environment.

When we place our attention in our core and develop our intuition, we can begin practicing transcendence. This is the process through which we create a spiritual shift.

The Library Man is sitting at a table with his sheaf of papers, tapping the bottom of the pile against the table top to get them aligned. He licks his thumb and applies it to a page, as if to look something up. He looks up at me with a slight smile on his face. He tries to look

---

[19] *New Self, New World: Recovering Our Senses in the Twenty-First Century*, North Atlantic Books, 2010.

[20] *Grandmother Dreams*, pp. 100-103.

at me earnestly but can't avoid expressing his playful feelings. He is struggling to maintain his professionalism. He is also very excited. Finally he stands up, tossing the paper pile into the air like confetti, and claps his hands together.

We have reached a critical juncture here. This is where science and spirituality connect.

(I have a strange energy sensation, like a bowl that has been dropped upside-down on the floor — it wavers noisily, around and around along its edge, faster and faster, closer and closer to the ground, until it finally settles flat and silent.)

Yes. This is how this business begins. You see, we will want you to entertain these ideas, to play with them, become comfortable. It must be like second nature to you.

(He is looking around, as if searching for words.)

So, here are the things you will know well. You will tell yourself that there is no other way to do this. You cannot go back to the way things were before you didn't have this information. That would be impossible. So now you are going along. And people will be asking you how this is. Some of this is skepticism, and some is curiosity. It does not matter, because they are asking. Asking is the next step. And this is what you will say to them:

There is a way of being that transcends this physical world. It does not leave the physical world behind, because you are necessarily in it. So it includes the physical world but also transcends it. That means that it expands. Being in the Zone means that the physical body, the energy of the physical body, has expanded to include more of the physical realm. The "more" is something that is not usually seen, because humans are not used to using this kind of seeing, this kind of vision. But it is always there, waiting.

Once you gain this kind of seeing, this kind of sight, other ways of being will become possible. These other ways of being are available, but few are using them. These other ways of being bring the Universe into sharper focus. You will find that you are a beautiful being in an amazing world where everything is connected in new ways. You will be able to see the energy that connects all things.

(I can see multicolored strings, energy filaments, connecting every

Point through the Zone.)

That is just the beginning. Because within each of those strings there is a rich luminance that feeds your soul. Not only your spirit. Your spirit is the way that you come to this luminance. When you enter the luminance your soul will be renewed.

Remember that your soul is the path that your spirit travels. It is timeless and infinite. When you bathe your soul in this luminance, you will be healing humanity. When many spirits travel with the luminance and many souls are healed, there will be a collective jump in the energy of the Universe. God-energy will be revitalized. And since you, yourself, are God expressed, you also will be revitalized.

This is what is being felt in the human world at this time. Other energies in other dimensions are aligning with this luminance. Humans have not cultivated this capability, and when they feel the luminance in nearby realms this creates a sense of dis-jointedness. The luminance is not going to decrease. It is up to humans to adapt to The Luminance. There are many ways to do this. Connecting to Nature is a good start, to recognize the spirit in all things. This resonance is not something that can be faked or pretended or hoped. It can only be felt. Resonance.

We are on a clear path and we are going easily. Hold these teachings in your cells. Bring them along in your day and see where you go.

The Shift is already happening. Reactions to this change vary depending on one's level of awareness.

The Library Man: *We were talking about The Luminance accelerating in other dimensions, where humans are not used to being able to "see" it. Even though it is not seen, it is felt, and that is part of the discomfort and edginess that some humans are feeling at this time.*

Not all humans are feeling this. As you are aware, some humans are very tuned in, and feeling the luminance increase. There is reason to celebrate these sensations, and people are following through on that. People are beginning to celebrate the common threads that link diversity. This is the kind of energy that honors the strings connecting everything. This will be a good practice for you — to see and celebrate the threads that connect.

The Canadian Aboriginal artist Roy Thomas was known for his colorful paintings of totem animals. I went to an exhibit of his work and was struck by the way he connected everything. Each animal's body contained an internal network of lines, like strings, and was also connected to every other being by threads of energy. I could actually feel the spirits inside and connecting the beings.

Use your spiritual vision to see these threads of energy. This is the luminance that is being discussed. It is everywhere.

Indigenous people all over the world know about this kind of energy. It is not something new. It is ancient. All humans were once indigenous people — these are our ancestors. We have lost contact with these energy vibrations. We are being encouraged to reconnect.

~

It is easy to get distracted from my spiritual work. There are negative feelings and events, in both my personal life and in the broader world. The "news" is full of tragedy. I struggle with things that don't even affect my life directly. I feel sick, physically ill, at the violent culture we are creating and the ways that people hurt each other. I sometimes lose my spiritual compass. People are suffering every day. How do I place this in spiritual context?

Universal Wisdom: *There is not much to say about this. It is a condition of being in physical form, that there will be suffering. There will be physical suffering and grief. There will be some who choose actions that hurt others. This is always happening on a personal level, in relationships. Sometimes it plays out in a bigger way, like a catastrophe. And then groups of people have to do similar work, coping on a mass level.*

There are always choices to make. Whether there will be Love and compassion, or fear and lashing out. Much Love and compassion was shown at the bombing in Boston (2013). As you have noted, Helpers make very real heroes. Everyone will have to choose what they will focus on. True leaders will help people see the way to human compassion. Your country is fighting a battle right now between fear and compassion. It can be seen in many social and political issues. These are the choices between Ego in service to itself (fear) and Ego in service to Spirit (compassion).

These are both individual choices and group choices.

Is this also the difference between Cranial Thinking and Belly Thinking. *This conflict between fear and compassion is the natural outcome of a long period in history when cranial thinking was held up as superior. The body has been discarded as a source of information and wisdom. This is related to a masculine-based culture.*

One of the reasons that you sometimes feel uncomfortable making your spiritual work public is because your culture is not ready to accept feminine function. Masculine thinkers are in charge of media and decision-making groups. The information about feminine thinking is not being presented or supported there. That is why it feels 'underground.' And that is how it will come to people.

As we have said, this is not a leader-follower commercial religion. People will be making this shift because it feels right, because they know in their gut that this is the way to move forward. People are tiring of the consumer-driven world, they are waking up to their relationship with the environment. Compassion is living in every person, they only need to wake up to it. Wake up to it and feed it. That is a choice.

Can you say more about cultivating this Belly Thinking. Is there another name for this.

There are many ways to think about this. Centered Living is a good way to see it. Centered Living means that the body and the mind are integrated. They are both in good working order, without the clutter and masking of toxins and distractions. This was discussed in the first book, the importance of reducing toxin intake and toxin focus. Physical exercise tunes the body up to the higher vibration of spiritual energy. Being out in Nature is a reminder of one's place in the world and what Harmony looks and feels like. The mind must be free of distractions, and open to un-knowing. There must be a place for new information to enter into consciousness, new information not in the form of factual bits but of global awareness. There needs to be a connection between the mind and the body, a connection that allows the sharing of energy and awareness. The connection needs to include the pool of Universal Consciousness, connected to All.

Yes, this is what you are feeling right now, both a concentration and a spaciousness. It is difficult to describe, because it is a sensation. When you are connected to Spirit, this is how you feel. Remember that Spirit is present in multiple dimensions simultaneously. So when you are connected to Spirit, you are connected to these other dimensions also. That is part of what creates the feeling of spaciousness—you have extended beyond the boundaries of the apparent physical world.

Spirit is also present in you, and you must be present to this energy in your body in order to feel it. That is the element of concentration that you feel. Simultaneously concentrated and spacious, physically centered and spatially centered. Centered Living. These are skills that are developed through regular practice.

I was given a vision which helped me to understand Centered Living and place it in a larger spiritual context:

One day during meditation I sensed a physical structure inside my body. It was like a bee hive — made of a very light but incredibly strong natural substance, a golden-colored papery material. It had a hexagonal honeycombed structure like bees use. It started at my core and built out, just slightly past the boundary of my skin.

As I placed my attention on the structure, it expanded several feet beyond my physical body and I began to have many associated realizations about bees and the honeycomb. The honeycomb is a place where bees birth and nurture their offspring. I understood that there are some kind of seeds to be planted in my honeycomb, seeds that I will nurture and send forth, that will go out to commune with the flowers and gather pollen, other ideas, and bring them back to the hive. There is a sharing, a partnership with other layers of reality.

Think about any life form — insects, plants, water — and what the world is like for them. It certainly is not the same as what humans perceive. Ancient peoples practiced a two-way communication with other beings, a sharing, a partnership, that benefited all. Most humans today are removed from that. We seem to think that we are the only beings on the planet, and that it's all here for us. Something is missing in that.

There is a parallel between the physical world and the spiritual world that is playing out in the current killing off of our pollinators. Physically, we have altered the environment in a negative way and we see that effect in the die-off of bees. Spiritually, we have altered our relationship with Nature. We no longer recognize that the bee is a communicator for us, dispersing the pollen so that we have plants to eat. We are no longer listening to our ancestors for the wisdom that will bring us and our children safely into the future.

I see a giant bee hovering in front of my face. This bee's body is much larger than my own. I can see the bee's fuzzy body, its jointed and lacquered legs, its compound eyes. It is hovering before me, and I hear the buzz of its wings. It turns and flies into the white mist of unknowing. I see it grow smaller and disappear. Then I am flying closely behind. I follow its pointed tail and we continue through the white mist.

I hear a humming ahead, the drone of many wings. We have come through the mist and arrived at a giant hive. It is so large that I can not see the perimeter of it. We are at a flat edge that has been exposed to show the infinite compartments that the bees have created and are working in. The leader bee turns to look at me, to make sure that I know I am to follow. We enter one of the cubicles. It is dark, but I can still see.

I have an awareness of the hive's context. The hive is made up of all these compartments, but they are also conjoined into one whole. Many bees are working in here, moving their wings and communicating in other ways. Each compartment and also the entire hive is made of a light papery material that vibrates. It vibrates with the sounds of the bees. The entire hive is alive with the communication of the bees. They can all feel it, no matter where they are in the hive or what they are doing. This is an expression of the part/whole nature of the Universe. Everything is simultaneously both its individual self and also part of something larger. The bees understand this. They each have a specific task to focus on and also a larger awareness of the workings of the entire hive.

The leader bee is looking back at me again. We are moving deeper into the hive. There is a maze of connected openings and tunnels. I am following the leader bee. We have come to a domed chamber, where the Queen resides. She is resting on a bed of papery sheets that cushion her large body. She is very wise. She knows all the ways of all the bees, the separateness and the connectedness. Her liquid, intelligent eyes are looking at me knowingly. A front leg motions me closer. I feel humbled, and bow down in front of her. She is honored and amused at this. She motions towards her left eye. I am to enter.

Her eye is a huge pool of inky liquid. I am very very small. As I enter the eye, I begin to tumble gently, floating and somersaulting. The inky liquid becomes the night sky, full of stars. I have passed into the Universe. Every one of those stars is a planet, a planet with bees. I feel my weightless body pulled to a planet, into its field, and down to its surface, where the bees are communing with the flowers. I am brought again to a hive, through the papery tunnels, to the Queen, through her eye, into the Universe, full of stars that are planets, then to a planet, into its field, into a hive, through the tunnels….

It is an endless cycle. The bees are maintaining it. Their drone is the humming of an entire dimension, a dimension that exists simultaneously with the one that we, humans, perceive. The dimensions are concurrent, and interdependent. They rely on each other.

I sense that the honeycomb structure I saw earlier, growing from own my core, is related to the Matrix, discussed in other writings. Those writings describe the blueprint of our genetic heritage, and how different structures can be built out using that blueprint, depending on the effects created by both the choices of our ancestors in the past and our own choices in the present. There are multiple dimensions occupying the same Space. What we "see" depends on where we place our attention, what coordinates we choose to focus on.

I am wondering how the dimensions are interdependent. The leader bee takes me through the hive-Queen-Universe-hive cycle over and over and over, at high speed, looking back at me to make sure I am following. Then I see that the dimensions are interdependent because changes in one will affect changes in another. In the hive cycle, I can see that if humans destroy the environment on the planet where the bees live, we will destroy the bees' ability to participate in that cycle. Of course, we will also damage our own food supply. Food is not just something that we put in our mouths. It is energy, that sustains us. There is a spiritual connection to our food. It is energy transformed from one thing to another, communication on a molecular and atomic level that is necessary for Life. The leader bee is nodding, Yes.

The Bee wishes to speak: *It is important to understand your connectedness to all things. Humans are living in a kind of isolation now. As a group, you have passed through a time when you felt you could control Nature without honoring the innate wisdom of the Universe.*

There is a way that things happen, a beautiful organization. Like snowflakes, there are no two alike, but their creation follows an underlying energy pattern. Science is trying to discern this pattern. Good scientists are aware that every time they travel the tunnels of the Matrix and come to the Queen's chamber, they will always end up back in the infinity of the night sky.

At some point, humans will be aware of God, which is the total of everything. When you allow this awareness into your own body, then you will be living a spirit-centered life. This is the correct alignment of humans in the Universe — to be aware of the larger context of Life, and to function there while acknowledging the gift that is physical form.

Awareness. Your place in the Universe. The vibration that occurs when everyone is doing their specific work. Humming up. You will be able to feel this. Not just one individual, although each adds to the whole. But the vibration of the whole. Vibrating with the resonance of God. You do not have to figure this out to understand it. Feel it in your core, where the vibration builds the structure of the Matrix that supports Life. The vibration is connectedness, Love.

Go now. Place some flowers in your home. Be aware of the bee energy in each flower and the flower energy in each bee. "Bee" in touch with the vibration of the Universe. Let it be your guide.

"What you need to do is something I haven't done, something no one's done, because the whole idea is to increase the level of knowing, raise the level of consciousness."

~Joseph Rael

~ 3 ~

Be The Change

We are, by our very existence, already participating in the ongoing creation of the Universe. Our actions create vibrations — in our lives, in our ways of being, in our personal energy. Our actions also affect the way we travel in the human dimension and the impact we have on others and our environment. Our collective interactions also create vibrations in concurrent dimensions and the greater Universe.

The Teachers are asking us to add to the current energy shift of the Universe. Taking the next steps in our spiritual evolution means becoming aware of our actions and choosing how we participate in creating vibrations.

Taking action, just doing something, is a limited goal. Choosing to change requires that we look at how we are changing. The **Library Man** came to me to discuss this. He has a sheaf of papers in his hands, as usual, and is waving me over.

Let's start our discussion today with the word "likeness."

Likeness means to be like. Go ahead and look that up.

The dictionary describes "likeness" as a representation, or similarity of appearance. So, it's not the actual thing but something that looks like it. It sounds kind of surface — how something looks.

Yes. Some things can look the same but not have the same qualities. This is something we need to talk about.

People can think they are doing a correct action because of how it looks. It is a way of looking at your own self and your own behavior as if you were outside of it — what would others think if they saw me doing this or that. It is a perspective that holds a considerable amount of judgment — the judgment of one's own self and also the internalized judgment of what you believe others think. This is a very off-center way to behave. If you are thinking all of the time about how this will be perceived, then you do not have your energy aligned in the present moment. It is directed into the future of what people will think.

The reason we want to discuss this is because you are holding yourself in this future trap of thinking. Culture encourages this kind of thinking, because if you are concerned about what other people think then you will be insecure and keep working to normalize yourself. That is very profitable commercially. We do not need to be concerned about commercialism at this point. What we want to do is counteract this tendency to think in the future. We want you to be able to focus more on your inner intuition, asking yourself if this is the correct action based on whether it is the right thing to do.

You have had discussions with other Teachers about this topic. What is different today is that there is nowhere to hide when you are operating through Spirit. There is nowhere to hide, there is no need to hide. When you operate in this way you will feel peaceful and at ease.

What makes this possible is being in Point and Zone simultaneously. This is something you need to practice again.

I can feel it when I do it. I call it Love and Let Go. It is centering in the point of my physical body and also expanding into the zone of Spirit. Both grounding and expanding at the same time. I need to do more of this, practice more regularly.

Yes. It needs to happen many times every day. We need you to be in this arrangement as a way of being. There is work ahead that will require this kind of energy balance. You need to be in shape for that, you will need to be able to tolerate certain amounts of "pressure" — other people's energy trying to direct you.

You have had some tests, situations where the behavior of others affects your functioning. Think about those and then go to Point and Zone. You need to be able to return to this balance easily.

I notice that I am unable to manage Point and Zone when I am using caffeine — my energy is not under my control. I need to get better at resting when I feel tired instead of reaching for more stimulant.

I very much enjoy the days when I am self-directed, when I choose what I do and when. I need to somehow be able to manage my work environment in a similar way — be more relaxed and flowing, practice Point and Zone balance while I am there. I see that I am not going to want to keep doing that job in the future.

Some things will have to shift in order to make room for the other work for which you are needed.

I know that something is going to change. I am on the path of these books. I can not see around the corner to what that entails. This is a journey I have chosen. This is part of my purpose in life.

Just Be.

Western culture encourages a lot of doing, staying busy — not just doing one task, but careening between multiple tasks all day long. It could be called multi-doing. It's all head work. Control. Management. Non-sensate. It limits my ability to slow down enough to make connections with myself and the Universe. Choosing to refocus my attention may begin as a cognitive process, but ultimately it requires that I change how I *feel*.

Universal Wisdom: *Humans have the opportunity and the ability to make this shift. It does not appear to be an easy transition. For most people, letting go of the need to figure it out will be an obstacle. The new way is something that is sensed. That is part of why it can be difficult to describe. You are a model. Part of your job will be to create the sensation.*

Use Grandmother Dreams *to describe it. The book is a guide of how to get there, but most of it has to do with sensation. What do people feel when they read different parts. What do they feel when they hear you speaking about it. Resonance. Resonance is the key. It is what will get people motivated, and it is what they need to connect with to make The Shift.*

It is a way of going Home. Indigenous people all over the world lived in this way for thousands of years. It is what made survival possible. It is what will make survival possible again. "Civilization" is coming full circle, having made incredible advances using left-brain-type thinking, but also having gone so far that it is out of balance. There is no one at fault here. Group momentum brought humans to this point. Group momentum is what will create the shift back into balance, with increasing emphasis on right-brain-type action. (Of course, there is not strictly a right and left brain, but that is a description that Westerners can relate to.)

Someone talked before about The Shift having a source in other dimensions.

This is true. It is also true that these dimensions are not separate from the "human" dimension. Humans are currently limited by the five senses. They assume that any other dimensions are outside of that. Really, they are concurrent. Other dimensions occupy the same space. They are just not perceived. So a shift in one of these concurrent dimensions will necessarily affect humans, it will change the vibrations in the space around and inside them.

Is there a way to understand The Shift as it is occurring in these "other" dimensions. How is it that Teachers are lining up to get access to the human dimension.

These are two separate questions. The Teachers are always there, they are only waiting to be asked. At this time, there are not many requests. The Teachers have information that will assist humans in making the transition to a broader spiritual context. Human religion has focused a great deal on ideas that describe what happens when your body ceases. While this is an interesting question, it is not the foundation of spiritual functioning.

The foundation of spiritual functioning is made up of the choices humans make every day. Choosing spiritual action, like compassion, for example, moves energy. It is why humans have been given a physical form — to amplify the resonance of positive energy movement. It is not governed by a set of rules. Best Action is evidenced by the feelings of resonance that it creates. Resonance in the individual and in the action created. What we are after here is Resonance. Resonance moves energy in all of the concurrent dimensions. In the space that the dimensions "occupy." The Zone. Moving energy from one Point to another Point or Points creates energy in the Zone.

Your job is to be a Point and move energy in the Zone. When energy

is moved in the Zone, other people near you will feel it. Then they will understand what you are trying to get across.
"Get across," literally — I will be creating Resonance Between Points. *Do not be distracted by people who talk too much. Words can create resonance. Too many words create a mental barrier to sensation. Words can also be a way to pull energy towards Ego. Make sure your own actions embody Spirit. Then they will be "heard" (felt).*

What the Teachers want us to be doing is creating an energy experience. It is not something that you can buy. It is not something that you can just talk about, or do with your brain. It is something you feel. What is felt is energy. The following is an example of moving energy:

During the summer months, I set up a table at my local farmers' market and open myself to meeting people and discussing spiritual topics. I never know just what is going to happen there. It's an experience in un-knowing, in letting go. I feel vulnerable but also excited, because I usually meet very interesting people. On a typical day, there is a wide variety.

One day, I spoke for a long time with a man who was traveling the country "Looking for God." It was an exciting conversation. Imagine all of the people and viewpoints he would come into contact with! My interest shrank, however, when he started hitting on me sexually and then also revealed that he was partnered. I learned that someone can be traveling the country on a God project, but still be functioning a lot with their ego.

Just then, a woman came up to my table and looked at the books. She recoiled, clasping the Christian cross on her necklace, exclaiming that her faith was strong and that this was satan's poison. She wasn't mean about it. But she was ruffled that she'd accidentally come into contact with it, as if it was evil. The traveling God-searcher was still standing there and he rather forcefully attacked her thinking, reminding her that Jesus had gone into the wilderness for 40 days, that Jesus was a mystic. While his thoughts were relevant, his attack scared her even more.

Interested in soothing the energy at my table, I pulled her attention to me and calmly explained that there was nothing harmful in these books, that the Spirits were giving me the same messages as Jesus — about Love and about creating compassion for each other. I moved my energy into Love and Let Go (transcendence). We were facing each other and I put my arms out slightly, palms up and open. She smiled and relaxed.

I learned that it is important to be able to reach out to people of religious conviction and find common ground. I was reminded about developing the Bigger Church. People with religious convictions already have faith in a higher power. They have many resources, but those resources tend to steer them away from independent thinking. People without religious convictions have more freedom, but fewer resources. Everyone is limited by cultural and technological clutter.

That same day, I met a man who talked about people who are accessing other dimensions. He said that we can be judged by other people as being "crazy" because they don't understand us. He talked about musicians, and all kinds of artists, who have to surf the edge and embrace disorder in order to be creative.

Bob Dylan wrote about this in relation to his creativity. He said that early in his career, "…it dawned on me that I might have to change my inner thought patterns…that I would have to start believing in possibilities that I wouldn't have allowed before, that I had been closing my creativity down to a very narrow, controllable scale…that things had become too familiar and I might have to disorientate myself."[21]

In order for something to change, something's gotta change. There has to be movement. Even though the new way is better or more helpful, I won't be well practiced at it. I'm going to make some mistakes while I learn. I will feel discomfort when I give up the old way. Feeling

---

[21] *Chronicles, Volume One,* Simon & Schuster (2004), p. 71.

anxious or fearful or irritable or sad is not a sign that something is wrong—it might just be a sign that something is changing.

I learned more about this on a personal level when I went through the tumultuous journey of cancer treatment. In just one year I gave up my body as I knew it, my health, my stamina, some of my cognitive skills, my job, a 30-year career, and my income—all while maintaining a single-parent household. It was a lot to deal with all at once. I was worried about my future, but I had no choice—I had to let go and see where I went. I had to learn that I can't control everything. After the dust settled, the only clear thing was my new path as an author, but I had no idea how to do that. I had to be able to let go and Trust.

A'riquea: *That's right. We would not invest so much in your process and then just let you go. We are still in this with you. We want this to succeed. You made a commitment, and we did too. It is true that you are going to have to take some action. But right now you need to get back into your physical presence. This is a long road, all of it. And as was said before, there is no linear finish.*

There is so much going on simultaneously. Think of how your body has changed, but also how your feelings and awareness have changed. Everything is in motion. That is why this is a good place to be making a change. It is easier to make a shift when things are already stirred up. There is less attachment. There is more freedom.

As we have said, worry pulls you into the future—a future which has not happened and is therefore unknown. It can be remade between then and now. It is worth thinking about, so that you can be making helpful choices when opportunities arise. But you cannot make choices in the future right now. Pull back to the tasks at hand—healing and return of energy movement. Awareness will come in time.

As I traveled the path of channeled writing, I understood that what I was being asked to do was assist myself and others in making The Shift. I knew that it would require following unexpected opportunities and using them to move consciousness. I could use the skills that I had developed as a community health nurse—communicating, teaching, connecting with people. But I was challenged to place that in the context of my current upheaval, to put a label on it.

A'riquea: *You are working hard to make this fit into a known quantity. It is natural to want to do this. It can give you a sense of security, something to hang onto. It is important for the process to be fluid. You will need to follow the unexpected. That cannot be measured against the name of your work. It has to fit your sensations. It has to resonate. You will want to keep yourself as free to resonate as possible.*

What about some of the people around me who are interested in also doing this work.

This is a place to be careful. Most have good intentions, and some good connections, and then they also have an ego, just like everyone else. It will be rare to meet anyone without this. You will have to navigate a world of humans in order to do this work. You will need to trust your intuition and then do the best with what you can. Look for those who have some of the same goals that you do.

I was encouraged by the words of Joseph Rael, the visionary Native American artist and shaman. In his book *House of Shattering Light*, he talks about the need to let go of managing, and learning to listen well: "It seems as if the Universe always gives me something right around the time that it knows I'm ready to go to the next level. I don't necessarily have to like it, I just have to do it. Then comes the next thing when it's time for that to happen...That's the way I live. I never know how the things I do are going to turn out. I just show up and do what I'm told. This energy follows me around, but I always know if I don't do what I'm told I will be unhappy. I used to tell my students, be sure that you follow your guidance because that guidance is in your higher interest. From that, other experiences will come to you that will enhance your growth."[22]

～

Uncertainty is a fact of life. We don't have control over everything that happens to us. An illness like cancer, for instance, doesn't

---

[22]Council Oak Books (2011), pp. 109-111.

make life uncertain — it just exposes the uncertainty that is already there. As I went through treatment and watched every aspect of my life unravel, I had faith that this was what needed to happen to lay a foundation for a new way of life.

I could have fought the changes and tried to fit them into the form of my old life. But that's not how transformation works. It's about starting over with what you have. I was feeling a little afraid, however, because I couldn't see the new way. I didn't see the way to go, the path to take.

A young woman came to me in a vision: She motions for me to come and join her. She is moving, along with others, on something like a conveyor belt of energy. She is bubbly and laughing. She is pointing to a spot open in front of her.

When I get on the energy belt, I turn and look ahead. I can see that there is a long line of other beings on the belt. It's a little like being on an amusement ride, we are moving into a scene of incredible technicolor and movement. People are dancing and moving and talking and laughing. This is exciting for them. I am looking around trying to figure out what the scene is, and the young woman rolls her eyes in exasperation. Why am I trying so hard? Just let go!

When I let go I feel my body lay back, and I travel the technicolor tunnel at high speed, the colors blurring. I am also rotating, like a spindle. The tunnel is all technicolor along the top, while below it is dark, it is the night sky full of stars. I have somersaulted away from the tunnel into the night sky, floating in a ball with my knees tucked up to my chin, my hair streaming around my head. I am enjoying the weightless float. The young woman is still on the energy belt, and is motioning impatiently for me to quit fooling around and get back there. So that is where I am supposed to be, on the energy belt.

I go back to my place on the belt and watch the colors go by, like clouds sweeping along. I wonder if the belt has to do with my intentions. The young woman is nodding vigorously. I have set energy in motion with my intentions. Right now I am riding on that energy. I am heading somewhere. It doesn't matter that I cannot see the end of where I am going.

I am reminded of the Malaysian plane that went into the ocean in 2014, and people just disappeared. The Oso mudslide, also in 2014, and people just disappeared. There is so much uncertainty. Every day could be my last. Every week or month or year, could be my last. I know this now. With cancer, I know it in a way that I never could have before. That's why you make the best with the time you have.

That has been hard for me, because I am trying to deal with so many changes at once, all while my body is full of the poison of chemo. But maybe that is what I need to be doing now. Maybe surfing the change and accepting it is what I can do. I have been reaching people and affecting them through my blog. I have been feeling that this is the kind of exposure I will need, eventually. Or now. Whatever. It is not for me to figure out. The young woman is motioning me back onto the energy belt. Yes, why can't I just enjoy the ride. Things will work out, one way or another. I cannot possibly see all of the ways that the future will be affected by what is happening in my life right now.

I need to be on the energy belt of my own intentions. It is interesting that others are on this energy belt also. Are these the ones who are going to help create the next layer of spiritual evolution? The young woman nods her head Yes, and she points ahead. Far ahead, at the end of the tunnel, is an opening. We are all moving towards that opening. I peer ahead, trying to figure out what it is. She has her arms folded across her body, tapping her foot and looking up at the ceiling in frustration. Obviously, I still have work to do in letting go. I am chronically trying to figure stuff out that I either don't need to or can't. I need to enjoy the ride more. Let go of Points. Experience Space.

I don't want to be stuck in my head, trying to figure things out all the time. I also don't want to be drifting around aimlessly. I want my effort to be balanced.

My **Grandmother Millie**[23] is pointing to the keyboard.

---

[23] **Grandmother Millie** is my paternal grandmother. She passed on long before I was born.

There is more to talk about regarding the way you move in the world. You have gotten into the habit of getting pulled along by one thing and then the next. You feel tired because you are always dealing with something that seems to be externally generated. It would be good to find a way to bring yourself more into the present. You will need to set some goals and develop steps to achieve them. Each day, ask yourself, "What am I doing to work towards this goal." Things will begin to arrange themselves around those goals, until your life is traveling on the stream of energy that that has created. It is the same principle as setting an intention and letting it create itself, except that this is more direct. You will make choices that support your goal.

I am being asked to arrange my activities around a goal and travel on the energy stream, the energy conveyor belt, that those activities create. And then I need to let go of controlling the outcome, to trust the Universe and how it works.

∼

Cancer was a cleaning of the slate, a total starting over in almost every area of my life. All along that path there were difficult decisions, and I just had to trust that things were lining up, even though I was unable to understand what the outcome was going to be. I could have gone a hundred different directions with anxiety, but those all undermine Trust.

If Trust is an action, what is it that I am trusting? I don't believe in a God that is some singular personality up in the clouds directing the life of every individual human. I am comfortable placing Trust in the God that is Universal Energy — that somehow there is energetic support for the flow of thought, intention, choice, action.

I first heard about "the Spirits that support the Creator" in a Native prayer, and it immediately caught my attention. These spirits are what I call The Teachers. They are supporting the God in me. They are supporting the thoughts and actions that move energy. Not just any energy, because they are certainly interested in the movement of Love and compassion, certain kinds of energy. They are interested in actions that move human evolution along. I would like to hear about the Spirits that support the Creator.

Universal Wisdom: *Why do you think you want to know this.*

I would like to be ordering my prayers and intentions appropriately, for one thing. I also would like to better understand this arrangement of multiple dimensions. Spirits seem to be supporting me directly, but I assume they are also supporting others, as well as doing other things. The actions of humans seem to be both affecting and affected by energy in other dimensions.

While I am typing this I can see a hazy blue world, inhabited by beings that appear to be hazy white. The beings can step into technicolor manifestations, so that I can see them more clearly. They can also present technicolor, apparently three-dimensional, environments. So that is all about presentation, making energy appear as objects that I can relate to from this side of the veil.

"Things" do not have the same appearance in other dimensions. They are made to resemble your dimension.

So, energy beings in other dimensions can see or understand this dimension. Or they have been here before? Or is it my mind that orders the information that way? I definitely see the Teachers as individuals with personality characteristics.

You do not need to know these things to continue.

I have to smile. My questions are not part of the current program. Why do I even think I need to know this. Kind of funny, that I thought I would be directing this. Okay. Is there something you would like to address today.

We would like you to know that the journey you are traveling will not be easy. You hope that everything will fall into place just because you are following directions. It may not be so. Other things have to line up, things that are not in your control.

It is true that you make the best of the circumstance you find yourself in. That does not mean that the reward will be the beautiful golden future you imagine. The way to do this is to make the best choice in any situation and then move on. You have been thinking about this in a linear way, that one thing follows another. You know, of course, that things happen out of order, and sometimes the action of another changes the whole direction.

~

Another Teacher came to encourage me on my path. I first saw him in a sleeping dream. I thought he might be my father's father, who passed on while his sons were very small, long before I was born. In the dream, he was a tall man with closely shaved, whitish hair. He was wearing a gray sweatsuit, looking very comfortable. I could tell that he was an athlete, muscular and strong, with a confident posture. I was sitting in front of him and I had a book on my lap that I was writing in. The paper was thick and brownish colored. There were entries in different colors, like a spreadsheet, handwritten. We were about halfway down the page and the last one was circled. I realized that I was keeping book (baseball game stats). I looked down at myself and saw that I was wearing a worn vest of red wool, my grandfather's semi-pro baseball uniform from the early 1900s.

Now he wants me to type. He stands with his arms folded, a very authoritative presence, somewhat impatient with my dithering. So I will move ahead and see what he would like me to write.
Can I ask who you are?
You can ask. (He is smiling.)
He leans forward and opens his mouth wide, swallowing me. I am tumbling down, down in the white mist. It is a pleasant state.

Now I have landed, on damp, green grass, a great lawn surrounded in fog. When I stand up I can see the bleachers above the top of the ground fog. The stands are empty now, but I can hear the echo of voices across the ball park, the crack of batting practice. I feel alive when I am here, like I have come Home. The man in gray has a huge grin on his face, his head thrown back in a belly laugh. I know he likes it here too, and is tickled to see me enjoy it. It is a shared love.

Now he is looking off in the distance, extending his arm to point at something. I turn, but can not see through the fog. Now he stands behind me, his arm pointing over my shoulder to something ahead. My eyes follow his finger.

A small hole has opened in the fog. Through the circle I can see a batter at the plate, just finishing a tight swing. He is looking out to the field, and then taking a home run trot around the bases. The basemen are congratulating him as he passes them. He waves to the centerfielder. Just as he rounds third he picks up speed and slides headfirst into home. He lies in the cloud of dirt laughing, with his hand still on the plate. He stands to dust himself off and jumps onto the plate with both toes before heading for the dugout. His suit is white with pinstripes, and he turns back to wink at me jauntily.

There must be baseball in heaven!

He smiles, sitting on the bench now with his cap tipped back on his forehead.

You are a happy man.

I was never happier than when I was playing ball. It was my whole life and I loved it. I wanted to give this love to my boys, but they missed it. Life was too hard for them after I died.

He looks down now, rubbing his eyes with his palms.

There really was nothing I could do about it. Their mother was a good woman who suffered for my love of the game. And then she suffered when I left. It all ended with nothing. Look at how my boys lived, in poverty and isolation.

You have something else, though. (He is looking straight at me.) You have something else in the way you walk the Earth. You have a gift, the gift of knowing. You can go where I never went, and pull us all along with you. When you come in to the Zone, we are all united. We are back together as a family, as one big family. We can understand each other. Because Zone is a common language. Don't be afraid to function from there. Sometimes you feel like you are losing your mind, and that is just because you are connecting to something other than Time. Don't worry over it. You need this skill. I couldn't do it. I got sick and died.

But the skills are the same. Stay focused and relaxed. Wait for the opportunity when it comes to you, and then use your concentrated energy to swing hard. Take off on the trip Home, connecting with those who are at the milestones along the way. Never give up. If you need to, slide headfirst when you get Home. Enjoy yourself. Don't be afraid to get a little dirty. It's all the same: baseball, Life.

Yes, I am your **Grandfather Wilhelm***. I want you to remember me this way, in a ball uniform. Don't give up. Just like baseball, Life is made of mostly failures. But you can't get a hit if you don't swing the bat. And none of it's any good unless you're having fun.*

I'm going to be talking with you some more. But right now I want you to go off and think about what I've said. Work on your attitude. Live your life like you're playing ball. Get into the game. Laugh it up.

∽

I understood the need to organize my life along a spiritual path. But I struggled with the daily challenges of being a single parent and working fulltime. I felt like I was fitting my life into a structure that was not nourishing me. What would my life look like if it was organized to feed me instead of drain me? I want to be riding the edge of the spiritual world. I have to focus on bringing that into the physical world, and using the teachings I receive to be a spiritual activist.

No.

Huh. I thought it would be selfish if I just kept having visions and experiences but didn't share them.

A'riquea*: Having the experiences is, in itself, a valuable process. It adds to the energy of enlightenment on a broader scale. Do not downgrade the value of the experience itself. It is true that the information needs to be moved, what you call spiritual activism. But it is not a specific experience that forms the information to be moved. It is the change and the learning that needs to be moved. It is important to have the experiences so that you have greater understanding, but also because it moves the energy patterns in physical form.*

It changes the vibrations.

It changes the vibrations in you, and that is what people are reacting to when they are excited about the information. That is why it was important to create the physical object of a book, but also to be prepared to work at moving that information in person. Person-to-person.

I am uncomfortable being in the spotlight. I shrink from it. But then I think about the interactions I've had around the book. I am nervous about doing book readings, for example, but when I get there I feel relaxed and present. The actual task is lovely. The anticipation of it is what was uncomfortable.

That is the difference between Ego and Spirit. Your ego was concerned about judgment and fitting in. Your spirit knew the way.

I seem to be floundering with the next part, the redesigning of my life. What is the next step here.

The next step is to get ready. Use this time to prepare.

What am I preparing for? I think my world is going to change in a big way once the books really get moving, and I should enjoy this time now, before the world comes into my life — appreciate the simplicity of how things are now. I tend to think of my life as too complex, but really it's just too busy with things that are not my primary focus.

Yes. You need to practice living your life in a spiritual context. Make sure that the things you are choosing nourish your spirit.

Ego in correct alignment, enjoying what Spirit chooses. Spirit needs to do the choosing. If the shoe fits that foot, then I will continue to walk the spiritual path, and that will feed me. There are so many physical-form complications. When I practice Love and Let Go, my spirit becomes more visible.

Don't be so hard on yourself. You feel you have made mistakes, but that is no reason to stop having fun. Remember there are two parts: Love and Let Go. Let Go. Of expectations, of anxiety, of Ego.

The world is about to open up to you. You will not be able to experience that if you are running away from it. Keep looking at that behavior. In order to Let Go, you must be present. You can do this. Go back in the first book and read "where does the fear go."[24] You are letting fear have too big a voice. Remember that you are preparing for the next part of your journey. Practice new behaviors that will help you Open Up. Practice being Open.

---

[24] *Grandmother Dreams*, p. 148: *"Fear, itself, is not a bad thing. It can be a tool. The realization of fear is, literally, a call to attention — pay attention to what is happening and shift your attention. Not away from it, but towards something else. Fear is a notice that disconnect is occurring. It is a reminder to reconnect. To reconnect, not with ego, but with Spirit."*

~

Being open invites new ways of seeing and feeling. I can use those new ways to make a change in my life, but only if I also make a commitment to making a change.

I dreamt one morning that I was at a school, a school for Indian people. Class was out and I was moving on. I was looking for a place to go to further my education. In my mind I was looking around the landscape of the state. I saw a college but resisted it, because it was not a Native school.

I was setting up a place to stay while I looked. I went where there were already other tents. I was dragging some 2x4s to make a platform under my tent. I was checking inside my tent, and saw that it had gotten wet inside when the door was open overnight and I was gone somewhere else. I saw a young Indian woman go by carrying a water container. She was going to a spigot to get water for me, to help me set up my camp. She was very glad to be doing this.

I see the smiling face of this beautiful young woman in front of me now. She is very happy, enthusiastic. She wants to cross over to me. She steps forward now, towards me, her smiling face looking downward as she approaches my body. She has my face in her hands. She looks me in the eye gently, talking to me sweetly and convincingly.

I am your **Flower Stream.**[25] *We have been waiting for you to become whole with your Indian Self.*

(I am overwhelmed at the thought of my Indian Self, I am crying.) This is one of the places I am stuck. Not understanding how I can belong when my skin is not brown, when I am not part of the community, not able to prove who I am.

But you are part of the community, the spiritual community. That is all that is important. The rest is something that is out of your control.

---

[25] **Flower Stream** is a young Indian woman. She is the manifested personality of my spirit form. Her gentle voice is soft and whispery, like flower petals.

We have been waiting for your return. We are happy to see your camp here. All you need to do is occupy it. The rest is already in place.
This is about Trust, and Faith.

And standing up in your own life, as you call it, walking straight. It is the Red Road, the path of Living Well. You know this path, you can feel it. When you trust those feelings, you will be traveling the spirit path. We want this for you and for us. We can support you, but you must make the choice to be on the path. You must make the choice every day, in every thing that you choose.

I understand this intellectually, it makes sense. But then I get pulled off and it is not so clear how to choose it.

How did you feel when you sat by your Spirit World husband in the Physical World on the pow-wow bleachers.[26]

I felt extremely alive. A little scared, but buoyed by the knowledge that it was the right thing to do. I needed to make that connection, to get it started.

And this is how to choose well — by how it feels.

She is looking above and behind her, to the clouds.

This is not so hard for me to understand — the spiritual realm. I am challenged to maintain that in the physical world. I have not done so well with my choices there.

You may want to think of a goal, like meeting your spiritual husband again. Try on the choices to see if they bring you closer to or farther from him.

Yes, he seems to be fading from my life lately. And I am also afraid of getting set up, of believing in something that really is not going to manifest in the physical world.

How will you know if you don't try. And if it does not manifest, for some reason that is out of your control, you will still have woven spirit into your choices.

Make your camp. Right now this is what you need to do. The next step will become clear only after you have made this choice.

I see the camp in the Dream World. Somehow, I need to weave that

---

[26] This relationship is explained more fully in Chapter 5: "Walking In Two Worlds."

into my physical world and the choices I make here.

Yes.

I did not sleep in my camp last night. I was gone and it was neglected. I became disconnected by a brief separation from my children. I felt abandoned, and I was aware that that was just a hook into my old negative patterns. Feeling lonely and isolated is a situation I keep recreating.

It is part of being human, this history. You have chosen to make it part of the definition of who you are.

I am clinging to it as an identity. It helps me to keep believing that I am not responsible for the situation I have created. Responding in this way is continually recreating the situation.

Yes.

So then, a response which does not drain my power into the external illusion would be....

To not take it personally. It may be true that someone has left you. It is also true that they have a life and are moving through it, and sometimes it overlaps with yours and sometimes it does not. You can choose to celebrate the times it overlaps. You can also choose to feel loss when it does not. This is the grieving of attachment that Buddhists work to eliminate — no attachment, no grieving. So there is something to be aware of in the celebration of being together. Are you celebrating "having" this person in your life, using this social connection to fill a void of longing or loneliness? Or are you celebrating the proximity of spirit — are your spirits touching each other?

Experiencing attachment and loss is externally focused. Celebrating spiritual connection is internally grounded.

And that is enough for now. We hope that you will choose to occupy your camp. I will be waiting there for you.

I see my tent. Eagle Brother, my spirit husband, is lying in there on his side with his head propped on his hand, looking out at me expectantly.

Once I began to accept the commitment, to occupy my camp, I sometimes felt small and vulnerable in the physical world. I wondered how to figure all this out. **Flower Stream** came to me again:

This is the way you need to be moving. You are going in a good direction. You are being sidetracked, however, by the need to figure it out. This is not a mental process, it is a feeling process. It is ok to help yourself with some labels for how you feel, but then needing to name everything becomes the process. Your Shift will be obscured. Focus on your heart. Ask your heart what it is feeling, feel the feelings. You do not have to understand them to move ahead.

Think of the wind. You can see the effect of the wind on the trees and the clouds, as it moves through your hair. You do not know where it came from or where it is going, and you do not ask to know. You just have the experience. Enjoy the wind in your hair. Enjoy the new feelings in your heart. Let your heart move with the wind. Listen to the song it makes there. Let the song guide you.

It doesn't matter if anyone else hears the song or dances to it. It is your heart, it is your song. For now, focus only on this.

Thank you. When I do this, I hear the wind in the leaves, and I feel my body swaying. It is very pleasant. It feeds itself. I feel a peaceful joy. *I am with you. Turn to me.*

~

Just making the commitment to change does not mean that I am suddenly lounging on a bed of roses. There will be continual challenges. I have negative experiences in the physical world, and I have to navigate my reactions to them—these are clues on my path.

I finally began to realize that a lot of what was wrong in my life had been my own creation. There was something about the way I had ordered my reality that was crushing me. Crowding out my spirit. I tend to think I have no choice, that I have to work this much and do this much and function this way. I had been convincing myself of that.

In *Anatomy of the Spirit*,[27] Carolyn Myss says, "From a spiritual perspective, the entire physical world is nothing more than our classroom, but the challenge to each of us in this classroom is: Giv-

---

[27] Three Rivers (1996), pp. 169-70.

en your particular body, environment, and beliefs, will you make choices that enhance your spirit or those that drain your power into the physical illusion around you?"

I had been beating myself up my whole life because I did not fit mainstream cultural expectations, because being "different" made me an outcast. I am judged as less-than because I am female, because I am a low income, single mother, because I am middle-aged and past the bloom of youth, because I have "extra" skills in dreaming. I have not been so concerned with changing myself, as I am frustrated that society has to be so rigid and judgmental. In the end, it is me that is being judgmental — about myself!

Universal Wisdom: *We need to tell you something that you do not want to hear. You do not want to hear this because it will change how you see things. You need to hear that Life is not all good. You want to think that Life is essentially good and you are getting robbed of this life by the outside world.*

You are still playing the victim. You have worked on this before, and that was important. Here is the next step: Life is happening. People are making choices. There are cascades of consequences all around you and everyone else. Living on this planet with so many people and so many choices, there is a lot occurring which is not in your control. The physical illusion is being maintained by many. The point of the books you are helping to create is that you may be able to open up some more people to increased awareness. This needs to happen. You need to awaken yourself, as well.

One of the things that you need to become aware of is how out of your control most of Life is. You cannot choose whether it is going to rain today or not. You also cannot choose other people's actions. You have been fixated on yourself as if protecting or defending or isolating yourself is going to make these "bad" situations change into something "good." You can only control your own perceptions, and you have been struggling with this. At some point, you have to give up the illusion that you have any control except how or if you will react to any situation or person.

It's not that things are hopeless, or that you are powerless. It's that you must focus that power on what you can control. The only thing you are in control of is Love. Love is the Life Force that needs to be moved. Everything that feeds Spirit is also something that moves Life Force, that illuminates Love. This is what your choices need to be based on. It is a very simple formula, not such a simple task. You will improve with practice.

This is exactly the difference between being spirit-motivated and being drained by the external illusion. It is the key to every one of my current challenges. My whole body feels alive right now. How could I have forgotten this? And, I am a little surprised to hear that I didn't want to hear this.

You are going to be challenged to start taking responsibility for your thought and actions. You have settled into a comfortable pattern of uncomfortable responses.

I am thinking about how long term these patterns have been wired. *It is important to be aware of the response pattern when it is in evidence. Sometimes, of course, you will not be able to see it. The most important thing is to make a conscious choice that moves Life Force, to choose Love, whenever possible. That is the practice part.*

All of the so-called negative feelings are clues — hurt, anger, defensiveness. Anything that pushes someone or something away from you. It's not that you need to accept bad choices by other people. What you need to be able to do is allow those choices to be in your world without eliciting a negative reaction.

It would be helpful to keep Zone in mind. All of those negative choices are in the Zone, they just are, because everything is. Their proximity to you is meaningless unless you return their negative energy, setting up a point-to-point pathway. A zone-to-zone relationship actually disperses the negativity, because it has nowhere to "land." Zone is continuous. Moving Love energy through it allows spiritual contact, connection. It reduces the impact of negative choices.

You are asking about the definition of "negative." Positive and negative are relative terms, of course. Some choices are consciously negative and others are unconscious. Most choices have some of each. This was discussed in the first book — most choices have some of both elements. What people call "evil" is purely conscious. Very few situations meet this criteria. Typically, you are going to be dealing with some of each.

You do have a responsibility to point out when someone's actions have been harmful, but it is not up to you to decide the consequences of their choice. It is up to you to function in the Zone and make sure that your own actions are as clean as possible, take responsibility when they are not, and not attract negative energy by reacting to the choices of others.

This last thing is key. You must first be able to open yourself up and move Love in the Zone. This weaves your spirit into the events and relationships of your life. You will know when you are functioning in the Zone by how you feel — open, expansive, loving. That is critical. Keep checking and make sure that Zone is your mode of operation. You have gotten very distracted lately by multiple Points. It is why you feel so tired, so drained by the external illusion.

You have finally given yourself some much-needed rest, but you have forgotten exercise. Exercise tunes up the body to an energy vibration which more closely matches Spirit. Don't be too concerned about making mistakes here. It is difficult to manage all of these areas at once until you develop more skills. The main thing is that you are aware of Zone and function in it as much as possible.

It is important to understand how choosing to make a change affects our lives. Every time we choose something, anything, we are planting a seed. The Buddhist concept of "storehouse consciousness" describes this. It reminds us that everything in our lives is either the fruit of a seed planted in the past, or a seed we are planting now for our future.

When we continue to repeat our behavior patterns, we are just planting the same seeds over and over. This means that we will continue to reap the same fruit over and over in our future. If, instead, I can interrupt my behavior and choose a better seed to plant for the future, I will reap a different fruit when that seed matures. It is a constant, daily, process. The following conversation explores this:

A long-standing challenge in my life revolved around my attempts to understand why I was single. I had managed to extract myself from a bad marriage and moved on. I was an attentive and aware single parent. I had a productive and rewarding job. I had a supportive community.

I asked: Really, do you get to have *every*thing in life? Why can't I just be happy where I am? I hear people say that they chose a flawed relationship because they didn't want to be alone. I'm not willing to compromise that much. Every situation is imperfect, but I need something that is at least a good fit. How much of this is about me being too defended, too closed, too unwilling, too picky? I feel like I'm driving in circles, not really getting anywhere that helps me deal with this challenge in a new way. The current way is old and tired. I need a fresh perspective.

There isn't really much to say about this. You have worked yourself up over a loss that you think you have. There may be a loss, but it is not what you think it is. You want your life to look like everyone else's, and you see everyone as partnered when that is not the case. Look around at the single men you see in the bars. Look around at the people who are married and miserable, who don't communicate. Everyone has things to work out, whether they are alone or "with" someone. You already know this. You choose to not see it.

You are not holding the edge of the coin. You are looking at one side. The edge is about relationships, all of them, and the collective of all of them. Go back to the foundation, your purpose in Life, which is to move Love energy. You can do this in an exclusive relationship, or you can do with a community of people. You are working in community right now, and things are beginning to move in a meaningful way there.

In both my job and the book.

The book is the most important place to focus. Your job is a way to practice what you preach. A relationship would just pull you out of focus. It is not something you need to be doing right now. Recognize your physical world, which includes the biological drive for sex. Keep that balanced with your spiritual world. You are right to be choosing a relationship that incorporates both. Realize that you are choosing. It is not that something is being withheld from you. Remember when you admitted that you were single because you hadn't found someone who was co-parenting material. That is a choice. So is this one. You are not the passive victim. Seeing yourself that way aids depression. Give yourself credit for choosing — not overly high standards, but health. This is where you need to be. You are not in the wrong place, you just are not seeing well.

This is very helpful. Exactly what I needed. Thank you so very much. Can I ask who is speaking today.

This is **You in the Future**, *a far distant future, reaching back to keep the path directed. You have done a lot of work, and it is much appreciated. Students are looking back from the future to see how this can happen. Clearly, there is a path which includes faith in the unseen world, connection to Zone. When you stay connected to Zone, you are recognizing the past and creating the future in the present.*

I can feel this. Zone has taken on a denser quality, more "solid" but still The Everything. More Presence. More energy. It's a good feeling. Not like pleasure-good, but like right-thing-good.

But I am confused. If I can choose to manifest this energy or not, doesn't that choice affect the future? How can the future be looking back if I am creating it now? Yes, it exists simultaneously, but how do my choices in the present affect the future?

Choice in the present affects quality in the future. There will be more discussion of this as you continue to learn.

Thank you. I look forward to more learning.

And, is there a name for me-in-the-future who is reaching back to me now. A name of some kind would help me to link. Or maybe not — when I said that about linking I felt a rigidity occur, a limiting factor which stifles energy movement in the Zone. I do not want to anchor Zone in this way. Me-in-the-future expands in all directions. Naming forms a linear bridge to a Point.

Expansion in the Zone is what you want to be doing. Eventually you will also learn to manage Point-to-Point energy in the expanded Zone, but this is not the time to do that.

I want to maintain an open space, not create limits. That is a recurring theme: allowing Space. This applies to all of my future, even one second from now. I don't need to work at creating or maintaining Space, I need to recognize Zone and exist in it.

I marvel at the beauty of this beyond-five-senses connection. I cannot imagine how anyone could function without this in their life. It is a great gift to me, and I am so thankful.

Honor the gift by following the path. Your feet will be light.

Thank you.

Be The One.

∼

Maintaining presence in the physical world and in the spirit world simultaneously, walking in two worlds, is a state of being. Various techniques or methods can be used to get to that state, but they are not the state itself. Techniques just help us learn to move our attention from one state to another. What is important is where we end up resting our attention, what we focus on. That is something we can choose.

Many people might find it hard to believe that we choose our state of being. But our state of being just describes an energy arrangement. Sleep is one state, for example, and waking is another. Anxiety is a state where we focus our energy on fear of the future. Task-driven Western culture encourages a series of anxious states, transferring our energy from one task to the next. We can ask ourselves, are we primarily constructing a conscious relationship with tasks, or with flow? With objects, or with space? With Ego, or with the Universe?

I had been struggling to deal with a coworker who was very passive-aggressive — sweet and syrupy on the surface but vicious underneath. She had intentionally created much damage in our work environment. For the most part, I managed to either avoid her or not engage her behavior.

One day, I was seated next to this person at a long meeting, and felt myself boiling with anger and judgment. To calm down, I had to examine my own behavior. I conversed with the Teachers as I sat there and came to see that I am not responsible for creating consequences for my coworker — that will happen in her own life.

I also heard that we are all, each one of us, God's creation. I could see everyone in the room, including myself and this person, as God's creation. Seeing all of us, singly and together, created a surge of tremendous spiritual energy.

A'riquea: *What would it be like if no one paid attention. If no one paid attention to what has been given. Everyone would be functioning as if they were the only person in the world. Stuck in their own bubble of pain and frustration, blaming everyone else for their circumstance in life, not taking responsibility.*

Responsibility means response-ability — the ability to respond.

The ability to respond to what. This is the choice you are given. We will respond to that which we have given our attention to. What we choose to focus on will determine our reactions and our actions. When you choose to focus on the behaviors of another, you have given up the ability to focus on your own behavior. This is a convenient dead end. It is difficult to focus on ourselves, because we will see that we are not perfect, that we are flawed. Yet this is what it means to be human. If we had no flaws, then we would have nothing to learn. Learning is what brings us closer to God. Remember that God is the energy of Life Force in motion. Being perfect is a stagnant state.

It is not that we should not put our attention on others. But what we want to see in the other is not the results of their human imperfec-tions — which is their behavior. We can look at their human imper-fections and Love them. We can see them through spiritual eyes, and offer compassion on their journey. We can recognize that we are all on a spiritual journey. That is our Soul Path. Spirit traveling the Soul Path.

Remember that our purpose in this life is to travel the Soul Path, to follow the energy of Love, creating Life Force through Compassion. The intention of the first book was to show the difference between Ego in service to Self and Ego in service to Spirit. The work of this second book will show Spirit manifesting on the Soul Path. This will require that you drop some of your external obligations. You have seen this, the white box of emptiness.

When I think about reinventing my life, it appears like an empty white space, kind of like the reply box on a text message, with the cursor blinking at me. It's wide open, and that feels like a huge freedom. I don't want to just fill it up, I want to choose what goes in there.

Yes, you will choose what to put in the white space, but part of the lesson will be about leaving the white space empty. Not making a life, but allowing creation to make you. Being open. You have to let go in order to travel in this way. It is another step. First you had to learn to let go of mental constructs, ways of thinking that limited your spiritual connections. Sometimes you will feel disconnected from the "real" world that others are experiencing.

I recognize this, that sometimes I am seen as "crazy." That is a term that others use to describe something they do not understand. But connection beyond the five senses, to Zone, means connection to the ancestors and the ways which will bring balance. Intuitive skills are needed, and the honoring of the feminine.

This is the balancing that needs to occur. It will be difficult for a world view that is built on masculine principles. Many people will be hurt as the masculine moves to extremes. These extremes are reactions to perceived threats, they are manifestations of fear. The masculine will need to learn how destructive these behaviors are. It will not be pleasant.

It will be very important to hold to the feminine principles in these times, not to join with reactivity and anger. Righteous anger is okay, but not angry behavior. Anger can be a limited motivator, but not the source of action. Be secure in knowing that the feminine is respected and welcomed. At first you will feel that there will be few who are ready, but that is the nature of starting out. Do not worry about this. Keep the faith that you are on the right path. We are with you.

Thank you so much. I feel grateful to be on this path, all with your help.

It is what you came to do in this life. It is good to be awake to that promise.

You do need to know that difficult times are ahead. For many. You will need to learn to use your voice. The first book is a voice, but so is your physical body. You will learn to use it. We will help you. Do not be afraid to connect. We all need to support each other.

~

In our everyday lives, we have many opportunities to choose where we rest our attention. We cannot control everything that happens to us. What we can control is how we react. How we react is determined by where we rest our attention.

I had a dream where I saw a group of Indian women sitting on the ground a short distance away. They were colorfully dressed, with feathers in their hair, seated on blankets. A woman's voice softly called out my name. I looked around to see who it was, but I couldn't tell. I heard it again, and stepped closer to the group.

The women at the edge had their faces turned to me, smiling in recognition. I ended up walking around to the other side of the group and sitting on the ground with them. I was colorfully dressed too. Someone was giving a teaching about muskrats and beavers. I was working on a project with my hands while I listened. I was tearing something into strips. It was noisy. Someone shushed me and I looked up in embarrassment, but the women were smiling at me with forgiveness.

The next thing, my parents were there. I was a spindly girl of 9 or 10. My mother was turning away from me in disgust, accusing me of being molested by a man because I had invited it. I was saying no, no, I didn't invite him! My father was there too. He was looking at me in disbelief—he wanted to believe me, that I hadn't invited the molestation, but everyone had said it was true. I felt misunderstood and blamed for something that wasn't my fault and had in fact hurt me badly.

I woke up from this dream knowing that these are two ways to be a woman—to be a sister or to be a victim. I choose where to focus my attention. I can be hurt by my mother's accusation and spend my energy trying to convince her to change her mind. Or I can welcome the blessing of recognition by my spirit sisters and accept their loving forgiveness. The choice I make, the place I focus, will determine the next turn in my path.

∼

It is not just each individual choice that creates my life, but the path created by the collective energy of all my choices—past, present, and ongoing. I reap the consequences of my choices. If I am moving blindly through my life, unaware of the choices I am making, I will continue to make choices without really knowing why. I will probably continue to bump up against the same problems over and over. I may even feel that life is treating me badly. Once I become aware of the choices I am making, I have the opportunity to alter the path I am on. Making choices with awareness means making choices with intention. Intention is the process of forming a purpose or aim for my actions.

I once had a dream that showed me how intention works. I had been desperately trying to find affordable housing for myself and my children. I was caught up in the stress of forcing something to happen, as if worrying and obsessing about it could make it happen. I dreamt that I was standing on a square plate of rock. The rock was floating on a small stream. I was riding this rock like a hoverboard, as it drifted with the stream's current. When I fixated on the rock plate, it began sinking. When I placed my attention on the movement, it continued through the water. As I woke up, I heard the words *"create an intention, and let it move itself."*

In other words, concentrate energy in the process, and then let the process unfold. Energy will follow the pathway created by my thoughts and actions.

Energy follows thought. We've heard this many times. Even Albert Einstein said, "Everything is energy and that's all there is to it. Match the frequency of the reality you want and you cannot help but get that reality. It can be no other way. This is not philosophy. This is physics."

I have used this process in my life to good effect, especially when I am making a transformation in my life. I make a list of elements that I would like to see as my life moves along. I focus on the quality of these elements, rather than a specific outcome, and then let the process work itself. Here are two examples:

I had taken a new job in a small town, but I had no place to live and there was very little housing available. I made a short list of qualities that were important to me in my new situation, including how much rent I could afford. I meditated on this list for weeks, making sure to focus on how it would feel to live in such a place. During one of the meditations, I was shown a field of wildflowers, a beautiful carpet of purple and red and yellow.

I moved to the area blindly, with just a carload of possessions. I stopped at the bank to open an account, and when I told the teller I didn't have a place to live yet, she offered me a rental cabin on her property. I met the qualities I had been meditating on. The rental price was exactly what I had requested. In moved there in the spring, when the snow was melting. By late summer, the field behind that cabin was awash with purple, red and yellow wildflowers — the flowers I had seen in my meditation six months earlier.

Another time, I was stuck in a high-responsibility, low-paying job with a hostile supervisor. I lived in a small city with few job opportunities, so I created a list of elements that would nurture me in a new job. The qualities included a rich cultural environment. And I wanted to be a spoke, not a hub, in a functional wheel of productivity and community support. I meditated regularly on this list of qualities, while carrying on with my life and remaining open to opportunity. One year later, I took a job working for The People of an Indian community. The foundation of the work was the good of the community, and my new building was set up in a circle, with the offices arranged like spokes in a wheel.

In both of these circumstances, the rental home and the job, I could not have foreseen the specific outcome. But I set an intention around a list of elements that would nourish me, and my path lined up to meet them.

Creating a list of elements means creating a group of qualities. When we say that something is "elemental," we mean that it is basic, or fundamental. In this case the elements, or qualities, are feelings. Focusing our attention on these elements means that we get used to how they feel and integrate those feelings into our everyday life. Then, when an opportunity presents itself that resonates with these feelings, we will recognize it as familiar. We will be able to say "this is it."

A'riquea: *Consider your elements in a way that makes them part of your life. It is not just a list. It is a way of seeing. It needs to be part of your vision, so that you will be prepared when opportunities present themselves. You need to let this settle in and become part of you. Take* *care of your physical self, prepare for your upcoming journey. Let the list become a part of you. Don't feel you have to rush.*

It is very simple. Once the intention is set in motion, you will be amazed at the ways in which it manifests. That is the beauty of living in the present, in all *of the present.*

～

Setting an intention is like creating a future memory. There is no Time measurement involved — it is not a linear process. There is only feeling, which is energy in Space. Each feeling helps in the formation of the intention. Then the intention floats along on its own current, making its way along an energy path. Setting a spiritual intention means charting an energy course on the Soul Path.

Universal Wisdom: *Believing in the intention and letting it find its own path adds to the flow. There are many energy currents at work. Humans, in their current state, cannot be aware of them. Being able to feel the current is important, because resonance with the intention's path will help you to recognize when choices are being made that harmonize with the path. It is not as passive as it appears. You are letting the path find its flow, but you are choosing elements that determine the path and also then making choices that resonate with the elements and the path.*

It seems as though the desired outcome suddenly appears on the path, but the path has been there all along. It would have to be for the outcome to appear on it. Many things feed into the creation of the path. Letting go of the old path is part of that. The elements are energy choices. It seems miraculous because you are used to thinking in a linear fashion. You are used to thinking that one thing comes after another until you arrive at a pre-determined concrete goal.

One thing that your cancer diagnosis is doing is taking you off of your usual path. You feel lost right now, because you feel like you have lost your way. This is just the suspension of your investment in the previous path. You already know the new way to go. It is a shift in energy. It is happening now. Keep focusing on the elements of the new path, the elements of your intention. These elements have a new energy resonance for you. Your spirit will align with these new energies. The path is being made. Focus on the elements to strengthen the new path. When you feel that your feet are being swept out from under you, it may be because the path has entered a swift current. Do not be afraid. You are joined to the path by your intention.

Cancer may seem like a drastic way to make an energy shift. It is a catalyst that some people would not be able to keep up with. Even though this is a big test in many ways, it is needed and you are capable. You are on a fast track. We are supporting you. Never doubt that you can do this. Continue to look for ways to move your energy into good alignment. This is an exciting time.

Bring the elements along with you. Try to feel the energy of each individual element. Understand where it resonates in your body. Your body is not just a house for your mind. It is an energy filter and an energy generator. That is why it is so important to have your body in tune. Good physical health leads to clear energy management, clear listening and voice. Love nurtures your body and keeps it clean. Loving yourself is an important vibration.

Mahatma Gandhi said, "You must be the change you wish to see in the world." In other words, I must make changes in my own life before anything in my external world can change, before I can ask others to make changes. And I cannot transform my own external life without changing the vibrations of my internal life.

Why would I resist change when it's what I want?
A'riquea: *Because it is new. It goes against everything you have been taught about being a responsible adult — to be independent, to see your physical security arranged in a familiar pattern. You know how this change business works. You have done it before. Set the intention and let it move itself. You will not know what it looks like until it presents itself.*
The best outcomes occur when I practice setting an intention and then letting it move itself. Instead of setting a specific goal, I create an intention based on the energy elements of where I would like to be, on how that feels. That gives me a measuring template for every action I choose — how does this feel? Is this vibration in harmony with the feeling of my intention? When I let go of the specifics and

trust the timeline of the Universe, I will travel a path toward my goal. I may be surprised when I arrive, because I never imagined that this is how it would look, but I know it is the right thing because I can feel resonance. In other words, I don't have to figure everything out, I just need to be aware of what the right thing will feel like, and make choices that match that feeling.

Charting a course into the unknown future can be unsettling. It's tempting to try to keep my old ways and just add on something new, to feel more secure with what I think I have than what I might gain. **A'riquea:** *Comparing will always lead you to disappointment, because it is a function of the Ego. A beautiful life is ready for you to step into. You have been waiting for this and now it is here. The larger context is waiting for you. By not comparing to your old life, you stay open to new opportunities to see yourself and others. When it is time to expand more, you will always have the benefit of your previous experiences to support you.*

Worry takes you out of the present and places you in a future which has not yet happened. It is a disconnect from being present. Planning ahead is a bad idea when there is great negative emotion attached to it. Fear is a reaction. Fear of the future is a reaction that has no space to move in. It has no outlet. It stagnates in a Point.

Imagine the focus of your worry in the expanse of Space. Realize that there are many paths to resolution. When you are used to thinking in negative outcomes, you imagine only those paths. See the many paths. Choose a positive outcome, and move your energy towards it. Experience Space.

∼

The following is a story that shows how it is possible to make a change that puts more meaning into life, to shine from the inside:

Grandmother Martha:[28] *I would like to tell a story. And you will be the listener. This is a story about the time I tried to be myself. I was a young woman at the time. I was working. It was the early 1940s and I*

---

[28]**Grandmother Martha** is my maternal grandmother. She was born in 1900 and lived 97 years. She began visiting me as a Teacher shortly after she passed on.

had a job doing some office work. I had some smart office dresses, which I sewed myself. I felt very happy with myself. I was meeting new people and I earned a little money. After the Depression days, it felt like a relief to be able to have a job. I really thought I had done the right thing. Then something happened that changed my mind about that. One day at work, I was looking in the mirror, and I saw myself in there. I was young and attractive and full of life. I was laughing. And then the other thing I saw in the mirror was that I was also a grandmother. I saw the elder that I would some day become. I wondered what the connection was between the young me and the elder, was I moving in such a way that I was honoring that elder. Suddenly, that whole office life seemed shallow. I was living a magazine life, fitting the expectations of my peers. I wondered what I was doing there, and I went home to think about it.

Having built up this idea of who I was, I didn't know who else I could be. I had children at home, and a husband. We'd built a little house and we were being a family. And I wondered about that, too. Was all of that just part of this idea of who I thought I should be? I felt that my whole life was hollow, that there was no substance to it.

Around that time my young husband had a heart attack, and had to stay home from work, which meant that I had to go to work full time. I was scared by his illness. But I was more scared by my new responsibilities. I decided that whatever I had to do for work, it was going to be meaningful. That whatever I did, it was up to me to put the meaning into it. It wasn't going to just happen by sailing along the way I had been.

I took a job at a radio station. It was still secretarial work, there wasn't much else open to women then, but it was something I could believe in. Back then, there was no TV. The radio was how people got all their information. During the war, the radio was a lifeline. I felt that I was doing something important. I chose to put meaning into my life.

"By accepting yourself, you will change. And though it may seem counterintuitive, it won't work the other way around. Acceptance is the key. Change is the door that can't unlock itself." ~ Holiday Mathis

~ 4 ~

Healing Patterns

Humans are pattern-seeking primates. Over the millennia, we have effectively used our awareness of patterns—plant and animal behavior, seasons, weather—to survive as a species. Along the way, there have also been individuals who were aware enough to see new or unusual patterns. That is how we came up with novel ideas like fire and the internet.

A pattern is a form of energy that is repeated. Changing a pattern requires the movement and transformation of energy. When we stay in touch with our inner knowing and follow through on it, we can use patterned behavior to our benefit, to set intentions and chart a new energy course.

Controlling behavior patterns is how social groups maintain cohesiveness. The rules for social behavior are often implied, but sometimes they can be very direct. We are reacting to these rules when we place more value on what others think of us than on what we know about ourselves.

Universal Wisdom: *One of the more difficult things about inhabiting a human form is that there appear to be rules about who you can and can't be. This is the driving force behind religion and culture—there are norms which create expectations which enforce the norms. Most of these rules work to reduce fear. Fear of the unknown or the unexpected. They appear to make reality stable and predictable. Disruptive thinking and* *behavior is acceptable only within certain environments. This is a limited outlook, of course, because Life is always in motion, always evolving.*

The world is entering a new era, when many of the old ways need to fall away. Creating a new sustainability will require destabilization. Many people will be threatened by these changes. Charismatic leaders will try to herd people into following them. But charismatic leaders cannot stop global warming and its effects. Each person will have to decide if they want to go down with the ship or get into a lifeboat. These are not easy choices. They all have risks.

You have a role in these changing times. It will be important to stay vibrant and vocal. This will not be easy, unless you place yourself in the larger context of The Shift. Ride the wave. Practice resting in your strength. This will help you, as long as you are drawing from your own strength, and not relying on others to support you. Your own strength comes from personal faith, physical vibration, heart-to-heart relationships. Maintain your awareness of Space. Place yourself in the context of Space.

In the past I have struggled to be vocal. There is an irrational fear of annihilation when I open my mouth to speak my truth. What can help me with this.

We have talked about this before, about the memory of danger that oppressed people carry in their DNA. Speaking out can be life-threatening. Everyone is oppressed to some degree, but some people have lost their lives by speaking out. This is the power that cultural structures have. They can erase whole groups of people with disruptive views, by silencing those who are intolerant of injustice.

The way for you to become more comfortable using your voice is to think about your words as planting seeds. It is not likely that you can change someone's view in one conversation. You are planting the seeds of disruptive thinking. You are giving them new things to think about. You may want to come up with some questions that might spark their interest. Some new ways of thinking about the world. These Books are important because they give people something to look at and think about in their own time, at their own pace. It cannot be taken in all at once. It is a gardening process — preparing the soil, planting the seeds, watering the little plants. Things will grow on their own, with the assistance of Life Force.

You can consider what will create the cracks that Life Force enters through. Hairline cracks in patterned thinking. Your own behavior is the best example, of course. This is why so many people are curious about the process that allows you to do this kind of meditation. They would like to be able to do this too. It will be a good thing when many are able.

I have found it difficult to describe. It is active listening with spiritual intent.

Yes. The first step is to begin accepting that there is a world beyond the five senses. That there is more to this world than what is easily visible. In this culture, one of the most difficult changes to make is letting go of the allure of commercial reward, that there could be better returns on spiritual activity than on physical consumption. There needs to be a pull-back from the current money-status structures of your culture. Not everyone is going to be able to do this.

~

Culture encourages us to follow predictable patterns of behavior. While this can help smooth overall functioning of groups, it can also lead us to get stuck. The following conversation discusses this stagnation. (It is also an amazing example of how The Teachers work in deeper levels of our consciousness.)

I had a dream where the word SULA appeared. I woke up perplexed — I had never heard that word. I searched the internet and found that it was the title of a book by Toni Morrison.[29] I went right to the library and checked out a copy.

The book is a richly woven tapestry of stories that explore the themes of black perspective, history, community, and relationships. This was all interesting and illuminating for me. Probably because of my own personal issues at the time, I was most interested in how the characters in the book behaved through the pressures of relationships. We are encouraged to pair up, regardless of the quality or consequences of such a union. Is there anyone who wants to speak to this.

---

[29] Alfred A. Knopf, 1973.

Universal Wisdom: *You are correct about this social convention, this idea that people need to be in pairs. A pair is a fairly stable shape. That is its benefit and also its failure. You have easily seen how a pair will create a bubble around themselves. That forms a sense of security. It also precludes new ideas and new ways of being. Stable, and stagnant.*

Toni Morrison showed these patterns, but her main point was to use these examples to show how people pattern their thinking and then have trouble seeing anything that doesn't fit the pattern. People make up their minds to stabilize their reality. That is the same stability/stagnation arrangement. In order to experience new ways, the mind needs to be open, which means that it is unattached to the usual patterns, that it is capable of forming new links.

You yourself can see the limits of conventional relationships, but you have not yet let go enough to be able to create something outside of that box. You are resisting this opportunity, precisely because it does not conform to your preconceived ideas.

Try to slow down the kind of thinking that attempts to place situations in a known box. Not that you have to rebel and be outside the box. Get the box out of the picture. Just let the elements exist and then see how they combine. There are things there that can be enjoyable and help you grow. Remove the box.

Removing the box and observing how the elements go together includes looking at my behavior. A lot of what we do as humans is patterned behavior, and we are not even aware of it. We choose things because we've been raised that way, and then culture reinforces those patterns. These patterns create vibrations, and the vibrations affect all of our relationships—with ourselves, with others, with our community, the planet. The Teachers are encouraging us to look at the vibrations we create. The following conversation supported me when I lost my job due to illness, but also helped me to see how important it is to be aware of my own patterns and the motivation behind them:

I often feel like I am in an ocean of spirituality, swimming comfortably in deep water. Up above, I see crowds of people on the shore, their egos crowing and reacting in a cacophony of behaviors that use up energy, keeping them on the surface. They don't even know it because they are so busy doing it. I don't feel judgment about this. I have been there too, I also participate in it, and some of it is important learning.

I would rather be supported by the deep water. It's warm and inviting and soothing. It supports my body, mind, and spirit. It's freeing, and far more interesting. I can hear whales singing from far away, observe things floating along in gel-like slow motion, enjoy the shafts of sunlight streaming down through the water. Up at the surface it feels noisy and overwhelming, exhausting. The air feels good on my skin, and everything is sharper. But the human activity is like being at a crowded city beach on the hottest day of the year — swarming.

Universal Wisdom: *You are a fish. You are like a fish. The surface is not where you are meant to be. It is good for you to be seeing the surface in a different way, because you have been trying to function there. That is why you became so exhausted. Illness is making you slow down now.*

If you really want to know what is going to happen, you will need to suspend yourself in this medium for a longer period of time. It will be helpful when you accept your new home and choose to function there. Yes, you feel like you are being irresponsible, but that is because you are still connected to your old way of being. It will fall away over time.

The things you want to be doing now are taking care of your own body and mind and spirit. You will need to disconnect from cultural expectations to do this. It is easy some days, harder on others. This is part of the shift that is being requested, because over-working is one of your culture's addictions. Over-working is not necessarily defined by the number of hours or days that are used in going to work, it describes the kind of work that people are doing. Remember the information about Harmony and choices. Are the actions taken at work ones that feed the overall vibration of Harmony. Not necessarily the harmony of the work environment, although that is a factor. Most important is the harmony of humanity and the planet. Are choices being made that further Love and Compassion. Are we helping each other to hum up.

As you have seen, it is difficult to sort this out when you are engaged in patterns that do not add to the harmony.

～

In mental health therapy, there is a well-known model used to describe human behavior. The model describes a self-reinforcing cycle: Since this is what I believe, this is how I feel; since this is how I feel, this is how I act; since this is how I act, this is how the world treats me; since this is how the world treats me, this is what I believe. This closed loop repeats itself, over and over and over, creating a pattern.

Whether the outcome is self-enhancing or self-defeating, the pattern created by this cycle is comfortable because it is familiar. In order to change the pattern, the cycle can be interrupted at any one of its turns — belief, feeling, action, reflection, belief. When a new element is added and practiced, a new pattern is created.

I can choose to interrupt the cycle, to change my pattern. Sometimes, all that is needed is a change in context. The following is a good example:

I was feeling completely overwhelmed. I was working full time as a nurse and trying to be a good single mother. I had no social life, no free time, no energy. I was under chronic financial stress. One of my children needed medical care. Basic things were breaking down around me — my furnace, then my car. Just when I thought I had run out of things to whine and cry about, I was diagnosed with cancer. I kept thinking about my Grandmother Millie, who went through breast cancer all by herself, and died alone at age 48. I was miserable. **Grandmother Millie** came to me with her arms crossed over her chest, looking a little angry:
This isn't what you think it is. Some end to the world. It's just another thing to deal with. Just one more thing. You seem to think that you are the only person with a wheelbarrow full of woes. You forget that you could just put down that wheelbarrow and skip along without it.
That woke me up and reminded me that I could choose to change how I felt about my circumstances. I could change my perspective. Of course, in order to change my perspective I have to address my

feelings. I can't just pretend to be happy. Western culture is generally uncomfortable talking about or processing feelings. There is an expectation that we will act as though we are happy, and ignore feelings that do not fit this expectation.

A'riquea: *Why do you think there is something wrong with you if you are sad and crying. There is a time for everything. This might be a time when you turn inward and acknowledge some deeper feelings. Most of your daily life is pretty busy with tasks.*

You are sad about not having your needs met. You have worked most of your life to push your needs down, make them less important. One thing would be to acknowledge a need when it surfaces. You tend to see the need as a negative, because it brings up strong feelings and gets automatically channeled into the category of loss.

Make sure you are addressing your own needs. It will be easy to get tangled up with what you think others expect. It needs to be more pure to hit home. Practice being self-centered.

When people try to pretend that they don't have difficult feelings, they are actually just holding them in. They store the feelings until they build up, and eventually the feelings explode outward in ways that can hurt others.

A'riquea: *This is the nature of much human behavior. People do not want to have negative feelings. If they haven't learned how to deal with them, they may choose to hold them back. They are actually doing a good thing by not reacting in the moment, which could lead to hurt feelings in others. It is important to know that the person holding on to their feelings does not want to hurt others. Eventually, they are unable to hold it all back. In a situation of either safety or pressure, they blow. Then there is a lot of concentrated negativity around them.*

You might want to recognize that this person actually feels safe enough around you to let their negativity out. The challenge, however, is for the people around them to not react to the bath of negativity. You may feel hurt or angry, you may feel abused or disrespected. Try to understand that this is the energy of the other person's feelings. It does not have to be yours.

Sometimes, even if you manage to avoid reacting, it is hard to walk away without strong feelings. Know that your own energy field has been affected by the intense vibration of this outburst from the other person. Being affected is not the same thing as being attacked. Much of your own reaction is to the feeling of being attacked. Then you become defensive or feel like attacking back. Deep breathing and centering can help you get back to balance. You may need to take action, in your own space, to shake off some of that energy vibration. Strong exercise is a good way to move that kind of energy. Focusing on the injustice of such an outburst will only feed the negative energy. Be thoughtful about what you choose to feed that energy. Is it more of the same? Or is it something that puts it into a wider perspective?

People who experience oppression have to deal with this on a regular basis. They are subject to constant random attacks from others based on characteristics that are unchangeable: skin color, economics, religion, gender. There is a fine line between accepting the broader perspective, that the person attacking them has their own issues, and turning the energy of the attack into a catalyst for change. You are seeing much of this in your own culture and around the world now. There is a shift occurring and many people are uncomfortable in many ways. There are those who are saying they've had enough of the limits of the status quo and they want something different. And there are those who are safe in the status quo and don't want to see anything change.

Change is the definition of Life Force. Energy is moving always. Seeds are growing into trees, and trees are falling down to make the soil. It is ever in flux. Nothing is static.

Be the change that you want to see in the world.

Yes. It is important to embody the energy vibration that promotes the greatest harmony.

This is the message we are trying to get out. How humans treat each other and all beings on the planet will ultimately determine the survival of all. There is no room for selfish aggrandizement anymore. But it is also a time of change, and some will be more or less skilled than others. Patience is needed.

Humans are coming into a time of great upheaval. This is like turning the soil in the garden. It is necessary for health. It will not necessarily be pleasant, unless you look for the openings of light and air, the opportunities for positive improvement, and act on them.

When feelings, especially "negative" ones, are not allowed to be expressed, they can be collected and showcased in order to prove that they exist. They can be used, like trophies, to prove the strength of the ego. **A'riquea**: *You can build a world with it. You think that it proves you are alive. Pain is a feeling. When you deny yourself in the physical world, you are not able to accept the gifts that Life gives you. Collecting negativity is a back-door way of being in the world. It allows you an escape. When gifts are offered, when the chance to feel alive is offered, then you go back to these "trophies." You use this pain to say "Look, I already have feelings, I don't need more." You use pain as a shield, to keep you from having to look at Life in a positive way. You develop a relationship with the pain to avoid a relationship with Love. You use the pain to explain why you cannot receive Love — because you are broken, because you are damaged, because you're not ready, because you don't deserve it. Pain is a habit. It is an addiction just like everything else.*

Sometimes when I am with positive people, I find myself judging them as being Pollyannaish, as being not real, as if they have not experienced Life because they haven't had enough pain to know what "real" life is like. Real life hurts you. Real life makes you grow like a bonsai tree.

Of course, everyone has pain. Some people are better at denying it, or hiding it or avoiding it. I am wearing it like a banner. Look at me, I am alive, I am more real. Sometimes when I see someone who is homeless or drug-addicted and suffering a great deal, I criticize myself for not being as real as they are.

It's also true that some are more sensitive to pain.

I am sensitive in many many ways. I seem, however, to have a high tolerance for physical pain. Is that actually true, or do I just have effective ways to integrate physical pain, and not emotional pain?

It is all the same in the end. Pain is a feeling. There are all kinds of feelings. You can choose which kind of feelings you prefer to have. That will make your journey lighter or heavier. And it is not "having" the

feelings that is your Earthly experience, it is the movement of feelings.
This is back to the movement of Love, which is compassion. Holding pain
creates a block to any kind of movement. Moving pain creates a flow for
all kinds of feelings.

For anything to be a feeling, it has to have some physical effect in the
body — we feel feelings with our body. It is an energy movement.
Yes. And it is generated by the movement of energy between Points. As
we have discussed, the Points are not in a static arrangement. There is
constant flow in and out of them. This flow, through Space, in the Zone,
is what creates a feeling in the body. As the energy moves, it has contact
with other Points.

    Pain is a feeling, a movement of energy, that encourages Points to
close down. There is a defensive reaction. Holding pain hardens the points
to energy flow. Non-elastic points cause stagnation in the Zone. Good
health requires energetic vibration in the Zone. This is something you
need. Energetic vibration in the Zone. The Zone around every point in
your body. Find the places that are holding pain and release it. Choose
to live a Life of gifts. Choose before it is too late. Be the Love you need.

Painful feelings can be created when we are judged by others. We are
taught to be afraid of that pain. We develop roles and identities to
assure us that we belong, to avoid being judged as Not-Us. This fear
of judgment is a poor motivator for our actions.

    Our ego wants to judge in order to set itself apart, to make itself
more important. Sometimes I have been exposed to judgment that
is personally directed at me, from people I thought I could trust. My
first reaction was hurt. When I was able to step back from that, I
began to feel compassion for a person who must be struggling with
their place in the world or their relationships with others. I wonder
what else there is to learn about judgment and compassion.

A'riquea: *Judgment is one of the coping skills that pushes people away.*
In that way, it creates Space around the one who is doing the judging.
When someone is feeling irritable, they may need more space around them.

    Of course, it would be more productive to recognize the need for
space and create that without hurting others. Once others have been hurt,

then there is the opportunity to apologize and ask for forgiveness. Both recognizing irritability and apologizing for judgment are ways to function in a spirit-centered life. Every time negativity is aimed at another, there is the opportunity to change to a more positive direction — for both the one aiming the negativity and the one it is aimed at.

Judgment can be aimed directly at you as a person. It can also be aimed at groups of people or imagined groups. Do not believe that a judgmental comment aimed at a group that is not immediately present has no effect. It is the same as judging individuals.

All thoughts and behaviors have energy attached to them, and that energy contributes to the energy of the Universe. Humans have many choices to make every day. If you are making judgments, it would be good to step back and put yourself in the others' place. Ask how it would feel to receive this judgment.

I am thinking about the many judgments I make. I am trying to be mindful about who I spend my time with socially, for example. I want to be with people who support my path. I do not want to use my time being around those who can not relate to my path, or who actively belittle me. It's not that I want to reject people. It's that I want to move toward healthier relationships.

There will always be choices to make.

Being judgmental means that there are negative emotions attached to the choice. Being judgmental uses fear or anger to make a comparison. Being judgmental requires that the person doing the judging pull away from the situation, removing themselves emotionally. It is the other direction from compassion. Compassion recognizes the humanity in others, it makes way for more ways of being, it broadens the context and welcomes others. Judgment reduces humanity, it reduces emotional connection and focuses instead on emotional reaction. It is a kind of war waged on others.

This can be a fine balance. You can be focusing on being compassionate to others but then trample your own needs. Compassion also needs to be extended to your own self. Your needs are not more important than others, but they are also not less. It is important to be aware of what your needs are, of course. Meeting you ego's needs is not the same as meeting your spiritual needs.

Part of your healing path is to become more sensitive as well as less reactive. Your life will become richer.

In order to make room for new growth, some pruning is going to occur. I don't have to cut off contact with people. I just need to move my focus onto relationships that are constructive partnerships.

Judgment is an activity of the ego. It is a patterned reaction to a perceived threat — a way of dealing with fear.

Universal Wisdom: *We have talked about fear before. Fear is a tool. It is the signal that you are disconnecting from Spirit. You turn back in towards yourself to protect that connection. When you turn away from someone, you miss the opportunity for your spirits to connect with each other. You go back to your own spirit, the familiar.*

This difficulty in connecting with others occurs when Ego is feeling threatened, responding to the fear. Ego has a history, the story that tells the future based on what has happened in the past. Ego follows a pattern. If you have not had many connections with other spirits, you will rely primarily on this pattern. You will expect to have your spirit rebuffed, not just your spirit but also your personality and your feelings. That seems predictable.

You have built a sturdy core of independence so that you will not have to rely on being accepted. There are benefits to this, and it is worthwhile to be grateful for them. You have a certain fearlessness in new situations — you trust yourself, you know what pleases you or not, you know yourself and are comfortable with that, you enjoy time alone. A direction you can now move is to share that comfort in yourself with others, to be that comfortable self when you are in social situations. People will appreciate that comfort, it will help them to relax too.

You need not rush headlong into new spiritual interactions. You can socialize with comfort, use your intuition about situations, and then share as you feel safe. This is not just an idea. This is something you need to practice. You will need to be interacting with a wider range of people. It is important to expand your comfort with yourself into these social situations. The spiritual connections will flow from that in a surprisingly easy way. No worries here. The only problem would be to stay in your current pattern, to stagnate. That is the choice you have: to stay the same or move on.

Opening myself to others means that I expose myself to the fear of being hurt. I know I cannot Live without opening myself, but I have built a belief system that no matter what relationship avenue I choose, it will be swept away from me — that it always ends with me losing out.

I would like relationships that are solid and long lasting and honest. I am afraid to believe that this can exist. I am afraid that I will never be able to make this connection in human form — it's only a mirage, a myth, a mistaken idea. If that's what I believe, then that will be true. Is love elusive, or am I ?

A'riquea: *We want to think that Life will be smooth and easy. We go to great lengths to assure ourselves that it is so. But it is not. Real Life is complicated, because it involves other people, and everyone has history that informs their story. It is not desirable to have the stories match perfectly, because then there will be no opportunities for learning. If the stories are too far apart, then they will be unrecognizable and too easy to ignore.*

What we look for in relationships is connection. Often that takes the form of security. But that is not the only path that a relationship needs to take. Certainly, there needs to be safety. But the purpose of safety is not to shield one another from difficulties. The purpose of safety is to create an environment where growth is possible. One of the elements needed for growth is instability. There needs to be opportunity for change.

In the best of circumstances, people in relationship celebrate each other's changes. They make room for them and patiently stand by for unexpected outcomes. They accept mistakes. They recognize when one of those outcomes is pain, either in themselves or in the other. Pain is unavoidable. Pain provides an opportunity for spiritual growth. It opens up an opportunity for self-examination and responsibility.

When hurt has occurred, whether it is created by our own actions or those of another, we decide how we are going to respond. We can make choices that move Life Force. Moving Life Force will enhance our relationships. Avoiding it will create distance. There are always opportunities to

heal past wrongs. Some courage is required. Courage comes from the know-
ledge that moving spirit is the right thing to do.

   Be thoughtful when you are choosing a relationship. Are there ele-
ments that will expand Life Force. That is the reason to create a rela-
tionship, no matter how brief or how deep it is.

   Do not be worried by the small spikes and falls in interest. The longer
term is what will show how this is going to go. Be true to yourself and
honest with others. Enjoy the journey, wherever you go.

～

Being in the moment can be painful, as we are exposed to our own
beliefs and those of others. Sometimes we are able to make changes,
and sometimes we can only observe ourselves repeating poor choices.
Here is an example:

Because I don't have a TV, I sometimes end up watching the World
Series at a bar. I was sitting there when a stranger started telling me
about his Catholic-farmer childhood. He described how some neigh-
bors had discovered Indian graves while plowing a field. I could tell
that he enjoyed retelling this story, and that his listeners were usually
awed by the gore of exposed leg bones and teeth and skulls. But I
became physically ill, flooded with dis-ease throughout my body. The
sickness I felt was the pain of ancestral trauma.

   I interrupted the guy to ask if he would feel the same way if
someone went to his Catholic cemetery and dug up bodies, and then
used the story for entertainment. He'd never thought about it, and
his reaction indicated that he thought that would be different — he
believed that these "other" people couldn't be the same as his relatives.

   Even though I could see him considering a change in his beliefs, I
was too sick go on with the conversation. I turned away and ordered
several shots of booze. I could see that I was choosing to numb the
pain and I did it anyway.

   I sometimes crave the getaway that chemicals provide — I want
to disconnect from intense emotional responsibilities in the physical world. Clearly, what I need is spiritual connection and physical
grounding, but I choose escape instead. I am aware of what I am

doing. These are examples of Ego in service to itself.

Universal Wisdom: *You have been doing some interesting learning. These are the kind of things it is good to be aware of—what you are choosing and why. But it can not be a justification for continuing to do it. Believing that learning about emotional escape by doing it is not a good thing. The awareness is helpful, the activities are not.*

The idea that some ancestors are "ours" and others are not, or that chemical use is an effective way to deal with strong emotions, reflects a belief pattern. It offers a way to navigate our way through a maze of emotional expectations based on our personal histories.

It is good to be aware of similarities in relationship dynamics, how threats and intimidation steer your own behavior, how you learn to react to survive. Talk about the bread-crumb analogy.

I recently heard a bread-crumb analogy used as a good way to think about "bad" experiences. The negative experiences in your life give you something to work with later. They are like the bread crumbs you leave behind on your walk through the woods and later on, when you get lost, you can use them as stepping stones to find your way back.

How would that work for you.

Certain experiences in my life pushed me off center. I left "home" and then I was "lost." In order to return Home, to reclaim my spiritual center, I can go back over that path to see where I became lost. That helps me heal the parts that got hurt.

I started to become lost during childhood abuse, where my five-year-old thought patterns told me that this happened to me because I was a bad person. I was also parented by people who were constantly trying to push me into their box of cultural conformity. They had limited parenting skills. I was exposed to deep rage, constant criticism, and manipulative shaming and withdrawal of "love." I ended up feeling like I was no good, that I didn't belong on the planet. In order to survive, I tried to become invisible.

This same dynamic played out in my marriage. My husband blamed me for his serial cheating, and I felt I had to become invisible in order to save my children's home. What mother doesn't choose her children? Over time, I gave up on myself as a woman. Then I gave up on myself as a person. It all collapsed when I realized that domestic abuse had damaged my ability to be a good mother. I realized it had come to do or die — do or die spiritually, and I got out.

And.

And I am still afraid to stand up in my own life. I have been afraid to stand up as an author, to move the book into the public eye, because deep down I still fear that I don't belong, that I have to sacrifice myself for others in order to be worthy, to survive. These patterns are things I learned to believe about myself. These are beliefs that keep me from occupying my spiritual Home.

This pattern is a design which you are quite comfortable with. You have arranged your world to fit these patterns. See how you have defined yourself by what is missing. See how you feel isolated. See how you have become a servant by profession. These things are only true because you believe them. There are multiple other interpretations of your life, but you have been choosing to see it only in this way.

If you want to choose to believe something else, it would be good to start out by taking note of things in your life that don't fit your belief pattern. You think you are isolated because you live alone. Think for a minute about all of the people who connect with you, who know you and want to talk to you. You are not afraid to go up to them and start a conversation, because you know it will be interesting. No one is rejecting you. You are rejecting yourself. Start to look around and see what doesn't fit the pattern. Note that these ways of seeing are also true.

Don't think you that have to jump there immediately and force yourself into this new way. Be patient. You already do this with your children — when you think they are being judgmental about someone, and you point out what it is that could be hard for that other person or motivating them in a way that your children cannot see. They have learned a lot from you in this way, to be compassionate and see more. Extend that compassion to yourself. Try to see another way that might be hidden at first. Imagine that you could be explaining these things about yourself to your children. See what comes.

Thank you so much. What a relief it is to have somewhere to go where these things can get worked out. It is huge, addressing my belief patterns. It helps me get clearer and cleaner.

I also want to ask who I am talking to. The last few times I feel like I am interacting with "we."

We are **Universal Wisdom**. *We are all of the voices of God, coming through a receptive mind. We are available to anyone who listens. You have learned to be a good listener. It is good for everyone.*

Now go. Be.

～

Patterns are vibrations. They vibrate from *within* me. Negative patterns disrupt my ability to move energy cleanly. I can't create external harmony from a place of discord. I have to have my own house in order so that I can go forth with strength and compassion.

I had a sleeping dream which helped me to see a pattern that was disrupting my ability to be clear. In the dream, I was in possession of something special. It was shaped like two small boxes, or two books, connected together with a piece of paper. The connecting paper was quite flimsy, not strong enough to hold up to the weight of the two books. A short woman with dark skin was there in the dream. She was a woman of great power, and she seemed to know what I had in my hands.

I was holding it, and feeling rather special for getting to have this object, but I knew it wasn't mine. I noticed that as I handled it, the connecting paper was beginning to tear. If I kept this, it would be damaged. Then the woman said to me, *"Best give back what doesn't belong to you."*

I woke up feeling that this was an important thing for me to hear. I puzzled on what it meant, what it was that I needed to give back. The truth struck me all at once, and with great clarity: I needed to give something back in order to heal a trauma. The trauma was the violent end to my marriage and my children's family. The two books were the stories of two lives. What I needed to give back was the behavior of the people who had betrayed me. I had been holding on to their behavior as if it was something that I could control — as if I could get them to apologize, get people to see how wicked and intentional they had been — the truth could go public and everyone would know what really happened. But the only thing I could really control was my own behavior. I was being stubborn and petty and vindictive. I needed to give their behavior back to them, not hold onto it, and address my own behavior.

Universal Wisdom: *What we want to say about your relationship with your children's father is that there is more to this than you are aware. There are forces working to bring you together. This is uncomfortable for both of you. But it is what needs to happen.*

I have been thinking lately that no matter what my issues with him are, he is my children's father and I need to support them by cleaning up my own behavior.

Yes. This is part of it. That would be a good practice. There is also more to it than that, although it is not something you can easily see right now. It would be good to think about it in more general terms. What do you want ANY of your relationships to look like, to feel like. Nothing can really move forward when you have not done work in some areas, no matter how limited they are.

I see a bowl of oranges, and one of them is rotten. The rotten juice is oozing onto the fresh fruit.

Yes, this is the idea. Everything needs to be clean in order for everything to be clean.

There is a bigger program here. When I realize that, I feel an expansiveness, that I will be able to move further in energy practice when I am able to let go of this and move my attention to bigger space. Move farther into the Zone. This is what needs to happen. No matter how my ego wants to react to this one situation, I need to move beyond it to further my spiritual life. Place Ego in service to Spirit. This is what I want to do.

It is also important to incorporate what you have learned. You cannot just erase the past and say it doesn't matter anymore. You cannot move into the future without clearing the past.

And now I see something like an exploded view in space, where something large has been broken into very small pieces and they are all moving away from each other.

This is the expansiveness of Zone. And it is what you need to do with this situation—break it into smaller pieces and let each one go. You have been condensing it into one big mass, and of course it is not that, it is all of the things that make it up. Many of those things do not belong to you. Your husband's family history, for example. Your own family history does belong to you, some parts of it do.

This made me think about my own defensive behavior. I was raised in an oppressive environment, with little emotional safety, and now I tend to react defensively—even where it is not warranted. The situation of my divorce is another example. I am continuing to defend myself against something that happened years ago.

~

Examining my life history, I can see that intimate betrayal has been a well-traveled path in my relationships. It was repeated over and over throughout my life. I trusted someone who then stole my innocence, my self-respect, my self-esteem, my safety. It is a reoccurring pattern.

Now I also see that much of the difficulty in letting go of that is the familiarity of the love-pain cycle: I reach toward someone I think I love, and the closer I get the more danger I feel. I keep reaching for what I think I want, and then I feel the pain and recoil. As I recoil, the relationship disintegrates, and I say "see, that's how it always is."

I don't want to travel this path anymore. What can help me heal this energy pattern?

Universal Wisdom: *You would like this to work out, because it seems like a magic-wand solution to a very deep issue. This pattern has many tentacles, and attaches itself to more areas than you are aware of. We can help you loosen up the energy, but it is also important to practice making a new pathway. There has to be somewhere for the energy to go. It doesn't just disappear, it transforms. So you might want to think about where you want it to move.*

Of course, I think of more trust, being able to accept love from others, being more open and available instead of running away.

That is a good start. Also think of adding something to the loop that is already there, or changing some component of it.

Right now I think of it as the love-pain cycle: that reaching for love results in feeling pain, and feeling pain leads to running away. The *reaching* part could be changed to *allowing*. Feeling pain could be a signal to shift from Point to Zone, recalling my true place with God. Is there another way to get at this.

This is workable. You can see that it really is about perspective. Whether the thing you are doing is closing or opening, shutting down or expanding, Point or Zone. Sit with this for a while. Observe yourself. Don't hurry to change, just be aware of experiences.

Analyzing this is not going to help much. There is only so much cognitive activity that can be applied. At some point it is not about figuring it out, it is about doing things differently. Taking action.

⌐

A good place to start transforming patterns is to be aware of those that are useful and those that are not. Once I have identified a pattern that is not useful, I have the opportunity to change it. This often involves a change in my identity: in order to be something new, I have to stop being something I am. This can be difficult, especially when the thing I want to transform is ego-driven behavior.

A'riquea: *This is a good thing to be thinking about — how much Ego is in charge. This was talked about in the first book. Of course, we want Spirit to be the motivation for our actions. That is the spiritual core expressed. And Ego, the physical manifestation, is the vehicle for bringing that forth. Your question about identity is important.*

People have difficulty seeing how they wear the masks of identity because it requires that the observer take off the mask in order to see it. Taking off the mask is not easy. Mask, or identity, is part of physical presence. We spend a lifetime creating these masks. They are glued to what we think of as our body.

One way to think about a mask is to see it as a role. We develop roles in order to fit into social constructs, like family and community. These have positive effects on survival. It is not so important to discard the role as it is to be able to see it. Once it is seen, then we can choose whether we want to have this role or not. We can choose to retain the positive skills we may have learned while wearing the mask, and we may choose to let the negative, reactive skills fall away.

Naturally, one can have many roles, many masks, and they will each need to be peeled back in order to truly express the spiritual core.

One of the masks I saw myself wearing was that of the Giver. I am sensitive to many vibrations, especially to the feelings of others. This intuition is a positive skill. It has helped me reduce conflict, provide support, and Love others. But it has also gotten me into trouble. I sometimes jump in and accommodate situations that do not need my help. And I often over-give, taking care of others at the expense of my own self-care.

I have built my life around being a helper. I am a mother and a nurse and a community volunteer. Those are not bad things. But what started out as a positive use of my skills grew into an identity as a Giver. This identity began determining who I was, how I acted in the world. Then the pattern of identity becomes a mask, a role one takes on for survival.

A'riquea: *Compassion is the path you want to be on. But it's important to look at what you think compassion is. If you do something "nice" for someone and they feel better, there is no harm done. But if your motivation is to fluff your ego by doing the action, or the action you take fluffs the other person's ego, then that is not Compassion. It does not mean that it is not worthwhile, or that there is not truly a positive effect, but it is not the Compassion that moves Spirit.*

Remember that you are working to Move Spirit. That means moving Spirit in you and moving Spirit in the other. That is about creating more Love, more Life Force, not just making everyone feel better. In some ways, helping every one feel better stunts the process of Moving Spirit, because then Ego is satisfied and Spirit is forgotten. Again, don't think that you have to stop doing that. But do examine what your motivations are, why you are doing this, and just what kind of energy you are creating. Is it Life Force.

Try to think about the Giver as a vehicle. Help the Giver see what an important role it has as the vehicle for moving more energy. Examine the motivation behind your actions. Try to let Spirit see out of your eyes. Let others see Spirit in your eyes. Allow Ego (the vehicle) to see the benefit of spiritual fuel — more Life Force means a stronger physical presence, a healthier body with more stamina.

The body can get tuned up by allowing more Life Force to flow through it. The engine gets clogged with toxic buildup when it chronically runs on low-grade fuel, or for short trips. True Compassion is spiritual fuel, running at a cleaner energy level. Your body is tired because the Giver/Ego has been trying to maintain spiritual vibration, when that is not its job. Ego needs to maintain the physical body, provide a healthy vehicle for Spirit to operate through. Then Spirit can fully inhabit physical Space, and maintain the energy flow that Ego needs.

There have been times in your life when survival was threatened and Ego took on the role of warrior for your Spirit. Childhood rape is the most obvious, but there were also many other reinforcers. It would be good to thank your ego now for that important output of energy. And also to acknowledge that it is time to rebalance.

You cannot always be at war without draining your Life Force. Your body will benefit from a better balance between Ego and Spirit. Of course, Ego has developed reactive patterns. Continue to observe your energy, your motivations, and any imbalances. Be aware of the choices you are making. As you have learned from The People: honor the warrior, not the war. Also, balance that with honoring the Giver's role as Peacemaker.

Wearing a mask, performing a role as part of maintaining an identity, describes Ego in service to itself. It drains energy rather than create a flow for it.

A'riquea: *Your energy is too spread out. Too spread out for the amount of internal maintenance you are allowing. You might be able to spread out that far, but it would require support or a lot more staying Home. You cannot be Home and Away at the same time unless Home is in good shape.*

It is natural for you to want to spread out, because Life is so interesting and it is hard to pass up opportunities to be involved in it. Right now, however, you need to focus more on being Home. You know what I am talking about — Energy Home. You are thinking about your children, and how that feels like Home. This is because they are the closest to you of any other humans, and feeding them also feeds you. That is family. Energy Home is really about You. Your body is your physical Home.

A role is not necessarily negative. In the right context, with Ego in service to Spirit, it can be a positive channel.

A'riquea: *A role is a part you play. Just like in a theater production. Are you an actor playing a role, and the focus of your production is about you, the actor, the name on the billboard, the fame and notoriety you receive? Or are you an actor playing a role, and your production is about moving forth energy and information through your actions? There are choices to be made.*

Much of American culture has gotten side-tracked into celebrity culture, as if famous personalities are all about the fame. Whether this is about celebrities, or about you in the context of your own life, this kind of role is ego-driven. It is about the ego being in charge, making choices that appear to secure the physical presence. Real actors expand their role to include the expression of greater dimensions for the benefit of others. Their role is to use their skills to help people see new ideas, feel compassion for others, open up their perspective.

Everyone has these choices to make about the purpose of their own life. Do I want to focus on my own physical security at the expense of spiritual growth? Do I want to return to my spiritual core and use that energy to add to the spiritual evolution of humans? These two paths are mutually exclusive. It is true that skills are learned over a lifetime, and someone is not going to become a Dalai Lama overnight just because they want that.

What the choice involves is a commitment. Choosing to fulfill your spiritual "role" involves commitment on a path. It involves recognition of your True Purpose, the reason you are on this physical plane, the contract you came in on, and then using your time on earth to express this. Remember that Purpose is about moving Life Force, expressing Love. And it is a process, not an end-point. Not a point at all, but Zone. Ego-identity is about occupying a Point. Spiritual-"identity" is about occupying Space, expanding into Zone, and using your energy for the benefit of All.

So you see, developing a new identity requires an awareness of energy.

Continue the development of your spiritual role. You will have to decide how that looks and feels. Maintain awareness of your choices. Stay open. Practice Being in the Zone. Be the Spirit-Walking Journey. Step in to the next leg of your Journey. It is waiting for you.

It is comforting, inspiring, humbling, to hear that it is just waiting for me. All I have to do is choose it. Making a leap of faith is more like taking a step in a process. It's as if I am on a path in the woods, and there is a fork in the path. It's not so hard. I can take just one step, and there, I am on the new path.

Choosing to change is something we can do by ourselves. Taking action to change our behavior patterns involves transforming our relationships with others.

A'riquea: *Of course, it will not be so easy to put it into practice. It helps to have seen the patterns. Roles are more difficult to change because they involve other people. Interacting with others who expect the usual pattern will draw you back into performing a role. There is safety in the role. It is like a dance, where everyone knows the steps. When you choose to step out, people's reactions will tempt you to get back in line.*

There are applications to Point and Zone here. The usual patterns require linear behavior—one thing follows another in a predictable way. Stepping out means moving into Space, where all things are possible. Playing a role is the same as getting stuck in a point, getting stuck in one way of doing things, without honoring the creative process. When you step out, you will be playing with creativity. There will be complaints, and even backlash.

There are different ways to look at this. Creativity for creativity's sake, art for art's sake, is its own box of attachment. It is not unlike following the rules just to follow the rules. Both are thoughtless and heartless. Your challenge will be knowing what your needs are and making choices to feed yourself. Of course, we are not talking about Ego's needs, which describe attachment. We are talking about Spirit's needs.

And what are Spirit's needs? Moving energy, moving energy between Points, through the Zone. Moving energy between people. Moving Love energy, which is compassion and joy. We have talked of this before. Living involves sensation, being aware of sensation in the body, being aware of vibration in the body, and moving it in Space. You must understand your energy relationship to Point and to Zone, and work with both of them.

Looking for opportunities for positive improvement in relationships requires compassion for others. As an empath, my challenge is not how to be compassionate, but how to be compassionate without absorbing the pain of others.

A'riquea: *When you have a lot of energy moving through your personal space, it is understandable that you might feel like you are drowning. This sea of emotion surrounds human life. It is one of the gifts of being in human form. All of the feelings, not just the difficult ones, are available to sensate beings.*

You can tell how another person feels by feeling their energy. Feeling that energy is not the same thing as absorbing it. Your own filters are especially open. You have extra awareness of feelings. It is part of what makes you able to do this kind of work, because you are open to sensing energy.

This energy is all around. It is always available. It comes in many forms. It is not reasonable to think that you can manage all of this perfectly. There will be times when you are overwhelmed. It is important to balance this flood with other energy, to help put it in perspective.

I have been looking forward to a break this weekend, when there will be outdoor music and dancing and laughing.

This is a good environment, although, as you know, that has its own challenges. That also presents a sea of energy and feeling.

This all requires so much management!

It just means that you have to set priorities and abide by them. Think about what intentions you want to set.

I want to make choices in the moment based on my energy, but set general intentions based on how I want to feel — what *quality* informs my choices.

This is important. The quality of your energy space is what will feed or drain you. This refers to the energy space around you, but that is ultimately created by the energy space within you. This is the place to start.

It determines centering.

It determines internal centering, and that also works to affect your external environment. Staying centered in the Zone allows other people to have their own space and feeling without pulling you in. You will be overwhelmed when you let too much in. That is just a side effect of practicing. Sometimes you will manage it better than other times. It is the nature of learning.

Let it all be illuminating and interesting, not in a documentary way but in a feeling way. Let yourself be amazed at how rich and varied and wonderful this human life is. Even when it feels "bad," it is part of the All. It becomes "bad" when you focus on that negativity and hold it in a Point.

I saw this when I was working with a group that disintegrated in dysfunction. Everyone involved in the mess was really doing their best with the skills they had. Everyone. When I tried to pin down a certain behavior and label a person with it, it just created more bad energy.

That is Point to Point concentration, without the context of Zone.

It's a dead end, because then everyone starts arguing over the Points, which are really not as fixed as we'd like them to be.

Points are fixed only by perception.

It is a beautiful day. The sun is out and the sky is endless blue. Is that only a perception?

It is a perception based on past experience. You have attached the idea that it is beautiful based on a climate where there is always enough rain. If you lived in an arid region you might be happier when you see clouds. It is not what you see, it's how you see it.

Like seeing someone's behavior as unskilled, instead of deciding they are an asshole.

Somewhat strong, but Yes.

Sorry.

Apply these concepts and see where you go.

"Truth is, everybody going to hurt you. You decide which ones going to make you suffer." ~Bob Marley

We develop patterns of thinking over our lifetime. These patterns create belief systems that affect how we see ourselves and how we see our world. As I was growing up, for example, I was taught to believe that what other people think and feel is more important than what I think and feel. This perspective supports the belief that control of my life comes from outside of myself. It taught me to disregard my core, and always place the needs of others first. At the very heart of my being, I believed that I should always come last, or never. This is a common cultural foundation for many girls and women. The other side of the cultural coin teaches boys and men that they have to always be first. Both of these gender stereotypes are coping skills that encourage Ego in service to itself. They morph into rigid roles and expectations.

As I examined these patterns, I began to see how I had created environments throughout my life that perpetuated the idea that I should come last or never. It was how I functioned as a family member, wife, mother, and even in my work as a nurse. I believed that putting myself first was selfish, prideful, egotistical — all things that family and culture taught me to believe were wrong.

When I began cancer treatment, I realized that I would need to learn how to put myself first. It was not a question about whether I should. It was necessary for my physical survival. I could not put off taking care of my health until I had free time, had gotten my work done at home or at my job, had more money, or after my children were launched. Cancer and cancer treatment took away all the energy I had for those other things. I was left with only enough to support basic physical survival. I had to shed layers and layers of beliefs, identity, and expectation. I had to learn how to live in the Now.

It was not easy to change lifelong beliefs. When I thought about putting myself first, I felt uncomfortable. If I did not put myself last, then I was placing myself in front of others — and no one should be more important that someone else. My whole life I have seen the effects of people who think they are entitled to come first, or are using desperate means to either be or appear to be first, or use their supposedly First status to oppress others. This is not the position I wanted to be in. This is all based, of course, on linear arrangements, on hierarchies. And it is all about Ego positioning.

Ego needs to be balanced with Spirit, so that Ego is serving Spirit and not itself. If I ask, "Am I traveling my soul path by making this choice?" (to meet my need or push it away), I am tempted to be motivated by the greater good, and I will almost always put myself last again. When is it in the interests of the greater good that I do not push my needs away? When do I show compassion for my own self? Are "needs" even the framework I want to be working with?

A'riquea: *This is actually a difficult topic to address. There are so many factors involved, it is not easy to distill into a few statements. I think that what you want to be thinking about is how you are moving in the world. Is your movement balanced. Are you making choices that help others and help yourself. There are so many choices every day and they are all interconnected with other choices.*

I'm thinking about an example such as what I choose to eat. If I choose a given food, is it going to be nutritious, how much does it cost and how does that affect what I can choose in the future, where did the food come from and was it grown in a good way, who are the farmers and how are they treated, how did it get to me, what am I promoting by choosing this food and not another. Am I choosing this food because it really feels like the right thing to eat now or because I have some emotional need that this food is going to meet. I have gotten off track talking about this when I want to be listening. Excuse me.

We're doing fine. These are good questions. Every choice you make is like a pebble in a pond. Even not dropping it in the water is a choice.

It seems that what you are trying to straighten out is what it would look like to be on your Soul Path. This is a bigger context than just meeting your needs. What if the example you gave was about spiritual practice, spiritual food. You have gotten distracted by thinking of Me in the context of Ego. We would like you to be thinking about this in the context of Spirit.

You are making good choices in your daily life. You can also be making those kind of choices on a bigger scale, choices that place you in position to expand your spiritual life. There are choices to be made that will ripple out into the field of humans and the Universe. The Creator is waiting for this to occur. Things have been lining up to make this possible. At some point, you will need to make a change that will turn your life. Yes, cancer has accelerated the possibilities, but it is up to you to manifest the needed changes. It is time to become a mouthpiece, a teacher.

I have no doubt that I am being supported in this. I can see how I have been stuck in the daily routines of work and mainstream culture that reduce my opportunities. I have been thinking about setting goals for My Life After Cancer. Maybe I should be thinking about setting goals for My Life *With* Cancer.

It is not about cancer at all. Cancer is just the catalyst for rapid change. It is up to you to grasp the possibilities and move.

I can't seem to let go of the need for security — needing to know ahead of time how this is going to work out. I am afraid. Of course, the antidote to that fear is Trust.

Trust is important. You have come all this way and it has worked out. Think about the first day you agreed to write Grandmother Dreams. You had a title and an opportunity. You did not know what the book would be about or how it would change you. What if you had not accepted that unknown challenge. We are asking you to make another commitment.

The thing we would like you to do now is go out into the wilderness. Not the wilderness of Nature, but the wilderness of Mankind, of Humanity. There is great need and the time is right. Even though you are afraid, you are ready to do this.

Part of my fear of moving forward is the discomfort I feel when outside attention is directly focused on me. I am not skilled at putting Me first in social situations. What do "Me" and "First" actually mean? The words themselves are harmless, it's their connotations that make me uncomfortable.

The word Me automatically brings up some sense of Ego, but it doesn't have to. What if Me described the *energy* Me? Not necessarily my body, or my physical body only, but all of the energy that is me. That would include my spirit and my soul path and the Creator and the Universe — not just the vehicle but also the fuel and the track and the context. When I think of it that way, then I have a responsibility to be present and move my energy in a harmonious way. This is not the responsibility that is an obligation, but the responsibility that is a calling, what I agreed to when I came onto this planet. That takes the pressure off of Ego and places it in balance. Then it is easy not only to accept but also to be eager for this arrangement.

And what if First defined something that was not a linear item in a hierarchy? What if it described a location in space. It would refer to a center. Like a pebble dropping in a pool, there can be no concentric ripples outward unless the pebble drops. And it would not have to be a horizontal surface. It would more likely be a sphere, and the circles created by the pebble would actually be spherical rings. This is the kind of activity we are all being asked to do — encouraging the awakening of humanity through the expansion of our energy.

The following information helped me to see that embracing myself as a whole person meant locating myself as a center in the Universe:
Universal Wisdom: *The Crone is a role that has been given very little value in your culture. It is seen as a waning of power, rather than a shift in power. Bearing and rearing children requires a huge amount of creative energy. As children move out into the world, this creative energy is made available for other endeavors. When a woman is raising children, she is a center by default — she is the center of her children's lives. The transition into Crone consciousness requires the creation of a center in the self.*

You are ready for this. Part of your current exhaustion comes from trying to maintain the old lifestyle in the face of this transition. By letting some of the balls drop, you are acknowledging that there are other places where your attention is needed. Do not be alarmed at the turbulence you are feeling. Pay attention to the things that actually align with your path, choose where you place your energy.

And make sure you are looking up at the stars for help with navigation. Context is everything.

Repeating old patterns is tiring. It is a poor use of energy. But sorting out belief patterns is complicated. There are so many layers — personal, interpersonal, and cultural. Sexuality is one of those very complicated patterns.

Many cultures around the world encourage the view that women's sexuality is dangerous and shameful, that our sole purpose is to be the property of men and vessels for their children. In the West this message is especially confusing, because we are encouraged to be sexually attractive, but then only enjoy the pleasure we give males — not our own. This must be confusing to men, also. Although I have been a lifelong feminist, I am still challenged by internalized shaming around sexuality. Why do I continue to shame myself?

Universal Wisdom: *You think everything has this punishment angle to it. That is the shame you feel. And you are willing to do it to yourself—create the punishment. You don't have to be punished for loving your body and allowing yourself to enjoy sex.*

I am crying. Somewhere inside me is saying "yes, you do." I am flashing to childhood rape. How there was a positive physical response to some of the sensations, and how that needs to be punished now by all the bad feelings, the shame, that it was my fault for getting hurt like that. I know this is child-thinking, but there it is, embedded in my perspective. How can I heal this? I want to feel good without feeling bad.

You are feeling the pain of a lifetime of punishing yourself. You can honor that pain for protecting you. It has also stifled you. Ask the little girl what would help.

What would help this pain?

Child Me: *I would like to feel safe again. That I could have the good feeling without the owie. It is like having chocolate with tacks in it. Sometimes I just have to have that chocolate, even though I know it will hurt. But mostly I just stay away from the hurt. And then I don't get candy either. And I try to be tough and say I don't need candy. But really, I don't want tacks.*

I wonder how to make chocolate without tacks.

Universal Wisdom: *Buy the kind without tacks.*

I feel like I want to carry around some real tacks and some chocolate.

Both, but separately. And see what comes up there.
You could do that. Or you could just buy the kind without tacks.
Try to think of other things that are just good on their own.
That's interesting. I thought about loving my children. And immediately I thought of how that hurts sometimes, too.
So that's not helpful. You have to think of something that is just good.
Huh. And then I was thinking of stuff that is pure bad. For some reason I thought of vomiting, which feels horrible. But then you feel better after.
A lot of things have those two sides.
Okay. Walking in the woods, or swimming in the river. Those are all good. Skiing in new snow. Nursing a baby. I was going to say "eating chocolate!" So the bad feeling, the tack, is an association, not a characteristic of the experience itself. It's added on.
Yes. It's a choice. You can un-choose by letting go of it. By acknowledging it as something added on. Something added on in a particular situation. By shifting your attention back to the good feeling, focusing on what is good about it.
The great freedom of letting go. The incredible physical pleasure. The skin-to-skin contact. Letting it be okay to receive, to love the other person back. Oh. That is where the pain shows up, because I think that I can safely assume the other person does not love me. I assume they are using me for themselves. That is also a learned belief.

I had a dream that illuminated some of these personal patterns. In the dream, I saw two picture frames, two windows into myself. The frames were side by side and seemed to exist simultaneously, like mirror reflections of different parts of me.

In one frame I was standing stiffly with my arm stretching out away from me. There was another person there and I was pushing them away. There was both defensiveness and strength in my action. In the other frame I was sitting huddled up, with my arms around my legs. I was very cold, shivering, and my lips were bluish. I was turning to the person next to me and reaching out with my face, asking them to help me get warm. There was fear and pleading in my action.

I'm thinking that the two frames refer to two expressions of my brain. One side is my intellectual self, the part of me that reacts with defensive posturing. The other is my emotional self, the part that reacts with neediness. Both of these parts are operational at different times. They are learned reactions, somewhat dysfunctional. I wonder what more there might be to understand about this.

Universal Wisdom: *You would like to think that this is something you can think about and then clean up. It is not that kind of thing. It is something to understand and then observe. These behaviors are confusing to others, because they don't know which one of these will display at any given time.*

When someone gets too close to my personal or mental space, where I might feel threatened, I react defensively and push them away. I think that deep down I am that other, needy, one — the one that never really felt mothered enough to have emotional security. When the frightened child surfaces, however, the intellectual adult takes over and pushes people away. It is a protective action that keeps me from fully experiencing my needs.

And what would happen if your needs were filled.

I assume that it is not possible to have my needs filled by another. The adult feels that it is foolish to make myself that vulnerable for something that is not even possible. So the emotional self is kept imprisoned by the intellectual self. I can see how this keeps the intellect in the driver's seat — if the emotional self is kept undeveloped, then the intellect always has a job to do in protecting it. Really, they are separate things. I can't solve emotional problems with intellect, and vice versa.

What are these two areas? Am I really looking at two sides of my brain? *That is a very simple way to look at it. It is really about patterns. Patterns of behavior that are wired through different circuits. Other people who have experienced emotional trauma may have some of these patterns too. When the trauma occurs and the emotional self is injured or disrupted, the intellectual self may take over to protect or allow time for healing.*

If the trauma is significant and/or repetitive, the intellect may take over areas that belong to the emotional self. Over time, an imbalance occurs. You see this in the body when one muscle is injured or weak and a neighboring muscle overdevelops to make up for that. An imbalance is created. Without correction, the imbalance will magnify and cause imbalance in other areas or increase the chance of other injury. It is not easy to correct patterns that have developed over a lifetime.

What are some suggestions for rebalancing.

A different question is needed, because there is not a recipe or an exercise workout that will change this. A decision has to be made, a choice. The choice is between being in the moment and being out of the moment.

The intellect is not in the moment. It takes over because it is basing its action on the past, and assumes that the future can only be the same as the past — that it is not mutable. The emotional self can act in the moment if it is freed of the judgment of the intellect. When the emotional self is acting in the moment, new ways can be created.

Humans easily judge the emotional self as being "childish," because it has less regard for consequences than the intellect. But a childlike quality is exactly what is needed to create new ways. Childlike quality values curiosity and adventure and let's see what happens. It does not prejudge outcomes.

Of course, not everyone has this pattern. Some may need to begin considering consequences and more thinking. This is not typical in the West.

I often feel like I do not get enough creative outlet. I crave free time without task outcomes, free time without a deadline or end time.

Look for it.

Practice being in the moment, no matter what it is that you are doing.

◞

Looking at our patterns and practicing new ways takes time and patience. Sometimes, cataclysmic events occur in our lives that force change. Then the psychic upheaval is so great that we cannot possibly go back to who we were before. This is called trauma.

A'riquea: *Trauma itself breaks the connection to cultural conditioning. Of course, it can also spin the other way and become a bondage, but trauma provides an opportunity to see the world in a new way, it is a chance to shift perspective.*

It is more difficult to shift when someone is working to maintain a predictable path. Then everything that occurs must be made to fit that fixed way of seeing and Being. Experiencing trauma and healing from it bring Being out into the open, where exposure to other ways is not so threatening.

The very act of healing requires a new way of Being. That is the gift — that one cannot go back to the way they were before the trauma. That is difficult to see in the short term. There is an intense feeling of loss. Healing requires the embrace of that loss, the recognition that something has changed, and the courage to move in a new direction. Healing is a kind of rebuilding. Of course, people can choose to move in new directions at any time. Trauma is not a requirement. The opportunity is always there.

"Trauma creates change you *don't* choose. Healing is about creating change you *do* choose." ~Michele Rosenthal

Historical trauma is a massive upheaval that is experienced both by individuals, and by the collective group to which the individuals belong. Additionally, it is experienced not just by the group that is traumatized, but also by any group that *causes* the trauma. Both the cause and the effect have wide and long-lasting effects. It occurs in the past but is carried forth across generations into the present by culture.

I wondered about historical trauma, and how it fit with spiritual evolution. Native Americans, for example, did not just "lose the war." They experienced mass extermination of their communities and their culture, much of which was carried out with intention over centuries. Black history, too, is full of the brutal trauma of slavery and loss of home and personhood. White Americans carried out these hateful actions against their fellow humans. All of this is collective history.

There's Jewish persecution and the Holocaust. Although women's legal status has changed in recent history, their bodies are still treated as public property and items of social economics. Even white males have their own kind of history — created by the cultural cage of limited emotional expression, and the brutality that males visit on each other. Obviously, every person has the opportunity to grow through these experiences, to see a broader context and choose compassion.

A'riquea: *Everyone does have some kind of "negative" experiences in their past. It is not possible to be human and not have had some loss. Loss can come in many forms, of course. Loss of innocence, loss of trust, loss of family connections, loss of Home location. How an event will affect one person is variable, depending on their previous choices and learning.*

Trauma defines significant or multiple losses, something that stretches a person's coping ability in such a way that new ways of being are required to go forward. Look up trauma.

Trauma is defined as both an experience and its aftermath: it is an experience that is deeply disturbing or distressing, and it is also the shock (physical, emotional, psychic) that follows such an event. "Trauma" comes from the Greek word for "wound."

So it is a shock to the system. If it is literally a wound, then that is an opening. Openings in the skin are a place where either germs enter and destroy tissue, or new tissue is beautifully created out of Life Force to seal that opening. A scar is evidence of healing.

Yes, an opening is made. An opening is made in the way that a person thinks about the world. The opening is such that the person cannot go back to thinking the way that they did before the trauma occurred. Sometimes people have difficulty making the change, and it may take a long time. Sometimes the change is never made, and people choose to cover their confusion and loss with addictions.

Addiction is like keeping a dirty bandage on a wound. The wound will not be seen, but it will also not be healed. Healing a wound requires that one look at it, address it, take care of it. It needs to be kept clean, so that it does not collect harmful debris. It needs air and nutrition and rest. It needs Love. Everything needs Love, including wounds. Sometimes this is very painful. That is the new tissue forming. The scar is a sign of Love.

The same must apply to historical trauma, except that it affects a group. Groups must have a way of thinking as well.

It is a similar principle but applied on a more complicated level. Groups do have their own way of thinking, although sometimes this is not very visible. People in the group know that things are done in a certain way, but the reasons may not be clear. Many thoughts and behaviors keep a group identity in place and offer stability. Hopefully, these thoughts and behaviors also promote growth.

When groups of people are traumatized, each person has to cope with the trauma, but there will also be coping by the group. Just as there is the possibility of disagreement and dysfunction, there is also the opportunity for new ideas and more cohesive relationships. The trauma stretches the coping skills of the group.

Historical trauma, by definition, extends over long periods of time, affecting generations of people.

Anything not healed in one generation will be passed on to the next. There is always the opportunity to heal both the present and the past. This applies to individuals and also to groups.

It seems that trauma that is not healed and is passed on becomes less specific. The experience is less direct, and what is inherited is a feeling. People don't know how to address these vague feelings of pain and disconnect.

That is because the group has lost its place. The group has forgotten what specifically occurred. This can result in the pain getting attributed to the wrong cause. It can become generalized and develop into a victim culture.

You are wondering why such a thing would be necessary or desirable in the scope of spiritual evolution. It is not necessary or desirable. It is human nature. It is the outcome of the difficulties that occur when spirits inhabit physical bodies.

Every defined group has their own version of historical trauma. Some are more severe than others. But they all involve the need to redefine the group within the context of healing. There needs to be a return to balance. First there needs to be a desire to return to balance, which is a desire to return to the spirit-fueled life.

Dysfunction occurs, for both an individual and for a group, when the coping mechanisms rely on an ego-driven life. For groups, leaders are important. The group will choose a leader who is either ego-driven or spirit-driven. Individuals will choose whether they will be head-driven or heart-driven. It is all about the motivation for living.

This is one reason you need not be afraid in your Native community. People may not have the same connections to the old ways that used to guide their choices. There may not be the spiritual elders available to guide them. But choosing to travel a spiritual path, even though it is amateur, is better than choosing to not travel a spiritual path. You are traveling a spiritual path.

I was about to say that pretty much everything that I am learning is about traveling the spirit path. Acting with compassion is about moving Love energy, about clearing my own energy vibrations and harmonizing with the vibrations of others, and encouraging others to move Love energy too. I understand that humans are in a unique position to move Love energy because we have physical bodies. Is there another purpose to moving this energy.

There is more to come. We have talked about the need to increase the numbers of humans moving this energy. Individuals cannot do this alone. This is about creating a channel for energy movement. [The next part is something I don't want to type, because it makes me fearful, but I will go ahead.] *A time is coming when many will be leaving the planet. It will be best if as many of those leaving as possible have developed the kind of clear channel that will allow them to move into another dimension.*

I can see this, like the tunnel with the brilliant white light at the end of it. So, many people will "die." I feel fear because my own children may not be able to make this transition. They are in another place in their lives, not connected to this the way I am.

But there are many ways to be connected, and some younger people will not have to go through the same education that you have. They already have the potential to be more evolved just because they were born into another time.

And, of course, it feels like mother-hen behavior to want to try to protect my own children.

It is your job to try to protect your children. And you are teaching them through the example of your own living.

～

There are skills we can develop, tools that will help us as we grow through trauma and loss. These skills can also assist us in making the changes that add up to The Shift. The following four skills were given to me in anticipation of a major change in my life.

Universal Wisdom: *We have something else for you. You will need some preparation for something that is coming your way. You may be surprised when it happens, but you can be ready for the action you will need to take. If you knew what it was, then you would spend much energy trying to figure it out ahead of time, and this would not be helpful. This is a time when you must trust. We are going to tell you the skills that will be needed.*

Humility is one. You often think of humility as placing yourself in a lower position. You are used to reducing your power to deflect attention. What you really want to be doing is maintaining your power and using it to place yourself in context. You want to broaden your context to include yourself and everyone else. Do not shrink to avoid, but expand to include. The whole world is your family. You have many kinds of aunties and uncles, brothers and sisters — your spiritual family.

Another thing you will need to cultivate is Triumph.

I immediately recoil from the word. To me it implies a kind of dominating victory, arrogance.

Look it up.

Triumph is described in the dictionary as both a feeling—of joy and satisfaction, and as a highly successful example of something. So triumph is about celebrating success.

Yes. It doesn't have to be all about you. You can celebrate the success of something that you helped to create. You can celebrate with others. You can be happy for the success. After all, there was also the possibility that it wouldn't have worked out so well. So there is always something to be grateful for.

Thank you. Humility and Triumph. Is there anything else I need to prepare.

The other is Acceptance. You will need to accept an environment of not knowing. Not knowing what or when this is going to happen. Not knowing everything about what went into it or how it proceeds. Not knowing the actual outcome. Accepting the loose ends as part of the process. And experiencing Space — there will not be a linear finish to this. These are all things that you can do. Your directive now is to practice them so that you will be ready when it is needed. There will be great joy in your experience. More so when you have these skills in place.

Thank you. I appreciate the heads up, the opportunity to enrich my life.

You are traveling down several paths simultaneously. Some are more visible than others. Some choices are more visible than others.

Humility. Triumph. Acceptance.

And, as always, laughter whenever possible.

Ha ha. Yes.

Go now. Move outdoors.

Six months after this teaching, my world was rocked to the core when I was diagnosed with two cancers simultaneously. These four skills were invaluable, not only during the journey that followed, but for my entire life since then. They are universal skills.

~

Changing our patterns also means changing our vision.

It's right here. Everything you need is right here. We don't often have our eyes open to it, we are so ready to let our world be defined by what we are taught to see. Anything that exists outside that vision is discounted.

I am trying to figure out who is talking. I see Great Grandfather standing nearby but looking away on purpose. Now he has walked over and entered my body.

It is time to start talking about another area. This is something you may not grasp right away but it will make sense by the end.

Here is a new speaker. A younger Indian man, with shoulder- length, flowing hair. He is in his 30s, idealistic, energetic, agitated.

I am your **Great Grandfather's younger self**. *I am living in the 1800s. We can see the approach of the white world. We are nervous.*

He is wearing pants and shoes and a shirt, all are a little ragged, clearly the only clothes he has.

He is shaking his finger at me.

See how you define me! It is only what you see with your eyes, and you are ready to make a world out of it! That is what judgment is. It is a very dangerous way to live. Because you are ready to define something, or someone, based on very little information. This is what narrows your world. In every way. There is much in the world that is not immediately visible. You know this intuitively, but you are letting yourself close the world by labeling it.

It looks to me like that is his only set of clothes.

Exactly. You do not know if this is how I always look. Maybe I am disguised, to move more easily through the swarm of whites. They see someone in the distance wearing two-legged clothing [pants] *and they assume it is one of them. I become invisible when my appearance is what they expect.*

He is standing in the shade of a tree as he speaks, the bright sky behind him, occasionally resting his hand on a branch, but always glancing around furtively. He is on his guard.

Yes. I have messages to deliver, and I cannot be caught on the way.

I can also see him in his teepee village, with his family. He has a young wife and baby.

It is getting harder to go back and forth between these two cultures. I wear these shoes and they hurt my feet, but I get used to them. When I take them off my feet are too soft to go barefoot. I am trying to be two things. I am afraid I am becoming too white.

So this must be a challenge for Indian people today, too.

Yes. They have been wearing the shoes a long time now. We are trying to build strength by going back to the old ways, but our feet are used to the shoes. We are no longer touching the earth in the same way.

He is pointing directly at me, his eyes finding me at the end of his finger's aim.

You. You have a part in this. You are also confused, but in another direction. You were born with the shoes on, yet your heart knows the other way.

I feel at home on the Rez, but I also wonder if I belong there. It is a relationship that is always shifting.

When people realize that you are there to heal, not to steal, then you will be accepted. They are getting used to you. But you have another purpose. This is the thing you may not understand. You are a vehicle for some of the ways. You are thinking about your work with birthing families, and that is a good path, but it is not the thing we are talking about. We will be sending messages through you. We have already been doing this.

Just remember that we may not be what we look like. There are many disguises. You do not really know who I am, just that you are talking to me. There are many disguises. Think of how many disguises you wear yourself.

What advice do you have for me. How can I understand what is happening and be helpful.

You may not be able to understand. This is about spirit-to-spirit transmission. You will not necessarily be aware of that when it occurs. The depth of your life is going to increase. The best thing is for you to stay in tune, so that you are a clear receiver and transmitter. Move through your world with awareness and intention. Believe that there is a greater purpose to all that you do. Be ready for opportunities that present themselves. And never, under any circumstances, judge the other based on your limited vision. Allow for a bigger picture.

You are asking me to include the unknown in my vision.

Yes. Allow the Mystery to be present. If you are always relying on what you think is known, you will be eliminating most of what is actually possible. That is a narrow view. Including the unknown expands your awareness into Space, into Not-Time. Indian Time.

He is ready to lope away, to walk many miles. He looks back at me with a little smile and a wink that says *see you next time.* I am aware that I may not recognize him next time.

Great Grandfather's younger self came back to me again to talk about walking in the white man's shoes. He was walking in those shoes to stay under the radar as he brought messages over the land, and he was concerned that he was losing his Indian self along the way.

This choosing, of one path or another, is one of the tests of faith. There are many choices, all day, every day. They may seem small but they add up to the way your life will travel. Sometimes you choose the thing that seems wrong, but that is because it is wrong on a small level. The thing that may be wrong on a small level may be right on a larger level. There are many layers.

I am doing this walking, even though it is probably changing my Indian self, but I am doing this walking because the messages need to move and I am in a good position to be the messenger. I have these skills. This is the right thing to do for my People, even though it might not look like the right thing to do for me.

I hear myself asking about that, in terms of what I have learned about needing to put myself first now, that it's not good for me to put my needs last or never. And I hear that there are many layers of Me.

Yes. I may be hurting my Indian self in the short term, but I am also growing in other ways. And when I help my People, I am helping myself also. I am helping to create an environment where my People can continue, and I am one of those people who will benefit. So I am also putting myself first when I put my People first.

I see how, for me, with cancer, "my People" could also mean all the cells in the community of my body. I am also realizing that I have work to do long into the future. The *Grandmother Dreams* series is only beginning. I need to be strong and healthy to carry out my life's work. What will help me move along in a good way?

This is not always easy to see. It is important to pray, to pray for guidance and understanding. Part of your belief system has to include faith in the Universe, that your ancestors, your Teachers, will help you on the path that is a good way. You have started that journey, but you still have doubt. Your doubt is holding you back. Let your faith make the road for you. You can do this. You know that you can do this. Acknowledge the fear and then step into your path. There is safety on your path. Not the safety of knowing, because you have to let go of that, of course. But safety in conviction, which is a bigger knowing.

The face of Great Grandfather's younger self is very close to mine. I can see his eyes twinkling with the Spirit Fire flame. He has a big smile on his face. My body is full of the energy of the Universe. My eyes are full of tears. I am coming Home. I am crying with the relief and the beauty of it. This is the place I must be. He is laughing now, laughing at my innocence. I have been lost a long time! Why is it so hard to listen to my own faith?

There is so much distraction in the physical world. Many people think they know the way and are telling you things that go against your spiritual intuition. Part of what needs to happen is for humans to get in touch with their ancestral knowledge. This is something you will be encouraging. The plants and animals were made first. Since humans were made last, we are the least experienced.

This is true. Humans need to look beyond their own arrogance and realize that there is much to learn in the way they treat others. Not just other humans but other beings. Humans need to see a bigger picture, to understand the connectedness. Westerners are good at compartmentalizing, keeping things separate when, of course, they are not. Everything touches everything else.

So maybe I can see myself in the bigger picture, and hold myself in that context while I accept the chemo. I will have to be strong to hold that context. I have been given a good practice — to experience the elements of my intentions right now, to have the feelings that those elements will bring when they manifest. This is preparing my energy body.

And that is when you are more connected with Us.

He is starting to move away, waving goodbye as he backs away into the sun with jaunty steps.

"I must be willing to give up what I am in order to become what I will be." ~ Albert Einstein

~ 5 ~

Walking In Two Worlds

We navigate the physical world with our five senses—sight, sound, smell, taste, touch. We navigate the spiritual world with our other senses—intuition and energy awareness. By suspending our investment in the five-sense world and allowing our energy to expand beyond it, we can travel in the Spirit World.

Westerners have been hesitant to do this. We prefer to "fix" our reality in the physical world, and this limits our perceptions. Long ago, for example, most humans were sure that the Earth was flat. Once we were able to breach the horizon and travel beyond it, however, we began to see a world that existed beyond our view. The Earth did not change. Our perception did. Over time, so did our beliefs. Eventually, those ideas were challenged and changed too, by traveling off the planet and out into space.

We have similar opportunities to expand our spiritual horizons, to expand both our perspective and our energy. By opening to the world beyond our five senses, by moving into the unknown, we can create new ways of Being. The Teachers are asking us to do just this. They want us to increase our investment in the spiritual world, to integrate the physical and spiritual dimensions. We are being asked to walk in two worlds.

Compassion is an example of an energy choice we make in the Physical World that feeds both the Physical World and the Spirit World. Honoring the spirits is another way can we be walking in two worlds.

Aniimaakii:[30] *This is part of holding the duality of separate and non-separate, Life Form and Spirit Form. Think about the circle, which has no beginning and no ending. Things start as one thing, and travel around the circle becoming another, until they are the first thing again. On the circle, both things are possible simultaneously. You can look at just one piece, and you will see just one thing. And then you can look at the whole circle and see them both there. You can see the grandmother in the infant and the infant in the grandmother. You can see Spirit at work in the Physical World, and you can see Life Form at work in the Spirit World.*

You are not used to seeing Life Form at work in the Spirit World, so it is not so obvious. Humans have been discouraged from going this other direction. It is one of the limits of organized religion, the idea that God can come to you but you cannot go to God. Or that someone higher than you in the hierarchy has exclusive access to God. But it is important for the energy to travel in both directions.

The Spirits are the intermediaries, the ones we recognize as inhabiting the Spirit World. They embody certain energies that appear to you as Teachers. They are connecting you to the Spirit World. You need to honor them and recognize their contributions. Spirit intermediaries are needed because few humans have the skills to communicate directly with God. That is very high-flow energy. It can be like getting electrocuted, or radiated. Be cautious of those who claim to have this direct connection. Their behavior will tell the Truth, not their words.

How do you know when Life Form is at work in the Spirit World? This is something that needs to be understood. When the spirits are not being honored, when they are being ignored, imbalances will occur. The most obvious imbalance right now is environmental. The Physical World is reacting to a lengthy period of spiritual disrespect by rebalancing itself. If humans had been asking the spirits for guidance, different choices would have been made.

Connection with the Spirit World can be hindered by too much

---

[30]**Aniimaakii** is an embodiment of Thunderbird Medicine, which expands the boundaries that limit humans to the physical plane.

thinking. Needing to know is an intellectual process that uses the five senses to prove something. This anchors our perception to our current reality. Moving in the Spirit World requires that we let go of our usual mental constructions and allow something else, without knowing what that something else is. We have to enter into not-knowing.

The following conversation about not-knowing occurred during a time when I was questioning my identity.

I lived my childhood as a nomad — frequently uprooted and moving from state to state. It was very freeing, never having to conform to an identity created by my location. But it also meant that I was challenged to understand where I belonged. As an adult, I became involved with an Indian community, and many questions came with that. My physical body had light skin, but I was welcomed in the community and many spirits came to me. It made me wonder about my heritage. If I knew who I was, genetically, would it somehow explain these spiritual connections? Would it place me somewhere, or would it prove that I didn't belong? Why did I think I needed to know?

I asked for some help with this and **Great Grandfather** appeared, motioning for me to sit down next to him. He encouraged me to let go of the need to know, explaining it in this way:

This is the best way to go. In knowing, there will be distraction from your purpose, which is to learn by opening. Knowing will close down some paths. Remember that you are to have a foot in both worlds. This cannot happen if you lift a foot out of one. A foot in each world means just that — you have a foot in each. Be thankful for the perspective that that allows. You have the benefit of Teachers in many worlds.

He turns to point to the horizon behind him, where a burning sun is just starting to come up over the edge of the world.

This is the New Day dawning. Use your energy to prepare for the rising sun and the day it will bring. You are on the edge of this new beginning. As we have said before: grieve your losses and then place them in the context of your life. You cannot change the way you came into your journey. You can only choose the direction you will go forward on.

Go In Peace.

He came to me another day and pointed down at the keyboard. He was laughing quietly, a twinkle in his eye. He extended his arm, pointing to the horizon, his hand sweeping the expanse from side to side. **Great Grandfather**: *This is what you want to be thinking about. This is what the ancestors knew, and what you will need to know again. This is the crack in the world, the line of movement which we all must pass through. It is the joining of the sky and the Earth, in a line which can never be fixed by Time, because Time is always moving. Look up "Horizon."*

What I found is that the horizon is a line. It is a line that appears to divide everything we see into two sections — that which is part of the Earth's surface and that which is part of the sky. It both divides the Earth and sky, and it joins them.

This line that is the horizon is called a "line at infinity." Think of a railroad track extending into the distance. This, and any other set of parallel lines, will eventually converge and vanish at the horizon. The place where they converge and vanish is called a "point of infinity." The actual horizon is made up of all these points of infinity, all of these convergences, strung together into a line — the line at infinity.

Before the radio and telegraph, the visible horizon was the maximum range of physical communication. You couldn't learn about other people or places without going there, without going beyond the horizon. This explains the concept of "broadening your horizons," which means expanding the limit of your mental perception, experience, or interest.

Great Grandfather is shaking his head Yes.

We can challenge our limits, broaden our horizons, by disrupting our usual thought patterns. This disruption makes creativity possible. Creativity opens the potential for new ideas, new solutions, and beyond-the-box changes in how we think or behave. This can happen on a grand scale, when whole cultures make a shift in perception. But it always starts on a small scale, with individuals allowing for breaks in their thinking patterns. The New Wave, The Shift, is this kind of change, and any work I am doing now with these writing projects is part of this shift.

Sometimes I feel isolated, because people around me are not ready to accept this kind of thinking. They are not ready or willing or able to disrupt their own thought patterns. This can not deter me from my own journey. I have already gone this direction, I cannot turn back and unlearn what I know. My patterns have been disrupted, in a good way.

I may feel isolated but I am not alone. I can place myself in a context that is supportive and nurturing and feel a sense of belonging. It is not the hearth-and-home kind of belonging. It is the sense that there are many Points out in the wide world which are already connected with me. They are points of infinity, they are part of the line at infinity, at the Horizon. They are already there, I have only to discover them.

Great Grandfather is motioning toward the horizon, using his open hand like an eraser, as if to push our focus away. He points to himself and then to me. You and me, he motions. And he points to the stars in the dark part of the dawn sky.

You and I. You and I and all the stars, all the ancestors. That is who is on this journey. We are not fixed objects. We are traveling though Space. We are all connected by the energy in the space between us. We are all moving, and we are all connected. And we are all One. Look up at the stars and see how simple it is. We are just this. And we are everything that that is. Infinite. When you are able to expand into the Horizon, you will find that you are an Infinite Point on that movable line. You will be an angel dancing on that point. It is your dancing, the way you move yourself, that determines what kind of connections are made.

You are an Infinite Point on a movable line. You are an angel dancing. That angel dancing is your heart resonating, compassion being created, Love energy fueling the Universe, fueling Life Force, going back to The Seed, your True Self who is One with God. You will know this when the Earth is beautiful again. When you see that Heavenly Perfection is all around you. This is the Heaven that religious leaders speak of. It is not some place in the clouds that is attainable only after death. It is right here. It is created by the movement of your heart. The Big Drum.

I hear pow-wow singing, I feel myself dancing around and around and around the circle.

This is the way it will come, by honoring the Earth and All who walk upon it. Move the circle. Honor the circle. Now go, and put out your asemaa[31], and have your day, with the knowledge that all is moving. The Shift has come. We are in motion.

I feel powerful emotions, tears are in my eyes.

There is great strength available to you now. Keep your body tuned up, ready. You will be prepared when the time comes.

Go now.

The welcoming points are numerous and clear, like stars in the sky. When I say that, I feel a transfer of energy. There is energy moving towards me, cycling through my body. Circling and circling, power is being created. I can see some of the points, and they are places where *Grandmother Dreams* has already landed. That first book is helping to magnify the points and create connecting current.

"Everything the power does, it does in a circle." ~Lakota

The circle and the horizon are connected. Author Janna Levin is a professor of physics and astronomy. I heard Levin in a radio interview, talking about the idea that even though the universe appears to be infinite, it may be finite. It may have a limit. As an example, she described starting from a point on the Earth and walking toward the horizon. The horizon appears to be infinite, because if you keep walking in a straight line you will move toward the horizon but never reach it. The horizon is not an edge that you could fall off of. It is a movable line created by the curve of light and the Earth. If you keep walking in that straight line, always toward the infinite horizon, you will eventually come all the way around the Earth to the exact place

---

[31]**Asemaa** is a plant medicine used in prayers and offerings.

that you started. What appears infinite is actually finite.

This reminds me of the loop of light that is our soul's path. My current place in Time is a location on that loop, on that circle. Included in that circle is not only my present, but also my past and my future — they are all connected. Because it is a continuous circle, the past, present and future are also concurrent, they are all on the line at the same time. I may not be able to see beyond the horizon of my present, but I am definitely on that loop. This explains why healing in the present can also heal both the past and future — it straightens out kinks and bumps and allows energy, Life Force, to travel a smoother circuit.

When I think about Great Grandfather's discussion of horizon and add Janna Levin's thoughts on the finite nature of the Universe, I can see how all of the loops of all the soul paths are interconnected. My current lifetime is a result of the energy paths of all my ancestors. I am, in my "present," located on the future of their loops. In my current lifetime, my present, I am also located on the past of my great-grandchildren's loops. This is how my own healing can heal both my ancestors and my future grandchildren, and why I have a responsibility to take that on.

When you realize that we all come from common ancestors from hundreds of thousands of years ago, it is easy to see how we are all related, through the criss-crossing of soul paths. It's as if the entire surface of the Earth was covered by the loops of everyone's soul paths, and anywhere I stand is a crossroads connecting them.

The circle that we travel is continuous, and holds the past and the present and the future all at once. While I was resting in these thoughts, I had a dream. In the dream, I accidentally landed somewhere in the future:

I was in a large room lined with banks of computer screens. They were different than today's computers. Instead of a port for a data disc or stick, these computer ports were cubes, with each side measuring about six inches. What fit into that port was a cubelike box with screens on at least four sides (there might have also been a screen on one end), and a handle on the top. Each one of the cube's sides had a different person's face on its screen. Each face was live, speaking, interactive. The people on the port's screens were all different: female, male, black, brown, white.

The cubelike box could be placed in the port and then all the people in the room could interact with them. All over the large room full of screens, people were sitting in chairs. The people who were sitting in front of the multiple screens were just as diverse as the people on the screens. They were all interacting. It was exponential communication.

I was following a young man, trying to talk to him about this project. He took what he called his "Face Box" out of his computer port. The faces were still on the sides of the box, still talking. He mentioned that this project was named "Twelve Thousand Faces," and that the intent was to connect people. People were using Face Box to talk to each other, and the sharing had to do with learning about each other and connecting on a human level.

When I woke up from the dream, the young man was still present. He turned to me and wanted to talk. Can you tell me your name? *You can call me* **Orvid.** *We haven't met yet, but I'm going to see you in another Time. I'm not sure why you have seen this, because it's not going to help you in your Time. No one knows how to do this yet. You, your culture, is all caught up in amassing connections. This is useful, I suppose, because it's how we get to the next thing. But at the moment it is pretty useless. It is wasting people's energy.*

Face Box isn't due up until 2050. What we're trying to do is connect people. Not just connect technologically, but connect deeply as human beings. What is it that makes us human? What is it that we share with other humans? What do we have in common? It's helping the spiritual communication network to hum up. This will work better when each human is able to hum up. I think that is what you're working on now with your books. It's kind of a slow start. But you gotta start somewhere. That's what we're doing. It's not all perfect yet. That's why I was a little frustrated that you were here. It's not all smooth, like I'd want it.
So, is there something I can do now that will help this along later?

Well, I suppose there is. People have got to be tuned in. But that just is your job. Can't do one thing before the other, not ready. People need to see their own humanity, not be afraid of it. Which includes Spirit, of course. You've got a big job before you. But that's just what it is — the next thing. So, no worries, you know.

I'll be 90 in 2050.

Cool. I'll be about 35. Look for Orvid.

I'm curious. What's the significance of the number 12,000?

It's 12,000 Light-Years. Doesn't mean much now, in 2010. It has other connections in 2050.

And, of course, I'm marveling at meeting someone who isn't even born yet.

I haven't been born yet in Time. In Space, we're all here.

Oh, yes. And that is where I'm meeting the Teachers, like you.

Mmmm. Not like me. I'm just a person, but I suppose you're learning from me because I appear in your future. You might want to check this, but I think that the Teachers are generated in your cells, which is Space, of course. But Universal Wisdom flows in the space outside your body. Yes, all of this space is continuous, so we are kind of splitting hairs here. Anyway, that might be a good thing to clarify. Not sure why. It seems like you need to know this. People are going to ask and you will need to know the answer. And right there I am going to get out of it. I have other things to work on.

OK. Well, thanks. It was good to meet you. And good luck with your project. One last question: is it okay to talk about Face Box, in a general way? I'm thinking my kids might be interested.

Yeah. They won't really get it, because it doesn't exist. But they will see it some day. Maybe they can help support it....

Hey, thanks. See you again.

See you again.

It would have been easy to get pulled away into the details of Orvid's future. But that would have distracted me from my intended focus in the present. There are so many interesting things in this world — Life has so much to offer! Distractions are presenting themselves all the time. It is important, in a general way, to stay on track.

I can get off track even when I am doing what I think is right. I was examining my own daily life, for example, when I realized how out of control it felt. There was a parallel between the condition of my work life and the condition of my interior life. I had been hired to support the health of mothers and babies in a small community, to improve outcomes for the next generations, to help strengthen the community from the inside. But it had all become cluttered by distracting office details and paperwork deadlines. I'd lost sight of what I was doing there.

Great Grandfather: *This is one of the reasons you were placed in the reservation environment. You are connected to the Way of Women. This is one of your gifts. You have been very patient, and more patience will be required in the future. For now, it is good to be aware of your goal. Think about what it would look like if all of your goals were met. Go ahead.*

I haven't really put that together before. There are many pieces, but they all work together. Women would choose to breastfeed their babies. Women would be free of harmful substances during pregnancy and parenting. Children would be raised in an environment where their caregivers understood and supported their developmental needs. Women would support each other in raising healthy generations. Men and multiple generations would work together to make this happen. What is woven through all of this is the practice of expanded energy, the awareness of a larger context. When I come back to that, my body feels electrified. I am occupying Space with energetic intensity. *This is the place you need to focus. If you can feel this kind of energy, then you are moving in the right direction. Right now at work you are letting your energy get distracted by endless details. You will not be able to connect with spiritual energy under that condition. You need to open your life, focus on moving spiritual energy. Let the details take care of themselves.*

We need to talk some more about the Horizon. I am showing you this again — there are things we missed in the first discussion that will help you now. Look again at the Horizon.

(He has his arm gently around my shoulder. He is pointing out over

Lake Superior into the distance.)

The Horizon is a location in Space and it is also has no location. This depends on how you look at it, how you wish to see it. It is not one or the other, it is both. You will know you are moving in a good way when you feel the expansiveness that is without location.

Seeing the Horizon without location, you will be pulled into the crack of light between the Dream World and the Physical World, between the sky and the Earth. There is such a place, a place with no location, that is only defined by all of the space there is. It is the moment where the Great Mystery resides. It is a place that is not-there. When you move into that space you will never stop moving, you will be flowing and you will be the flowing. You will have fallen off the fin of the fish into not-Time.[32]

It is possible to make this journey while you are in physical form. It takes much practice. You will begin to be shown pieces of that practice. Pay attention to all that is put before you. Pay attention to the sensations created. Trust your response and allow it. More people are watching you than you know. The Underground will begin to reach for you.

I see a man from the community, he has taken my wrist and is pulling me into the circle, pointing to a seat. When I take the seat, I see people in regalia, I hear pow-wow singing and drumming. I am enthralled. When I stand up, it all disappears. When I sit, when I take my place, it returns.

Another of my Indian friends is sitting next to me, and he looks nervous, like I will judge him if things don't turn out well here. I am focusing on my seat, and allowing my place. I feel a circular flow of energy, cycling in front of me, through my crown, down my spine, through my feet, out and up again, through my crown, cycling, cycling. I see the regalia, I hear the rustle of feathers and dresses, the jingle of bells.

I see a young man in regalia, dancing well and moving energy. He is paying attention to his dancing and also to the energy context

---

[32] See *Grandmother Dreams*, pp.100-105, for a discussion of Time and the fish in relation to a quote from Louise Erdrich. In summary: Time is a fish and we are on the back of that fish for a while; then we fall off into something called not-time.

of his dancing. He is moving Life Force in his body and also with his body. He is integrating it all. He is turning the Wheel of Life. He looks at me and winks, and raises his staff and whoops loudly, celebrating the energy. I want to dance, too, but he moves his hand to signal No. He continues to dance, moving a little away from me.

I am standing, looking at the grass at my feet, the blades of grass rooted to the ground and dancing in the breeze. Small dancers in regalia are there, too. They are the size of the grass blades and dancing among them. The grass is happy. The Earth is happy. The dancers are focused and joyful. The sun is shining. My guide takes my wrist again and points to the seat. I take the seat and the young dancer is once again before me. Something is moving my life, a cycle of energy. *Now you will go outside in the sun and see the grass in a new way. When the seat is shown to you, you will take it. That is all for now.*

Thank you Great Grandfather. Chii Miigwech. See you again.

His shaggy head lowers and he turns away.

I continued to think about everything that Great Grandfather had said about the Horizon. During that time I also did some bodywork with an intuitive healer. I experienced significant cross-generational healing, and then I was pulled into the crack of light at the Horizon. This is how it happened:

I had been struggling with a head and neck ache for about three weeks. When I laid down on the energy worker's table, a spirit immediately flew into my body. It was my Great Grandfather, an Indian man with a big shaggy head of black hair, like a buffalo.

During the body work, I could see that he was carrying an injury. The point in my neck which held my pain was the same place where something sharp, like an arrowhead, had penetrated his neck. I could see its gray tip. And the area around my left eye socket, which had also been part of my three-week headache, was also his injury — some kind of crushing blow. During the body work, the areas of pain were removed and healed. I asked my Great Grandfather if he had survived those injuries and he said Yes, but people were afraid of him after that because he was so disfigured.

I did not talk about any of this during the body work, because I did not want to disrupt my Great Grandfather's healing. When I told the therapist about it afterwards, I was struck by how parallel my own injuries were to his. I had fallen on my head as a child, landing on my left eyebrow, with my neck taking the impact of my body falling. So these were my injuries and they were also his injuries. The past and the present, in the same place.

In the days after that healing occurred, Great Grandfather was always with me. He kept repeating an action and trying to tell me something. He kept pointing to the horizon. Typically, the horizon he shows me is a line of open sky between a cloud blanket and the big water of Lake Superior. Today there is light streaming out of that line of open sky.

Great Grandfather repeatedly swings his finger outward, indicating a direction. So I am not to just look, I am to go there. I am traveling towards this brightness, the meeting place of the land and the sky. The horizon itself is a line in my vision and I am zeroing in on a point in the line of the horizon. It appears like a dot, a small black circle like a period. As I travel towards the horizon, this tiny point, this circle, appears larger and larger. Of course, the horizon is a movable location, always distant, but this point is not. It is something that I am approaching. And then, of course, here I am and it is the opening to a tunnel. When I go into it, I can see bright light at the other end of it.

Like similar experiences before, I am flying in this tunnel. I am flying into a strong wind, my hair streaming back. I have my face full into this wind. I smile at the force of it. My arms are at my sides, and I am moving at a high speed but with a feeling of total relaxation. I am rotating onto my back and sides with ease. As I near the end of the tunnel, I am suddenly in zero gravity. I am floating in a blissful state. I am floating in thickened air, almost like gel. This is the Zone of the Universe. Now I am swimming forward towards the end of the tunnel, my hands pulling and my feet kicking through this thick medium, leaving trails where my hands have scooped.

When I come through the end of the tunnel, the gel ends and I am floating in light. The environment is light. It is not air or gel, it is light. Extremely bright. I am rotating lazily, no longer in control. Bright light is shooting out from around my eyes, my open mouth, every pore in my skin. I am made of the light and I am surrounded by it. We are one. (Sitting here typing, every cell in my body is vibrating in recognition and renewal.) I am drifting, and light is streaming out of the palms of my hands, the soles of my feet. Every strand of hair is a light string. The body I left the tunnel with is gradually dissolving as the light within me joins the light around me.

Now just the essence of my physical body remains, a ghostlike film of flimsy membranes. Now even these are gone and I see my skeleton, the source of this inner light, being eaten away from the ends towards the center, crumbling away and the pieces disappearing into the light, being absorbed. There is only my spine, twinkling with light, mostly blue with some red and yellow. The twinkly lights[33] are coordinating, to create a pulse. The pulsing spots of light each have an eye on them. The pulsing is each eye blinking. I hear happy laughter. The eyes are blinking, and looking at me looking at them. I am each eye looking, and each eye is looking at me. Now the eyes are turning away, and looking into the sea of light. An eye has detached and is floating away into the light, heading for another location. One by one, the eyes are detaching and drifting away. My own eye is pulled into the wisp of my spine that remains, and it floats away too.

I have no eyes at all. There is only my spine, which is a blue rod of light. Now the rod is a ribbon, and it turns toward itself and joins ends. A circle is created. A circle. A hoop. A spinning hoop with sparks crackling off of it. A black bird swoops through the light and dives through the hoop, collecting it around its neck. The bird looks at me. There is an explosive pop. Smoldering feathers and fluff float away, leaving the bird's skeleton with the sparking blue ribbon around its neck. The raven squawks and lifts into flight, leaving into the place where the horizon would be. Some memory of my physical self is

---

[33] These are like the twinkly lights I saw after my mother died, when she was absorbed back into the Universe (see Chapter 1).

still attached to the blue ribbon of my spine, and I am pulled along in the raven's flight.

Now the raven is standing in the grass, with a full black body again. It opens its beak and a human laugh comes out of it. The raven is rolling on its back, very well humored, and laughing uproariously. I am smiling. I wish I understood what she was laughing about. **The Raven** stands up and points her wingtip at me. *I was laughing at you, because you are so easily taken on a grand adventure. We have gone all the way through death and not once were you afraid or questioning. You will notice that something has changed today. Rest your awareness in that change. And now you will be reborn.* The raven tosses the blue ribbon and it fits around the memory of my body's neck. It unrolls and straightens to become my spine again. And the eyes are looking at me, the eyes are spots of light. My skeleton reforms and my body fleshes out. White light streams from my body. I am pulled back into the tunnel. I squish through the gel. I drift in the tunnel. The wind catches me and fills my lungs as I pop out of the entrance.

There I stand, looking at my hands, and then into the distance, where my Great Grandfather is turning away and motioning for me to come along now and journey with him. I am still stunned, but I run along after him.

Something that strikes me about Great Grandfather's teaching is that the Horizon is a location and it has no location. Not one or the other, but both things are true at the same time. This is a perfect explanation of how the Dream World and the Physical World are concurrent, occupying the same space. They are one thing, but seen in two ways.

Seeing the horizon as a location is a way to place it in the physical world. I can point to it and say "see, there it is," and you will be able to see it too. We can send a boat out into the ocean and keep watching it until it disappears. Even with a telescope, we will not be able to see it once it passes over the Horizon. The horizon is a definable location.

The horizon also has no location. It is movable, a concept dependent on the reference point of where you happen to be standing.

The Shift has come—a spiritual transformation is in motion. It means that we need to be able to place ourselves in a present which includes both the Physical World, a location, and the Spirit world, which has no location. The directive we are being given is to exist in both of these worlds simultaneously. This is a skill to learn and develop.

While I am learning, I will sometimes be more in one world than the other. But when they both come together, then I will experience Love And Let Go, centering and expanding at the same time, the energetic sensation of transcendence. I will be in my physical body, centered in my spine, and also in contact with All That Is, all of the Zone. Simultaneously.

This seems so complex, but it is really very basic. It is the movement of energy awareness.

Universal Wisdom: *So much of this is difficult because there is much pressure from others to conform. To keep "reality" in a manageable box. You have been witnessing this in high school students—the ability to deny oneself and many obvious pieces of evidence in the face of group thinking. It is why it's sometimes hard for you to speak openly about your spiritual work. It takes another kind of support to speak out.*

A fair number of people think I am crazy, some even believe I could be dangerous. But my first book is starting to move. The more that happens, the more people I connect with, the more I am able to open up—it creates a positive cycle. I often hear things coming out of my mouth that are already synthesized, before I even think about it. Sometimes I am learning from my own words.

This is why it is important to keep you body tuned. You want to have as much capacity for clarity as possible. Moments will create themselves.

I need to be present, to be living my own process.

You have been concerned about doing this "right" socially. The bigger question is how can you do this with the most spiritual depth.

Spiritual depth is fairly easy when I am sitting at home in meditation. It requires more focus when I am out in public, where I am subject to the judgment of others. As I was preparing for a book launch, one of my first public appearances to discuss spirituality, a Teacher came to help me:

There is something for you to know here. The book launch is not that important. It is a vehicle, yes, but not in the way you think. It is important to gain definition of the project and be able to speak about it. Whether you sell books or not is secondary. You are about to become a mouthpiece for the Teachers. You started with the written word and now you will move towards the spoken word. Yes, we sense your fear—you don't think that you signed up for this. But of course you did. You have been surprised all along the way, because it is not possible to always see ahead in the road, around the curves. We will help you. This is what we are here for.

It is important to experience Zone, what you are doing right now. You will need to be able to do this in public, with people watching and waiting. Think about being the vehicle. We supply the words, the information. You will be the physical presence that makes this possible.

Suddenly, fear has made it difficult for me to stay in the Zone. I am very aware of the physical environment around me. Fear has drawn my energy up, out of my center and into my upper body. I am having trouble accepting the new expectation. It is not so hard to comprehend. Of course this would follow—they already told me that moving the information would be important. And I am no stranger to speaking in public, teaching. So it is not the act itself that is frightening. What is frightening is that I will become more visible. I am afraid I can't do this on my own. And I also know that I can.

You can do this. It is what you came here for, and you are doing well keeping your contract. But it is not all about that. The contract you came in on is not so much about meeting an obligation. It has more to do with feeding your Spirit. Consider how much more alive you feel when you are doing this work. You are more grounded and vibrant. This is how we are meant to be in human form, because then we are able to move the energy known as Love, to create the resonance and harmony that is so important. It is not just an end, it is a means, and it is a way of Life.

If you want to join the River of Life, to connect with the Lifeways of your birth, then you must move with the energy of the spirit, which is spiritual connection. Keep recognizing the lines of spiritual connection between yourself and others, between events, between events and people, between Nature and yourself. Continue to put out your asemaa in the way you have, recognizing your connections and praying for good relationships with All. It is not something abstract. It is very real and present and living. Open your eyes, open your heart, open your arms. And then you must also open your voice. Words are the spirit speaking. The spoken word is much more powerful than the written word, because it creates more resonance, it moves more Love energy.

Try not to worry about this. Just let yourself entertain the idea right now. More will happen that will allow you to practice this gently and see the benefit.

Thank you so much. I am afraid, and I am also capable. I will do this. Can I ask who is here today.

I am the next Teacher. I am someone who is known as **The Speaker**. He offers his right hand, and I take it with my left, as we turn to face forward together. And there is the sun, shining directly on us, and the Earth, with grass and small flowers cradling our moccasins. And there, the wind, rustling our hair and bringing a sweet breeze. It is good to be alive.

He is turning to me and leaning down to look in my eyes. His eyes are gentle and deep. He is showing me the River of Life in his eyes. When he smiles there are happy wrinkles accenting those eyes. It is nice to see his smile. He is a peaceful warrior. When I say Ogichidaa, he looks forward again. Then he releases my hand and walks away. I am here in the sun, on the Earth, in the wind. All I want is to Love Life.

~

Cultural demands in a capitalist society are loud and many. Hermits and monks support their spiritual lives by shedding the demands of culture. For the rest of us, creating balance is not so easy. Many of us are trying to travel our spiritual path while also working to survive in the physical world. How can this be balanced?

Universal Wisdom: *Sometimes you fall into the trap of allowing yourself to function spiritually only after all of the other needs have been met—spiritual life gets the "leftover" time. There really is no such thing.*

Life cannot be separated into compartments that are purely physical or purely spiritual. You will always have a body to maintain, and your spiritual life is always present, even if you are not consciously occupying it. During depression, for example, you may feel cut off from your spiritual life, but it is still there, waiting to be activated. We have talked about that before. The spirit never leaves, but sometimes it is more active in other dimensions, and this is especially true if it is not being given attention in the physical world.

This balance between the physical and the spiritual is not as difficult as some might imagine. It does require practice. It requires the creation of an energy pathway. You are well aware of this path, but sometimes you are not using it. You are getting pulled off by intellectual tasks and physical overload. In any moment, you can ask yourself: how does this feel, am I connected through my intuition, through my spirit? What would help me make this connection right now? Breathing is a good practice. Stopping to breathe is even better. Stopping to breathe and connect is best.

Love and Let Go (transcendence) is the sensation that indicates a simultaneous connection to Spirit and to the Zone. Stopping to make this connection will remind you of your purpose. With much practice, one could go through each day and maintain this connection without effort. It would be second nature. This is what we hope for humans, that more and more people will be able to operate in this energy state. It is what is required by The Shift.

So rather than be frustrated by the feeling of being disconnected, I could recognize it as a gift, a notice that I need to move my attention to Love and Let Go.

This would be optimal. It is often difficult to get past the physical distress or distraction of being disconnected, or of being poorly connected. Attention needs to focus on connection. Moving back to connection is about shifting attention. As you know, it is easier to shift to something that you are familiar with, and that is what is happening when you practice.

I am thinking about how Time affects this connection. If I am bogged down by external demands that involve a deadline, or a time constraint, or time pressure, then I am allowing myself to be trapped in linear thinking. Is that correct.

Yes, and no. The clock has a tendency to link activity to Points, to fix energy in a static way. The discomfort of working against the clock is created by this attempt to concentrate energy into a static point. It is important to recognize that these Points only exist in the context of Space, that energy is constantly moving in and out of a Point through Space. The tick on the clock will pass, it is only a moment. The energy will keep moving. When your mind is focused on the Point, you will not be aware of energy moving.

Of course, the energy is still moving, whether you are aware of it or not. When you are unaware of the energy moving in and out of the Points, there will be a disconnect from "reality," and that creates the feeling of stress. It is important to find a way to allow reality to be fluid. To see that the Horizon, to see that the Universe, is both a location and not a location. Bringing the physical and the spiritual together means that you must be able to allow both to be true at the same time.

I am thinking of the time constraints of my job as a community health nurse: the funds have to be spent by June 30, the food program is on the 15th of the month, the client needs their procedure at 9:30 and 12:15 and 2:30 every day. So those are locations, specific points. And then there is the stuff that is not a location, like helping to establish a breastfeeding relationship between a mom and baby. If I have too many things that are points, or if I let my attention rest primarily on those points, then there is not enough room for the things that are not-points. There is not enough room for Space.

Yes. And all of that occurs in your mind, by choosing where to rest your attention.

There is also the structure of your work environment. You can only do so much as an individual. You may have to choose another work environment if your current situation cannot support enough Space.

I have been allowing myself to get pushed down by the hand of Time. What if I was able to feel more Space in all that I do.

It is a choice.

And I have not been seeing it as a choice. I have been letting myself feel more and more pressured. Maybe that is what my coworkers have been reacting negatively to — my stress level.

Yes. And then there are the challenges of their own lives. They don't want to deal with stress at work.

Isn't that interesting, because I don't either. It is what I have been complaining about, trying to get across—that I don't like this situation. I was hoping they could support me somehow, but maybe I wasn't clear enough in what I was asking for.

They don't want any of your work load.

Of course not. It doesn't sound very pleasant, does it. If I don't want it why would they. It feels more relaxing to go into this saying what my boundaries are, what I am willing to do and not do. Make the Space I need.

And now I am frustrated because I am spending so much time rehashing work issues.

But it ties into the ability to be in the spiritual world and the physical world simultaneously. It is a parallel. It is something you have to be able to create for yourself. Someone else is not going to come along and create it for you. Everyone has this responsibility, to create the environment in the physical world that will support a spiritual life. It applies to all areas: family, work, home, community, country, climate, planet. You start small, where you can see the effects. You have gotten your personal life and your family life pretty well aligned with your spiritual life. You are working on your work life right now. It is all necessary as a foundation for bringing your books into the bigger world. You need to be able to manage the smaller things first, build a lifestyle that supports spiritual activity.

That really puts it in context, that this work thing is not separate from everything else I am doing. It's all connected and all on the same path. I don't have any trouble accepting or believing that I want to do this. I just needed to step back and see it in context. Same Point and Zone discussion.

Walk away now and carry this into your day.

As I became more skilled in traveling across the veil, I began functioning in both worlds simultaneously. Learning to manage this was both exhilarating and frustrating. One hot summer day, for example, I was sitting in the bleachers at pow-wow and became aware of a man dancing in the circle. I did not know him, but was inexplicably drawn to him. Somewhere in the space between us, our Spirits met. I had other responsibilities and had to leave the circle for a few hours. When I came back, he was gone. The man, the physical person, was gone. But our spirits remained powerfully connected.

The next day I left the community for a conference. This man's spirit remained with me, urging me to interact with him. I drove six hours that day, and during the drive I was visited with many visions. My physical body operated the car, while my spirit body traveled great distances.

Early in the drive, in a waking vision, I was swimming in a lake. The water was cool and dark. I was in my element, effortlessly at one with the water. I came to the surface and the beautiful man from the pow-wow was standing on the shore. He extended his hand and motioned for me to come along with him. I was hesitant to leave my water world, but Great Grandfather had told me on another day to "take the hand that is offered." So I came out of the water and took the man's outstretched hand. I was happy to feel his skin. He pointed just over the tree tops, to a tipi village, and he led me there. I had so many questions! But he was silent and my speaking only muddied the dream.

He brought me to a tipi and sent me in. He indicated that I was to sit in the center, and he left, closing the flap. Inside it was dark. I did not want to let go of him. While I was sitting quietly in the tipi, I realized that he was asking me to accept my place in the Spirit World. I continued to drive my car down the highway in the Physical World, absorbing this spiritual awareness.

A little while later, the beautiful man came back and motioned me out of the tipi. I took his hand again and he led me farther into the village. I soon felt myself growing wings and flying high in the air. The air was his element. We were flying high above the land and seeing great distances. We were flying above the shore of Lake Superior, the mountains on my right and the sparkling lake on my left. I turned and flew Northwest. I flew over Winnipeg, then up the west shore of that lake, to its northern end. I flew farther into Canada, and then Alaska, and over the Arctic Circle.

It was strangely easy to have these amazing and powerful visions while also driving my car. I was transported to another world, yet remained in this one. The experience was kind of like listening to an engrossing book on tape during a long road trip. I stopped the car and got out, the visions disappeared, and I came back fully into the Physical World.

Back behind the wheel, the beautiful man again took me to the tipi village, and I was once again led to the tent and seated in the center. As before, the beautiful man came back after a while to get me. This time when he led me out I felt my body change shape, and I became an eagle. I was in an eagle body and flying over the lake. The beautiful man had carried an eagle feather in the pow-wow circle, and as I thought of that I became aware of his spirit name: **Migizii Niikaan, Eagle Brother**.

I also became aware of a clear white opening, like a shrine, in my chest. Eagle Brother stood in that clear space and danced, with energy and ease. His dancing brought me into my self in a new way, into my eagle body, and I realized that Lake Superior is my homeland. This realization about The Big Lake arrived full force as Eagle Brother danced in my heart.

This homecoming filled me with the intense sensation of being Touched By God, and I cried. (I had to do deep breathing to simultaneously stay in the Physical World and operate my vehicle.) Several minutes later, as I stabilized, I felt a tightness in my chest. I gave in to the physical urge to shriek, and it felt like the human equivalent of a raptor's scream. The tightness was released from my chest and moved up into my throat. I gave a shrieking wail and a few ululations and whoops. The tightness released from my throat and moved to the top of my head. A little high singing released it from there. I laughed out loud with the joy of it. I was integrating the Dream World into the Physical World. Time stopped. Time flew by.

Later that day, Eagle Brother brought me back to the shore of the dark, cool lake and pointed gleefully at the water—we should take a swim! He dove in first, and I followed. This water was my element, and I had him hold onto me while I swam. At one point, I was on the bottom of the lake admiring the jewels there, and I could see his silhouette against the sky above us. Then I had him get out on a flat, warm rock, and I sprinkled him with cleansing water and combed out his long, wet hair with my fingers. I washed his face. I dried him and wrapped him in a blanket. I wrapped myself in a blanket too. Then we went back to the tipi and laid together in the same blanket, our arms around each other, our skin still cool from the lake.

Sometime during our time together I had to exit the Dream World to maneuver in city traffic. I gave him my dream body to hold while I was busy in the Physical World of Time. The blanket-together continued once I was quietly in my room. Very sensuous and loving. Loving our dream bodies together. Once in a while I came up against an unnamed emotional discomfort of his. I wanted to love him, not hurt him. I understood the need to give him space. I was willing to wait and be patient.

I was accepting of the Unknown in the Spirit World, but I was confused by the Unknown in the Physical World. It seemed so odd — having a rendezvous in a dream with someone who actually exists in Time. I kept asking myself how much of this was really happening, and what might I be inventing? I wanted to know this man in Time, but I didn't even know his name in the Physical World. Eagle Brother, can you show me how to find you? He shakes his head No.

I would have to decide how much of this I could handle. For the moment, I was happy and willing to be patient. I felt committed. I felt crazy. I was okay with that.

Days rolled by, I struggled in the Physical World. I felt disjointed from my external environment. I just wanted to be with Eagle Brother. Sometimes we met, in the Dream World, on the shore of the cool lake. Or we walked hand in hand in the woods, talking about the leaves and the birds. Both Healing Grandmother and Great Grandfather had their arms folded across their chests, silent, looking away, not meddling. In retrospect, I wondered if they were allowing us to court.

I became more and more frustrated in Time. I did not know how to manage this. I was sad to not be with Eagle Brother in physical reality. He said he could not meet me. He is, apparently, one of my Spirit Teachers. But I felt like I was in love. I wanted to make physical contact! So I was living in the Dream World, and somehow functioning in the Physical World but not at home there. Who can help me? Great Grandfather is looking away. Healing Grandmother, can you show me? Her arms are still folded, but she is facing me and pointing with her eyes to the window of unknowing. I go through, crossing the veil.

I am swimming in the white mist. It is like swimming underwater, with my breath held, my hair floating around head. I see bubbles come from my mouth. I can see the sky up above me, like when I saw Eagle Brother's silhouette. I come to the surface to see him. The silhouette is only the cardboard cutout of a man, floating on the water. I am standing in the ankle-deep water. I drop the cardboard and look toward the village.

He is on the shore there, motioning for me to come along. I take his hand. He is talking excitedly. He is hurrying forward. I wonder if I am real. He is smiling, very animated. There is good news here. He gives me a hug with both his arms around me. Our cheeks are touching. I can feel this in the physical world. Tears are in my eyes. He is asking me what is wrong. I tell him I missed him today. He is exasperated, saying that he has been with me all day.

He is talking, excited again, and leading me to the village. Now I am caught in a little whirlwind of spider webs. I can see him walking towards the village and I can't get untangled from them. I call to him. He turns and comes back, considers the situation. He says that this is a mess I have made. I must undo it. I want to laugh, believing that he is teasing me, but of course what he says is true. It is the web of my own doubt. He pretends to think heavily, hiding a smile, saying he wonders what I could do about that. I know the answer is Trust. Yes, but trust in what, he asks with mock wonder. I guess trust in Love. No response. Trust in You. The web dissolves and we embrace playfully. He starts off again for the village. I'm not going, I say. Why not, he asks. I don't know, I answer. I am thinking that it is time for me to move on. I can't believe that this is coming out of me, it must be fear talking. He shrugs, and turns again. Wait, I say, fear rising, but I want to be with you. Then come on, he motions.

I know that I need to go to the village again. And there we are. In the open field of tipis. They are light colored, with drawings on their sides. He is marching along, sure of his destination. We stop in front of one of the tents. He opens the flap and signals me in. He gives my rump a playful slap as I head in, then closes the flap behind me.

I am inside now. There is a small fire in the middle, with two people on the other side of it, facing me. One is a beautiful young woman. The other is an elder. I am feeling silly, having just gotten spanked in front of them, but I need to focus on those before me. The young woman is wearing buckskin. Her face is smooth and fresh, her hair pulled back. She is looking away. The elder is a very old woman with white hair. She is very short and very wrinkled. She is mumbling to herself, and handling some herbs from a pouch. She is singing the song of these plants.

The young woman, Flower Stream, is looking away. She is struggling to maintain her composure. I wonder if she is sad, could cry, but suddenly she looks forward and down and laughs. The young woman thinks that I am funny, tells a little something to the elder. The elder smiles a little, continues with the plants.

Well, we have invited you here, Flower Stream says, *because we have something to tell you.* My mind begins to search. I need to quiet myself and just be a witness. *We asked you to come because you should know that I am going to marry your Eagle Brother. I am going to marry him when the sun comes over the hills.*

He has told me about you, that you laid on the blanket together. That you washed his hair. There is something that you should know. The only way to see him in the Physical World is to allow this marriage in the Dream World. Because then I will take your body and you will take mine and we will share a journey. You must agree to this before we can go forward. I wish for this to take place. Eagle Brother cannot know, because he is looking for you. But he brought me here, how can he not know?

He also knows my thoughts, so he will know. The young woman says, *we will use the plants, and no one will remember, not even me.*

I don't know what I am agreeing to. Is there danger in this choice? The elder is nodding her head. Grandmother, what do I need to know to make this decision. *You need to know that this is the path prepared for you. When you choose this you are agreeing to your path. It will not always be pleasant. There will be some great losses. There are great losses in every path. It is already decided that you will do this. It will help your sickness. The sickness in your heart. It will make you strong. There, it is done. The plants felt your willingness. Young woman is your helper now.* I am afraid—have I just given up control of my life?? The wise one says *Yes, and it is good.*

Eagle Brother has just come back to the tent. He looked in, saw that Flower Stream was inside my body, and angrily yanked the flap closed. Now I am outside with him, searching his anger, trying to understand. He has been trying to leave this young woman, and now we are stuck together. I don't know if I have been tricked. Now I don't know if he is loving me or Flower Stream. What can I do Eagle Brother? *You can go back to where you came from*, he says pointing to me. But I still want to be with you, I say calmly. He looks startled. *You do?* he asks. Of course. That is why I came here.

I can feel Flower Stream being absorbed into my cells, and I feel myself expanding, expanding, floating up into the sky. I can see Eagle Brother far below. His arms have stretched into the sky to reach for me, and he pulls himself up. We are in the clouds together. It is the white mist of Unknowing. I see Healing Grandmother on the other side of the window, smiling.

When Eagle Brother holds me, he starts to fall downward. When we hold each other, we are together, and he smiles. His wide smile makes me smile too. We are twirling, arms outstretched, laughing. He points up to the sky and I see the sun, burning brightly over the edge of the clouds. The sun is over the hills, he says, and that means we are married now.

He pulls me up close. He is soft and happy. I am thankful. We embrace gently, and land back on the shore of the cool lake. We part for the night. He walks jauntily to the village, whistling, and I dive into the cool lake, remembering our time on the blanket. I swim to the window of Unknowing. Healing Grandmother is there and motions me through. I come through to her side. I see myself glowing, like the white mist. I am like a ghost in the darkness. This is my spirit self. Healing Grandmother nods.

The night world is dark, and I am very bright. My whole body is a weaving of energy trails, as though I am transparent and made of illuminated string. Smiling increases the glow around my face and neck. Love is another color, pinkish. Anger is yellow, healing is blue, harmony is green. Here I am, in the Physical World, with an illuminated energy body.

Part of the marriage ceremony involved Flower Stream joining my body. She soon came to me to complete that integration. She floated up into the sky, motioning for me to come, and my spirit followed her up towards the milky moon.

She takes my hand and swims, her hair loose and streaming behind her. We swim in the water of the sky, which becomes the water of Sparkle Lake.[34] We swim down deep into the lake, all the way into its muddy bottom. We burrow under the brown mud together and curl up there, pale and white, like a sleeping seed.

When she swims straight up to the surface, we are one. We break through the surface and it is night. Above is the night sky, full of stars, my ancestors. There is one very bright star above me. Very bright, and large. I am swimming to it through the air. I am swimming right into the center of that brightness. I am going very fast, with my hands out ahead of me, parting the stars. My hands separate a vertical line in the sky, and each hand pulls a side of this vent open.

Behind the sky there is blackness without stars. I poke my head through and look. The blackness is what is beyond the stars. It is textured and soft, like fleece. I rub my face on it, like a baby looking for the breast on her mother's chest. Suddenly I am smaller, and my

---

[34]Reference to a previous re-creation of my being, from *Grandmother Dreams*, pp. 100-101.

body fits easily through the opening in the sky. I move through. I am looking around. I am the glowing whiteness, like the sleeping seed at the bottom of the lake. I am dancing side to side. I can hear Paul LaRoche singing.

Now I am spinning, with my arms over my head, and I become a cylinder of white floss. This cylinder is the hand of a clock, moving counterclockwise. Time is reversing and going forward at the same time. The clock face is stretching out, becoming another cylinder with a clock face on each flat end. This cylinder, with a clock face on each end, is a hand on a bigger clock face. It is rotating counterclockwise. And making a cylinder. A repetitive pattern, with the clocks getting bigger and bigger and bigger. Macro scale. Time is expanding. Each time another clock face becomes evident, I feel my body expanding. It seems like I could burst.

The clocks keep multiplying and multiplying and multiplying. There is a loud sound, like waves whooshing, lapping a shore. I am standing on a shore at night. The shore is on the Earth, and the Earth is a clock face.

Flower Stream: *Everything is bound up in Time, and Time is unfixed, ever moving and reshaping. Time is a mirage. Dream World acknowledges that. Physical world denies it. The key is to bring the Physical World and the Dream World into balance.*

I see the yin-yang symbol — the blending of different yet complementary systems. Each a part of the other, each its own separate world. *Animals bridge this balance. All beings do. Humans seem to be stuck in the physical. But the Dream World is always at work.*

Begin to talk with others. Find out who is aware by asking about their dreams. Those who look you in the eye when they answer are also looking for you. Be careful. If you open yourself too wide, without knowing who you are dealing with, you will leave yourself vulnerable to damage. Yes, you have missed some opportunities by being too slow, but there are always more opportunities. They will keep presenting themselves.

Your man at the pow-wow grounds is looking too. That is why you connected. Feeling the presence of another clear being. Do not be so worried about one chance that is over. Yes, time is fluid, but in the Physical

World you can not change something that has already happened. In the Dream World it is still happening. Continue to look there. Don't be so sure that you will know what it looks like when you find it. Shapes shift.

Stay open in the Dream World. Be cautious in the Physical World. Go slow. Wait patiently and observantly. Go where you are called. You can find Love in the Physical World, but it is difficult to maintain. You are on a good path. Trust yourself.

After our marriage in the Spirit World, I readily accepted Eagle Brother's medicine in my life. Many times I felt myself looking out into the world from an eagle's face. On long walks outside, I walked hard and fast, very close to beginning a run which would launch me into the sky. On those walks, I felt the need to have my arms out, and often let my outside fingers flutter, like the steering feathers on wings. I felt a lightness, like my bones were hollowing. I often had visions of myself as an eagle high above the shore of The Big Lake, and I could see very long distances from there.

At the same time, I struggled to integrate the idea that Eagle Brother is both a Spirit Teacher and also a real person — someone I experienced in physical time. Over the next few years I saw the physical man who is Eagle Brother, but I only saw him at pow-wow. I learned his name and approached him, thanking him for his help in the Dream World. (He seemed only a little surprised, since the Native community readily accepts that the Spiritual World is active).

I have been challenged to understand, especially in this case, how the Physical and Dream Worlds intersect. Before this, I somehow assumed that the Physical World and the Spirit World were totally separate. This seems foolish to me now, but my assumption about them being separate reveals some of my doubt about the "truth" of the Dream World. My experiences there seemed so out of the box compared to everyday life, to the mundane management of the Physical World. I had a hard time believing that some of what happened in the Dream World was not just an invention of my desires. I also know that this is not just my invention, because the things that happen in the Dream World are often an unforeseen surprise, creating a little shock of learning. If it was really just fantasy, then I would be controlling it. In fact, I have to let go for it to happen.

So that is one question, about just how separate they really are. I know that the farther I get on this path, the blurrier the line between the Physical and Dream Worlds are, in my own comprehension and functioning. More specifically than that question, though, is that I want to be faithful to my spirit husband. Does that mean that I am also faithful in the Physical World, that I forgo any other physical relationships? Even though I may never have a relationship in the Physical World with the man who is Eagle Brother? This is a good example of the split, or not-split, between the physical and the spiritual.

Eagle Brother has been here quietly listening to my questions. *This is an interesting thing you are asking, because I am thinking about this too, he says thoughtfully. How can I have this life with you in the Dream World at the same time that I am also having my own life in the Physical World.* Of course, this makes me wonder if I am also accompanying this man in his physical world but am unaware of it.

Aniimaakii: *Yes, you are. You do not yet have the skill to manage all of this at once. It is one thing that you will need to learn. How to be more than two places at once. You are challenged to be in two places, this is what you are learning now. Accept your Eagle Brother in your life, bring him along in your travels. Learn more about how the Spirit World and the Physical World blend. You are already aware of how they are separate. Practice letting both ways be true simultaneously — both separate and not separate. You must be able to hold this duality before you can move on. Do not worry the details.*

This needs to happen. You will need to negotiate your relationship in the Dream World. Do not allow the games of the ego. Feed the spirit, the spirit of your relationship.

Many days Eagle Brother came to encourage me to occupy my camp in the Spirit World. One day he came and was excited to show me something. He was pointing ahead eagerly, happily. He wants me to look. He is flying, with his hair streaming back, smiling. What a smile—I just want to look at him. He wants me to quit fooling around and look ahead.

I see a hill. At the bottom of the hill is a row of huge trees, lovely green-leafed ancient trees. Under the trees the grass is short and smooth from human activity. It is warm summer, and the grass is dry. We are sitting in the branches of the old trees, looking down. A red fox comes under us, under our feet hanging high off the ground. The fox puts a front paw on the trunk, lifting itself up to get a better sniff. Then the fox jumps up and is sitting with us in the old trees, comfortable as I stroke its back. The three of us are looking down at the dry grass.

There is nothing there and I look to Eagle Brother, using his English name. He looks surprised that I know his name in the Physical World, but points down again. He is disturbed that I used his name. When I say My Husband, he grins. He points again.

The toes of some red shoes appear at the edge of my vision, and then there is a man in red regalia looking up at us. My Husband is looking at the man and pointing to me. I come down from the tree to greet him. My Father, I am pleased to meet you. His head rears back in a little surprise, that I recognize him. He looks up to my husband and then to me. I have many questions, but wait to be spoken to. I look up at Eagle Brother and the fox sitting in the tree, looking down at me. Eagle Brother's Father moves away, thinking, and rests against a nearby trunk.

A woman with a cane approaches slowly from a distance. She is wearing a buckskin dress. I kneel down and sit on my heels to wait patiently, eyes downcast. I see myself, and I am Flower Stream. When Eagle Brother's Mother is a short distance away, I join her, walking side by side. I can hear her breathing, it is labored. We walk slowly. I am silent. She is talking quietly to me about berries and birds. I feel young and patient, full of Love.

We have arrived back at the Council Trees, where Father is waiting. He is happy to see me. He reaches out a hand in welcome. I keep my eyes down, demure. He gently guides me around a large tree to a campfire. He motions for me to sit at the fire. He gives me tea in a tin cup. As I sip, I see my face reflected in the surface of the tea. I also see the branches of the trees above me. I see Eagle Brother and the fox watching from some distance away. My Husband looks on eagerly.

I turn back to the tea, which is now a cup of red beads, now a cup of red berries. I am stringing them, stringing the red berries. They are brilliant red, and I tie the string of red berries around My Father's neck. He is smiling. I don't know what is happening, but it is good. I sense that I am meeting Eagle Brother's parents for approval.

Now Father is asking me, where do you come from? I answer that I am from the Great Lakes, the Great Lakes have been my home. He looks somewhat puzzled and asks about my People. I say that I hardly know them, that I have not lived near them for a long time. He wonders how this can be, how you can not be with your People. I say that this is hard for me to understand too, because sometimes I feel that I am without a home. But then I know that my home is where my spirit rests, and right now my spirit is resting in Gichi Onigamiing. He seems to accept this.

He is thinking again. He has one arm across his chest, with the other elbow resting on it and his hand fingering his chin in thought. He seems to be asking, what do you want in this family? I answer that it is only to be Loved as I Love you, an Opportunity to Learn and continue to find my place in All That Is. I see My Husband and he is looking down. I don't know if he is disappointed or just concentrating.

I am not interested in saying something to my Father just because it sounds right. It has to be right—it has to be in my heart. I hear my Spirit Self say: *I did not know that I would marry this man in the Spirit World, I was led there by Grandmother and Grandfather and I trusted them and did as I was led to do. I am very pleased to have been given this honorable path. This is my one desire in this Life, to follow the path of Spirit, to open to all of the worlds that are available and to use the wisdom from these travels to assist others in the physical world. I have been given gifts and talents. It is my responsibility to bring them to good use. With an open heart, These Are My Words.*

My Husband is looking up, incredulous. My Father is still looking at me through the fingers at his chin, but I can see a slight grin behind his seriousness. He has to smile, so he looks away to the side to regain his composure. I look down to the tea in my hand. I see that the cup is filled with tears, and one has just dropped from my cheek to join the others. I will taste this tea, and know that it is very sweet.

My Mother comes to me and takes the cup. She replaces it with another tin cup, this one full of a thick red liquid. It reminds me of blood. I dip two fingers in and then streak two red lines horizontally on each of my cheeks, and two vertical red lines on my forehead between my eyes, and also down my chin. She takes the cup of red and now I have a cup of crystal blue. I throw the contents into my eyes, and they become filled with twinkly stars. My mouth is filled with lightning bolts.

My Husband is swinging down from the tree, the fox hopping down behind him. He walks toward us, looking down as he comes. He is wearing a dark blue shirt. He has red marks and lightning bolts on his face that are the same as mine. He stands before me, takes my hands in his and looks into my face. His eyes are also bright with stars, too brilliant to look at, yet we are looking each other in the eye. We step toward each other and our transparent bodies pass into one another. When we come through the other side, we turn and look: we are back in our physical bodies. The other bodies are our spirit bodies.

He is relaxed and happy. He motions for me to walk with him. Our hands join, and I can feel the smooth warmth of his skin. We leave the council trees together, the fox at his side, an eagle flying above us. My Husband stops to point ahead to the mountain top. He takes me in his arms and we fly there together. We are up there, lying next to each other on the rocks, warm in the sun, looking up at the sky, admiring the clouds. Everything is as it should be.

~

The Physical World and the Dream World are not separate, they are intertwined. Our purpose in this Life is to follow the path of Spirit, to open to all of the worlds that are available and to use the wisdom from these travels to assist ourselves and others in the physical world.

It is possible, with practice, to walk in two worlds at once. We are both a human being and a traveling spirit.

One night I had a dream that showed me how this works. The dream took place in the house where I had lived before I was divorced. Over many years, my former husband and I had cleared that land together and built a house that I designed. Gardens of flowers and trees, that I had planted, surrounded it. I had raised my children there, one of them had even been born in that house. It had been very difficult to give it up, but it eventually became so toxic that I could not possibly live there. After a while, the "other woman" moved in. It seemed the final coup d'etat — she had destroyed my marriage, taken away half of my precious time with my growing children, and now she was even living in my house.

In the dream, I was walking through the rooms, and I could see that my children were living there with this woman. I fell to the floor, face down and naked, sobbing, saying "this was my Home," over and over. In that instant, I simultaneously became two beings. I was both the physical body sobbing on the floor and also a gentle spirit standing next to the crying figure.

The Grieving Me was sobbing in a way that I have never heard before. It was primal, deep, coming through my spine. I could hear the sounds in my ears and feel the vibration in my body while I slept. Sorrow was being expressed from the very root of my being.

In the dream, my former husband approached. Immediately, the Grieving Me stood up in angry defiance, fiercely focused and ready to fight. The Spirit Me gently said, *This is not what is needed here. What is needed here is compassion for this Being.* My Ex disappeared, and I crumpled back to the floor and continued sobbing. Spirit Me stood by with a soft hand placed on Grieving Me, embodying non-judgment, witnessing the grief with total compassion.

I woke up completely aware of what had transpired — a huge well of sorrow had been released under the most supportive of circumstances. I had been both the griever and the supporter. This was a monumental shift. A gift.

I was reminded of this integration of the physical and spiritual worlds again while I was going through cancer treatment. I had had my first infusion of chemotherapy—powerful life-killing drugs, and it had not gone well. I had a dramatic physical reaction, complete with crash cart and a dozen medical personnel, during which I'd had difficulty speaking and responding. I was aware of my brain being erased. This was only the first of many visits to come, and going back felt like I was knowingly returning for another rape of my body and mind—delivering myself into the jaws of the shark. I was afraid.

To prepare for the next rounds, I prayed: Ancestors, please help me have the strength to face this. Help me to focus on the parts that I have control over. Help me be thankful for the good things I have in my life. Help me to remember that you are with me, that I will not be there alone.

Universal Wisdom: *This is the way it needs to be right now. This is very hard to understand, of course. You want to just go on with your life. But your life is moving on a new trajectory. Part of the journey on the way there is about stripping away some of the old ways. It is like removing layers of skin. It is painful. Healing will be required. And takes time. The thing you need to be aware of, in every minute, is that you are strong enough to take this.*

Be the two beings of your Releasing Dream. Be the human being, who is suffering. Allow the suffering to move through you. And also be the Gentle Spirit, who stands by with Compassion and Love. You are both of these. God is in the moving of the energy. The moving of the grief and the moving of the Love. They are both sides of the same coin.

And holding to the edge is....

Holding to the edge is faith. Faith that there is purpose in living. You are a spirit-walking journey. You are traveling in many worlds simultaneously. When things seem unstable in this world, they are moving in other worlds. They are especially moving when you are releasing grief and embodying compassion. You can be doing these things when you are in the environment of the infusion center. This is what you must practice. Moving the grief and moving the compassion.

This means that I would have to be very present.

Not necessarily. You could be in the Dream World when this happens.
If I am experiencing fear, then I am not centered enough to be in the Dream World.
Remember that fear is a tool. It will tell you when you are detaching. It is a reminder to return.
And it is helpful to think that there is something I can do, instead of being a passive victim of the situation.
Let yourself be with God.
That is a little worrisome—wouldn't I risk staying there and not coming back.
Except that we will bring you back. It is only a renewing journey, not a permanent one. As hard as it may be to comprehend, this is part of the grooming for your new life.
A special kind of travel.
Another kind of travel.

Being with God is a matter of perspective. It is a place to rest my attention, it is something I can choose.

I had a dream where I was seated before **Aniimaakii**. His outfit of soft, tanned leather included leather wristlets and a headband with feathered lacing hanging on both sides of his head. His bare chest was smooth. I was seated in the manner of a student before a teacher, and he was asking me questions that I answered.

We had been talking about plant energy, when he lowered his head and his voice and it became difficult for me to hear his next question. I politely asked him to repeat it. He answered quietly, and I had to ask him to repeat it again, two more times. I was starting to feel foolish, but I finally understood that he was asking me "where are you from?". I told him that my ancestors were from a nomadic tribe in eastern Europe. His expression soured, and he got up and began walking away. Immediately, I realized the true answer: I am from the heart of God. When he heard my mind thinking this, he stopped and nodded in agreement.

I have danced around Identity my whole life. Now I can see that it is an important question, but I have been looking for an answer in the wrong place. I have been looking for an answer that serves my ego, not my spirit.

I am from the heart of God. That means that I am made of Love. I am the vibration of Love manifesting in physical form. When I serve my spirit, when I live a life of Love, I am resonating with this Original Form. This physical resonance is a vibration that my spirit recognizes. When I resonate with Original Form, I am emanating a vibration that other spirits recognize, too, and that encourages other humans to join in. Because it is a vibration, it can be shared.

～

I must be open to these gifts of spiritual travel. I have been given the gift of a physical presence, and through it I receive the energy and wisdom of the Universe. I must share these vibrations with others, to empty my hand again and again by sharing these gifts. Only the open hand receives. By giving and receiving Love I honor the blessing of my existence.

Universal Wisdom: *And become the spirit-walking journey that God has given you.*

I am blessed. My spirit has been given the added dimension of a physical body. I am walking the Earth with the energy of God. I am the journey, the movement, of a spirit traveling. The place where I travel is the Universe. My blessing is in that space.

It is in that space, and so is everything else. When you step into Space, you allow All That Is, which includes your blessing and everyone else's too.

Remember who you are. You are a spirit-walking journey. You are a butterfly dancing on the perfume of flowers. You are on the path which God has given you. And you are not alone.

~ 6 ~

Tools For Transcendence

I have benefited immensely from channeled writing. With the help of this tool, I have experienced amazing personal and spiritual growth. From the very outset, however, The Teachers have been clear that this information was not just for me. This information is to be shared, and others are to be encouraged to use channeling themselves.

Channeling creates an energy pathway. Currently, this pathway is like a little rabbit trail in the woods. Some people are using it. But in order for it to become a recognized superhighway, easily available to many, more people need to be traveling there. When many people are accessing this information, we will have made a leap in our spiritual evolution.

The energy pathway of channeling is a link to ancient wisdom. Imagine what our world would be like if thousands of people were accessing and using this kind of information! In this chapter I will offer some tools so you can begin channeling yourself.

What is channeling? Channeling is not magic and it's not a technique. It is a skill, a skill that can be learned. It occurs in a state of alert relaxation that allows access to knowledge beyond the five senses. It's like tuning a radio dial—radio waves are all around us, even when the radio is off, and we just have to learn how to tune in and become a receiver. This spiritual tuning in occurs through Transcendence.

Transcendence is an energy state. It is a trance-like arrangement that integrates full physical presence with intuitive energy expansion.

In other words, it simultaneously incorporates both the Physical World and the Dream World. It combines Point and Zone, which is the body and the space around it, in a state of being both grounded and expanded at the same time.

It can be overwhelming to try to imagine this. But it is not something that we make happen with our intellect, our cranial brain. We can not will it into being. It is something that we allow, by creating the energy environment where it occurs. There are two parts to this—the physical and the intuitive. And there are several ways that either of these can be enriched.

The key is practice. That's why it's called spiritual practice. It's something we work on over time. Like any kind of training, a receptive energy state takes attention and investment. If I want to become fluent in a foreign language, for example, I can't just buy it. I have to do it. I have to want to learn more. I might start by reading books about it, or engaging a teacher. I'll need to replace my old vocabulary with new words and ideas. I will want to go to the place where that language is spoken, so I can understand its context and be surrounded by it. Eventually, I will find that I even dream in this other language.

Channeled writing is like that, too. You start with a desire to expand and then learn through practice. Over time, you will become immersed in it. Once it becomes second nature, and the feeling is recorded as a memory in your body, you can easily come back to it over and over.

Below I offer suggestions for learning. You do not have to do it all at once, and you do not have to do it this way. You will find what works for you. When I first started, I did 45 minutes of grounding and meditation before writing. Now I can be in transcendence anywhere, without preparation, even in the canned goods aisle at the grocery store. It is always available. When you begin, I suggest that you choose some of the areas listed below to work with, and make adjustments as you go.

One of the areas you will want to look at is physical presence—how grounded am I in the physical world, in the current moment? The spiritual world, the world beyond the five senses, has a higher vibration than the physical world. "Higher" does not mean faster or more intense. It means more open, more spacious and free. In order to access the spiritual world, I will want my physical energy to more closely match that higher vibration.

I choose the vibration of my body by how I live every day of my life. That vibration is determined by my lifestyle. A sedentary lifestyle, with much time spent sitting, tends to slow down my physical energy to a lower vibration. A "lower" vibration is more dense, sluggish, and bound up. A lifestyle which includes intentional activity and vigorous exercise tunes up my physical energy to a higher vibration. I recommend strong exercise every day. By strong exercise, I mean rhythmic, aerobic movement that increases the heart rate for about an hour, hopefully longer. This moves nutrients and toxins, and leads to physical balance. Exercise that is repetitive and rhythmic also re-arranges my thoughts, taking them away from cranial functions such as planning ahead and emotional rumination. Exercise breathing is deep and rhythmic, like the breathing of meditation, and creates energized relaxation. For my activity, I often choose walking, hiking, cross-country skiing, or swimming. If I make them a priority, they can be accomplished on a lunch break. Many of these choices have the added advantage of being outdoors.

Nature itself is functioning at a higher vibration, in tune with the Universe. Immersing myself in Nature helps me to recognize the circle of life and my inclusion in it. It helps me cultivate gratitude for the gift that is my lifetime. Exercising in Nature is most helpful if I can slow my mind enough to really see the planet I exist on. There is also great benefit to quiet time alone in Nature, sitting in solitude. That helps me practice Being, rather than Doing.

Of course, I also need to look at what I am putting in my body. It is a privilege to be able to choose what I eat. I want to choose foods that come directly from plants and animals, rather than from factories. There is already a lot of information available on this topic. The short version is that the vibrations present in what I eat affect the overall energy vibration of my body.

I also recommend the practice of mindful eating. I have a singing bowl on my table, and when I sit down to eat I bring the bowl to resonance, as a form of prayer. While the bowl is singing I give thanks for everything that went into my meal: the plants and animals themselves, the food they ate and the water they drank, the air they breathed, the sun, the farmers who made the food possible, the trucks and truckers who brought it near me, the grocery store workers where I purchased my food. It is all related. I also thank my own body, for choosing and preparing the food, for taking it in and bringing its vibration into my cells. I continue my gratitude as long as the bowl is singing. This can be several minutes. Then I enjoy my meal even more. Some Buddhist monks practice a similar vibrational devotion with meals. They start their prayer, however, with an empty bowl—before the meal is served. In this way, they are also mindful of the possibility of not having food, and how that is a reality for so many people around the world.

If I want to be a clear channel, I will also need to look at my chemical use. Regular intake of alcohol and other drugs, including nicotine and caffeine, moves my body away from its natural state. In many cases, I develop a relationship with the substance that precludes a relationship with Spirit. I can also be addicted to myriad behaviors that are not specific chemicals but have the same effect. Clearing any of these out is guaranteed to be spiritually worthwhile.

A little-recognized obstacle to spiritual connection is lack of sleep. Western culture invites frenetic jumping from task to task, encouraging busyness over ease. But sleep is the Rest-and-Repair part of living. Skimping on it invites stimulant use to get us through the day. Caffeine and nicotine do not create energy out of nowhere. They borrow it, from the body, and when the energy loan comes due with interest there are often health consequences. I've heard people justify their overdoing by saying, "I can sleep when I'm dead." It seems they don't recognize just what they are inviting!

Everything in Nature is cyclical. The seasons, a lifetime, each day—all have a beginning, a middle, a decline, and an end. Humans are no exception. Our body needs the down time of sleep to clean and clear. Our brain needs sleep to rest and reorganize. And our spirit needs space to travel without the body. Sleep itself is an altered state that is somewhat like meditation. Think of sleep as a spiritual practice, and give yourself this gift.

The other part of traveling the path of transcendence is energy expansion. Energy expansion goes hand in hand with physical presence, because having awareness of the body will help with awareness of what is beyond the body. This is the intuitive, nonphysical part of spiritual practice.

We all have intuitive feelings. They are often stifled or discounted by Western thinking, which would like everything to be provable using the five senses. You will want to begin paying greater attention to your intuition. Be aware of how your gut (your belly brain) responds. The more you listen to, honor, and act on intuition, the more you will be in tune with your spiritual life.

A good way to begin working with energy expansion is through physical movement that incorporates energy awareness. There are many forms available, and they tend to have Eastern origins. Qigong is the ancient healing practice from which all martial arts developed. It is gentle and nourishing. Other forms include T'ai Chi and Aikido. Yoga is now a mainstream exercise. All of these are best when practiced with awareness of energy movement. After learning the basic movements, regular home practice is important. Home practice prevents one of the pitfalls of ego engagement—competition with other practitioners. Energy movement works best when you do it with and for yourself.

Breath is an important part of all meditation and movement. Attention to breath is a useful way to practice moving your energy. The following exercise was given to me to help relieve stress. You can do this any time, anywhere, for any amount of time, for any reason. **Universal Wisdom**: *You can help yourself be more present, to yourself and others, by monitoring the energy of your being. Take a minute to scan your body and see where you are holding your energy.*

If you are stressed in some way, then your energy is probably con-

centrated in your upper body and your head. This kind of arrangement places you off balance. Literally. Your upper body is heavier than your lower body, and muscle rigidity is required to keep your energy self from tipping over. Bringing your energy into your pelvis, lower in your body, creates stability and freedom of movement.

Try to breathe, not just with your lungs, but with your energy. When you breathe in, let your energy move into all the space inside your body. When you breathe out, let your energy move into all of the space around your body. Focus on your torso, the part of your body that includes your heart and your belly.

Breathe in, breathe out.

Feel the energy inside your body, feel the energy outside your body. Inside, outside.

Concentrate it, expand it.

Breathe in, breathe out.

Experience density, experience freedom.

Bring it in, let it out.

Breathe in, breathe out.

Another way to expand our awareness is through meditation. Meditation simply involves moving our energy into the space within and around us, the space that connects us to The One With All. I use a Circle of Life guided meditation in my channeled writing workshops, and I will share it here. It is best if it is read to you, by another person or on a recording, so you can focus on moving your energy rather than on reading. You can also go through the process on your own, choosing words and concepts that have meaning for you. What you want to be doing is placing yourself in context, and practicing moving your energy with awareness.

Start by creating a quiet location, free of all distractions. (Turn off your phone.) Follow this by creating a quiet place in your body. Do some gentle exercise or movement to bring your energy home. When you are ready, get in a comfortable position with your eyes closed. Begin with breath awareness. Observe your breath. Moving in. Moving out. Moving in. Moving out. You do not need to control your breath, just notice it. Moving in. Moving out. Enjoy this awareness for several minutes.

In a moment, you will be asked to move your attention outward, into the space around you. We will be using the cardinal points — East, South, West, North — and the way they travel as our Earth rotates. In most indigenous cultures, the cardinal points are directions. They are not the single points noted on a compass. They are directional areas. If you are the center, facing South, then the East is the entire area to your left that is not the North and not the South. The East is one quarter of the circle around you. We will begin in the East. Decide where you think East might be. You do not have to be accurate, you just need to create a reference.

Place your attention in the quarter of the circle that is the East. The East is the beginning. It is the place where the sun comes up each day. Light dawns in the morning and spreads over the Earth. We give praise and thanks for the East, for the sun, for the beginning of each new day. Now move your attention to the South, the quarter of the circle that is the South. The South is where the sun stands at midday. The sun's rays are bright and warming. We give praise and thanks for the South, and for the sun's strength. Now move your attention to the West, to the quarter of the circle that is the West. In the West, the sun slowly goes down, bringing us to the close of the day, when we begin to slow and ease into rest. We give praise and thanks for the West, for the end of each day. Now move your attention to the North, to the quarter of the circle that is the North, where the light of the sun is quiet and the night sky is revealed, full of stars and galaxies and endless space. We give praise and thanks for the North, for the quiet time of day when we rest and reflect. Now move your attention again to the East, where the dark of night-time retreats and the sun returns at dawn.

Every twenty-four hours we travel the circle of the sun. We give praise and thanks for the cycle of our days. Everything the power does, it does in a circle. Rest your attention in the East, the quarter of the circle that is the East. The year begins in the East, with spring. Spring is the time when the light returns and awakens the Earth. The birds return to sing as the flowers and the grasses raise their heads from slumber, and water begins to talk in the rivers. We give praise and thanks for the East, and for the season of Spring. Move your attention to the South, which is the summer, when the sun is strong and its heat draws life from the earth. Animals tend their new families, feeding them from Nature's bounty, and trees celebrate with the rustle of leaves. We give praise and thanks for the South, and the bounty of summer. Move your attention to the West, the quarter of the circle that is the West, where summer turns to autumn. In the West, the sun begins to give way again to the darkness. The plants turn in on themselves, and release their seeds of hope onto the ground. The wind comes and combs the leaves from our Earth mother's hair. We give praise and thanks for the West, and for the autumn. Move your attention to the North, to the full quarter of the circle which is the North, which is the winter. Winter is the time when the earth rests under a snowy quilt. Sap gathers deep in the roots of trees and the bears sleep. All is quiet, resting. We give praise and thanks for the winter, for the North.

As the circle continues to turn, we return again to the East. Human activity follows the seasons. It follows the circle. In the East, in spring, we plant our seeds for a new growing season. Rest your attention in the East, in the planting of seeds. As the season turns, rest your attention in the South, where the warm sun of summer nurtures and strengthens the young plants. Rest your attention in autumn, where the plants are mature and fruiting, where we harvest the energy of the spring and summer in the foods we will eat all winter. Rest your attention in the North, in winter, where the ground lies fallow and resting, waiting for the next turn of the seasons. We give praise and thanks for the turning of the seasons, and the food that is provided by it.

Rest your attention again in the quarter of the circle that is the East, the new day, the spring, and see our own lives in the cycle. In the East, we are born, and our spirit joins our body. We are born of the Earth mother and nurtured by her as infants and children. We are born into our lifetime. Now rest your attention in the South, in the summer, in the midday, and see how everyone grows from children into young adults, full of fire and heart energy, the next generation emerging. The circle turns, the seasons follow. Rest your attention in the West, in the evening, in the autumn, where we mature into adults, our many experiences bearing the fruit of wisdom, as we enjoy the quiet beauty of sunset. Rest your attention in the North, in the winter, in the night sky. In the North we are elders, having lived a full cycle and sharing the wisdom of our living. We learn endurance and patience as our bodies turn inward. At the end of our winter, we rest in the Earth, in the night sky, and empty our bodies before beginning again, as ancestors holding the stars. We give praise and thanks for the seasons of the Earth, for the circle of our lives.

Everything moves in a circle. We rest our attention in the East, and we see that everything has a beginning. Relationships, careers, projects, all have a beginning. They start out as ideas, fresh and new. We move our attention to the South, and we see that everything has a middle. We see our ideas develop into plans and adventures. We move to the West, and see that everything has an ending. Our plans and relationships are carried through. We realize their failings and their gifts. We move our attention to the North, and we see the empty time, between the ending of one thing and the beginning of the next, in new form. In the East, we start again, but from a different perspective, having already traveled the circle with it. Nothing is permanent. We give praise and thanks for the flow of the Universe through us, constantly moving.

We travel the circle in everything we do. Everything around us is traveling the circle also, sometimes joining our circle, sometimes traveling its own. The circle is turning and turning. We are turning and turning. We are a circle. We are on the circle. The circle moves through us. It is all One.

~

A meditation such as the Circle of Life is a good way to start a channeling session. When you begin channeling, you will need a quiet place and open time. Choose a place without distractions and give yourself two hours without any other commitments. Begin by practicing energy movement. Do some yoga or Qigong or stretching. Focus on your body and use gentle movement to increase your awareness of energy moving through it. Your goal is to become physically focused. Once you are grounded, you can sit quietly to practice energy expansion. Move your energy out into the space around you through meditation or guided meditation.

Practicing both grounding and expansion creates a state of alert relaxation, and will help you move toward transcendence. When you do this regularly, the amount of time needed to move your energy in this way will decrease.

People do all kinds of channeling. It doesn't have to be writing, but that is what I know best so that is what I am going to describe. The advantage of writing is that it provides a record. I sometimes don't understand the teaching until I have reviewed it later, or have studied it several times.

It's best to start out writing in a private place. Sometimes the teachings will be very moving, you might be crying, and you don't want to limit your emotional expression. Commit to writing continuously for at least one hour, so that you can move through any places when you might feel stuck. Begin writing and do not stop. The point is to get some flow going. Notice when you are judging what you are writing, but do not stop. If you get stuck, keep writing, even if you have a whole page with "I don't know what to say" written on it. Best results usually come from starting with your own feelings or issues (just like journaling). Write about that for a little while and then ask for guidance. Rather than yes-or-no questions, use open-ended questions, like "What would help me with this?" or "How could I go about that?" Keep writing. Listen, and allow any answers, even if they seem ridiculous or don't apply. Inserting your own agenda of disbelief, or steering what you think the answers should be, usually hinders or shuts down the process.

Use italics or underlining or capitals or stars, or whatever you like, to note when you think you hear something that is not your voice. Don't be concerned about who it might be — intellectual intrusion clamps down the process. You want to be operating as much as possible with your intuitive energy, not your head. Do not focus on spelling and grammar so much as intention and content. This is not a test. It is an opportunity. It is a chance to allow creative energy to flow through you. You want it to be relaxing and refreshing.

Always end your writing time by saying Thank You, regardless of the outcome. Express gratitude for the spiritual space that has been created. The following is a gratitude prayer that can be used either at the beginning or the end of your channeling time:

I give praise and thanks for everything that makes our journey on this planet possible.
I give praise and thanks for my physical presence and that of others.
I give praise and thanks for all our relations.
I give praise and thanks for all the animals, the four-legged, the winged, the swimmers.
I give praise and thanks for all the insects.
I give praise and thanks for all of the plants.
I give praise and thanks for the air.
I give praise and thanks for the water.
I give praise and thanks for the soil and the rocks.
I give praise and thanks for the planet that we stand on.
I give praise and thanks for all the planets, and all the stars, and all the galaxies.
I give praise and thanks for the Universe.
I give praise and thanks for Life Force.
I give praise and thanks for all the unseen forces, for the spirits who support us.
May I also give myself this same gentle support.
May everything I do honor the journey of my spirit walking the Earth.

When you have finished your channeling time, create a gentle transition back into your daily life by taking a brief walk or enjoying some other five-sense experience, such as drinking tea.

It's likely to take some practice to get in the groove of channeled writing. The more often you do it, the more likely you will tap into the Dream World. To create a channel, or pathway, I recommend that you schedule regular writing time several times a week. It helps to put it on your calendar, just like you would other appointments, to make it a priority.

Real life happens, of course, and sometimes you will miss your writing time. Be gentle with yourself. In your calendar, note what you were doing instead of the writing. Pay attention to what you are choosing. (Driving a friend to the hospital instead of writing is different than, say, scrolling through social media.) Think of your writing time as a mini-retreat, a time to relax and get away from your busy life.

As you continue to practice, you will create an energy memory of how it feels to be in transcendence. It is positive and refreshing. The more you do it, the more you will want to do it.

Once you are in the habit of channeling and the pathway becomes established, you will see it evidence in other parts of your life. Sometimes you will experience compelling dreams while sleeping. You may be shown something in a waking vision, rather than in words. You may hear sounds or music or see colors. You may be moved to draw or paint or sing. Welcome it all without judgment, and marvel at the amazing potential of the Universe.

⁓ 7 ⁓

The Next World

Channeling, writing, and editing is a continual process. In *Grandmother Dreams, Conversations Across the Veil*, the Teachers shared information about leading a spirit-fed, rather than an ego-driven, life. As I came to the end of that book, I was given a glimpse into what the next steps would be. That became the second book, *Traveling Light, Moving Our Awareness Beyond the Five Senses*, which you have just read. It outlines the journey of traveling the soul path. As this book approached conclusion, I was given information about a third book.

Universal Wisdom: *You would like this to have exact answers and neat endings. There is no such thing. Life is constantly being made. You use a meditation in your class about the wheel of life, the wheel constantly turning. It is possible to be on different points of the wheel in different places of your life. In every ending there is a beginning, every beginning there is an ending. It's where you choose to place your attention, how you integrate the changes into your everyday life. You can focus on a point, or you can focus on the wheel. You can focus on the path, or focus on the journey.*

Point and Zone. It always comes back to that.

First is the awareness, then the movement of awareness.

And after the movement of awareness?

First is the awareness. Then the movement of awareness. Then the movement of awareness between Points. Consciously moving energy from one Point to another, with a conscious vibration of energy.

The movement of awareness is transcendence. The movement of awareness between Points is?

The movement of awareness between Points is traveling in other dimensions. Not just being in them, but actually traveling there and creating change.

I am barely able to comprehend this.

Because you have not really done this yet. It is something you will learn.

I find this exciting, and daunting, of course.

It is all as it should be. Do not worry about this. Move forward as you have been. It will come in time.

It seems so simple, and so clear. Of course, I have this capability too. I just never considered it. This is why I need to continue to create the space and time to keep learning. Sometimes it is necessary to break down barriers of consciousness. I will carry on, and listen for what I need.

There is more to come. Things that you cannot imagine now. Your directive is to stay open. Being worried or depressed pulls you into the future or the past. It limits your ability to be present to what is.

Just allowing myself to feel the possibility of the third step, moving awareness between Points, opens me to new possibilities in energy. It means transcending, and then allowing the space created by transcendence to be energized. I have felt something like this before, usually just before falling asleep — like having a giant exploded-view experience of my body, where all of the parts have extra space between them. It's like seeing an engineering schematic drawing: I see all of the parts, separate from each other, but shown in a way that explains where they fit and how they are connected. It feels larger than Life.

And in the space between all of the parts there is the potential for active energy to move and change, to transform.

This is amazing. Unexpected. Beautiful. Inspiring.

Here is the next world.

The Next World.

That is the title of Book Three.

There is always more. Think about how you are using your time. Be wise.

CPSIA information can be obtained
at www.ICGtesting.com
Printed in the USA
BVHW071920180222
629285BV00001B/5

9 781734 198713